How Should the Army Use Contractors on the Battlefield?

Assessing Comparative Risk in Sourcing Decisions

Frank Camm, Victoria A. Greenfield

Prepared for the United States Army
Approved for public release; distribution unlimited

RAND ARROYO CENTER

The research described in this report was sponsored by the United States Army under Contract No. DASW01-01-C-0003.

ISBN: 0-8330-3736-6

Published 2005 by the RAND Corporation
1776 Main Street, P.O. Box 2138, Santa Monica, CA 90407-2138
1200 South Hayes Street, Arlington, VA 22202-5050
201 North Craig Street, Suite 202, Pittsburgh, PA 15213-1516
RAND URL: http://www.rand.org/
To order RAND documents or to obtain additional information, contact
Distribution Services: Telephone: (310) 451-7002;
Fax: (310) 451-6915; Email: order@rand.org

Preface

The Office of the Assistant Secretary of the Army for Manpower and Reserve Affairs raised a concern that the Army's use of contractors on the battlefield did not stem from any clearly articulated policy and could well be inappropriate. It asked RAND Arroyo Center to identify the policies and processes that appeared to be driving Army decisions to use contractors on the battlefield and offer ways to increase the likelihood that these policies and processes would yield outcomes consistent with the Army's high-level goals.

Arroyo's analysis proceeded along two parallel tracks. One looked from the top down at the risks associated with using contractors on the battlefield and what could be done to manage these risks more effectively. The other examined one of the largest contracts supporting deployed Army forces to understand better how Army use of contractors works from the bottom up. This report details Arroyo's findings from the first track. Arroyo's findings on the second track are reported in *Risk Management and Performance in the Balkans Support Contract*, by Victoria Greenfield and Frank Camm, MG-282-A, forthcoming.

This report should interest policymakers and analysts responsible for identifying and assessing the risks associated with using contractors on the battlefield and for making sourcing decisions based on such assessment. Decisions that affect the Army's use of contractors occur in many places discussed in this report—outside the Army; in its services acquisition, force development, and system development communities; and in the support planning staffs that support combatant commanders in individual contingencies. This report focuses on the Army context but addresses issues relevant throughout the Department of Defense. Much of our treatment could be generalized as well to sourcing support services in nonmilitary organizational locations or "venues."

This report does not address or recommend specific changes in sourcing decisions. Rather, it focuses on how to improve the Army's understanding of the benefits, threats, risks, mitigations, and ultimately the residual risks—the risks that remain after all mitigations have been implemented—associated with using a contractor rather than a military unit on the battlefield. It recommends specific ways and places to apply the Army's doctrinal approach to assessing operational risks to risks associated with using contractors on the battlefield.

This research was sponsored by the Assistant Secretary of the Army for Manpower and Reserve Affairs and was conducted in RAND Arroyo Center's Manpower and Training Program. RAND Arroyo Center, part of the RAND Corporation, is a federally funded research and development center sponsored by the United States Army.

For more information on RAND Arroyo Center, contact the Director of Operations (telephone 310-393-0411, extension 6419; FAX 310-451-6952; email Marcy_Agmon@rand.org), or visit Arroyo's web site at http://www.rand.org/ard/.

Contents

Figures

Tables

Summary

Using contractors on the battlefield is risky, but the U.S. Army has relied on contractors on the battlefield throughout its history. Beginning with the Vietnam War, a variety of factors have led to growing dependence on contractors. Given the risks that contractors impose, is this increasing dependence appropriate? Throughout history, Army leaders have decried the risks associated with using contractors even as they continued to bring them to the battlefield to provide critical combat service support (CSS) activities.

The Office of the Assistant Secretary of the Army for Manpower and Reserve Affairs (ASA [M&RA]) was concerned that many parts of the Army may make decisions that affect the use of contractors on the battlefield without adequately considering the effects of their decisions on military readiness. ASA (M&RA) asked the Arroyo Center to examine this issue and recommend improvements.

This report identifies the major decisions that shape the Army's use of contractors on the battlefield. It explains the arguments that have shaped these decisions. Drawing on the Army's own approach to assessing risk, Army and other Department of Defense (DoD) documents, field interviews, literature by Army personnel about their own experiences with contractors in deployments, and a detailed case study of the largest contract supporting Army deployed forces at the time, the report offers a conceptual framework the Army could use to revisit these decisions. The framework should make the connection between these decisions and their sourcing consequences more visible and lead to Army sourcing decisions more nearly consistent with its strategic goals. The report focuses on a choice between contract and military sources, but the framework could easily be applied to a broad set of alternatives. We collected the information used to build this framework before information about the Army's experience with contractors in the 2003 war in Iraq became available, but the framework appears to be consistent with this recent Army experience.

The report should interest policymakers and analysts responsible for identifying and assessing the risks associated with using contractors on the battlefield and for making sourcing decisions based on such assessment. Decisions that affect the Army's use of contractors occur in many places discussed in this report—outside the Army; in its services acquisition, force development, and system development communities; and in the support planning staffs that support combatant commanders in individual contingencies. This report focuses on the Army context but addresses issues relevant throughout DoD. Much of our treatment could be generalized as well to sourcing support services in nonmilitary organizational locations or "venues."

The Standard Army Approach to Assessing Risk

The Army has a standard method for dealing with risk (Chapter Two). The field manual, FM 3-100.12, clearly explains how a decisionmaker can

- identify the hazards relevant to a decision,
- identify the risks associated with each hazard,
- mitigate these risks, and
- assess the residual risk associated with any decision—the risk that remains after the decisionmaker has implemented appropriate mitigating controls.

The manual explains this approach in the context of operations, starting from the premise that a commander does not seek to eliminate risk but to avoid unnecessary risks. A great deal of the commander's operational art is embedded in identifying what risks are unnecessary, but the basic framework provides a clear way to apply that complex art to specific decisions on the battlefield.

As FM 3-100.12 explains, the approach described can be applied to any decision that a commander faces. It is well suited to the decisions of where, when, and how to use contractors on the battlefield precisely because these decisions are integral parts of any field commander's support plan. These sourcing decisions are most appropriately made as an integral part of the commander's development of a basic course of action on the field.

This report proposes using this standard Army approach to structure risk assessment that compares the residual risks of contractor and military sources of CSS on the battlefield. It refers to the *relative residual risk* of using a contractor as the risk of using a contractor, relative to the risk of using a military source, after the commander has applied all appropriate mitigations for each source. That is, the report compares two courses of action. Each course of action includes the choice of a contractor or military source and the choice of the mitigations that accompany the use of that source. Mitigations remove unnecessary risks associated with each course of action. The approach prefers the source with the lower residual risk and recognizes that the commander's job is not to eliminate the risk associated with choosing a source but to manage it appropriately within the constraints that the commander faces.

A Disciplined Way to Assess Risks Associated with Using Contractors

This report applies this approach through the following sequence of reasoning.

First, commanders use contractors only if doing so offers some advantage (see Chapter Three and Appendix C). If no apparent advantage exists, the issue of using contractors on the battlefield never arises. We need to understand what advantage a contractor offers. The report identifies two classes of advantages: inherent advantages relative to a military source and relief from policy and resource constraints that the commander faces.

Second, the use of contractors on the battlefield presents specific risks (see Chapters Two and Four). We need to understand what risks the commander should worry about. The report identifies four relevant risks: shortfalls in mission success, the safety of contractor employees and their equipment, resource costs, and other specific but broader goals typically outside a field commander's immediate military concerns, such as total force management or compliance with administrative law.

Third, the risks relevant to any specific sourcing decision in this context stem from key hazards associated with the intensity and predictability of military action during a contingency, status of international agreements on the status of forces, status of contractor employees under international law, the Army's ability to control a contractor, the Army's responsibilities to protect and support a contractor, and a number of other factors (see Chapter Three and Appendix B). These hazards are interrelated. Some may be influenced by efforts to mitigate the risks associated with other hazards.

In the fourth step, the Army has extensive opportunities to mitigate the effects of hazards associated with using contractors to provide CSS (see Chapter Three and Appendix B). The risks that the Army faces when using contractors in any particular circumstance ultimately depend on the extent to which the Army takes advantage of the mitigations available. A sourcing decision is as likely to depend on the mitigations anticipated as on the severity or probability of the initial hazards themselves.

Fifth, even if the Army takes advantage of all the mitigation strategies available when it uses a contractor source, some risks will remain (see Chapter Five and Appendix B). Inherent differences between doing work in-house and depending on an outside source create unavoidable risks. These risks are well known; the Federal Acquisition Regulation (FAR) is designed explicitly to help manage them. In the end, however, the Army must compare such remaining risks with the benefits it gets from using a contract source and with the risks and benefits of using an in-house military or government civilian source.

In the sixth step, when the Army applies appropriate mitigations, the relative residual risks associated with using contractors are likely to vary across CSS activities and contingencies (see Chapter Four). Their levels are likely to depend on five basic considerations: the type of activity, the type or identity of the contractor, the nature of the contingency, the location and battle phase for the contractor on the battlefield, and the quality of government oversight of the contractor.

Seventh, an analyst conducting a standard Army risk assessment can weigh the factors above in a systematic way to determine whether a contractor or military source is preferable for a particular activity under particular circumstances (see Chapter Four). Using a "simultaneity stack" of missions—a set of missions that defense planning guidance suggests the Army should be able to execute simultaneously—such as that used in each Total Army Analysis (TAA), an Army analyst can use a standard assessment to determine what mix of contractor and military sources is appropriate for any CSS activity in the Army force as a whole.

Lastly, it is very likely that this sequence of reasoning will yield a mix of contractor and military CSS, in part because contractors have inherent advantages in some circumstances and in part because contractors help the Army overcome constraints imposed for reasons unrelated to sourcing policy in other circumstances (see Chapter Five). The sequence of reasoning above can support a risk assessment of relieving these constraints and thereby reducing the Army's dependence on contractors (see Chapter Six). The form of such an analysis differs from that for a sourcing decision subject to constraint. The risks and information required to assess the implications of loosening a constraint also differ from those discussed here.

This sequence of reasoning identifies the information an Army decisionmaker needs to apply the standard Army risk assessment framework to a sourcing decision. The approach proposed here is not simple. Complexities discussed here directly reflect the complexity of operational art on the battlefield and of the multiple risks relevant to a sourcing decision. Application of the standard Army framework to more traditional operational questions is not simple either. Ideally, sourcing decisions in a particular contingency would be made as an integral part of operational planning for the contingency. However, the same basic sequence of reasoning can help support decisions made at a higher level, elsewhere in the Army, and outside the Army.

Where to Assess Risks Associated with Using Contractors

Where should risk assessment relevant to Army sourcing occur? Such assessment should support decisions that significantly affect Army use of contractors, wherever those decisions occur (see Chapter Seven). Decisions in five distinct organizational locations or venues appear to be important.

Outside the Army. The size and operational tempo (OPTEMPO) of the military force affect the use of contractors. As military end strength falls or OPTEMPO increases with a fixed end strength or monetary budget, the Army is likely to rely more heavily on contractors to provide services that the military simply cannot provide. Airlift capacity affects the use of contractors. As airlift—military or contractor—capacity increases, the Army is likely to rely less heavily on contractors that use local nationals or forms of transportation not available to the Army. Troop ceilings and policies on military presence in a theater affect the Army's use of contractors. As restrictions on the presence of military forces in-theater increase, the Army naturally turns to heavier use of contractors. Decisionmakers outside the Army choose the policies relevant to each of these factors, albeit with input from the Army. But historically, sourcing concerns in the Army have not shaped the decisions made here. Perhaps they should.

Army Services Acquisition Venues. The policies the Army uses to choose contractors, design contracts and quality assurance plans, and oversee and support contractors in-theater heavily affect the residual risks associated with their use. Joint training of military and contractor personnel, application of these policies in-theater, and active integration of contractors into planning in-theater also affect residual risks. The more the Army uses the policies called for in its doctrine on the use of contractors on the battlefield, the more desirable contractors become relative to military personnel on the battlefield. This part of the Army's doctrine has emerged primarily from the logistics community. Decisions to apply the doctrine will occur there and in the operational community ultimately responsible for training the force and integrating logisticians with operators during contingencies. Formal risk assessment can help Army decisionmakers understand how such changes are likely to affect the risks that the Army faces on the battlefield and the implications of these risks for Army use of contractors.

Force-Design and Management Venues. The TAA determines which required CSS activities the Army will resource from the active-duty, Guard, and Reserve military components. These decisions affect the use of contractors. Diminished active-duty component capability to perform an activity can encourage contractor use to alleviate rotation constraints. Less reserve component capability to perform an activity can encourage contractor use to avoid the political costs of repeatedly mobilizing a small number of units and personnel within these components. The Army uses operations and maintenance (O&M) funds to get other support services, including contracting services. Decisions on how to use O&M funds occur in the Planning, Programming, Budgeting, and Execution System (PPBES) and major command (MACOM) resource management processes. Such decisions on the application of O&M funds affect the Army's use of contractors directly. The sequence of reasoning offered here can help decisionmakers in the TAA, PPBES, and MACOM resourcing processes to understand the effects of their decisions on Army risks and their implications for Army use of contractors on the battlefield.

System Design Venues. System requirements officials and program managers choose the support concept for a new or modified system. This encourages dependence on contractors when the support concept envisions a long interim contractor support period or requires highly skilled support personnel on the battlefield over the life of the system. More generally, officials use spiral development to field systems early and collect operational data on them from the battlefield to refine their designs over time. This encourages the presence of contractors on the battlefield. The sequence of reasoning offered here can help these decisionmakers understand the effects of their decisions on Army risks and the presence of contractors on the battlefield.

Specific Contingencies. Given the decisions made in the venues above, a combatant commander (COCOM) calls on existing Army capabilities to assemble a force. The sequence of reasoning presented here flows directly from this decision setting and is likely to be easiest to apply in this setting. That said, this is the setting that has received the most attention in recent Army doctrine on the use of contractors on the battlefield. Despite its direct applicability here, the sequence of reasoning above may well improve decisionmaking more in venues that have not received as much attention.

In each of these venues, the sequence of reasoning proposed here asks decisionmakers to assess risk by comparing the residual risk of using a contractor source, with appropriate mitigations, with the residual risk of using a military source, with appropriate mitigations. Unfortunately, the decisionmakers in each venue control only a portion of the mitigations relevant to their decisions. They must make assumptions about mitigations that other decisionmakers will apply. Standard Army guidance could help all decisionmakers coordinate their decisions against a common set of assumptions. In the absence of such guidance, the decisionmakers in individual venues will likely apply their own priorities or plan for the worst, assuming mitigation will be inadequate elsewhere. The joint effect of such behavior could easily be underutilization of contractors and hence a higher level of risk on the battlefield than is necessary. The approach suggested here would be grossly incomplete without Army-wide guidance to coordinate decisions in different venues.

Today, decisions relevant to Army use of contractors on the battlefield are made in many of these venues without regard to such an effect. In other places, decisionmakers recognize that their decisions affect the presence of contractors but do not use a risk assessment compatible with the Army's standard approach to risk assessment to address the effects of their decisions. The Army literature on using contractors on the battlefield and, most particularly, its doctrine on this topic recommends repeatedly to assess the risks of using contractors. We offer the sequence of reasoning in this report to help decisionmakers respond positively to that recommendation in every venue significant to the Army's use of contractors on the battlefield.

Can the Future Differ from the Past?

Even when Army leaders have preferred not to use contractors on the battlefield, why have they repeatedly found it necessary to do so? This report suggests that this may have occurred throughout the Army's history in part because contractors have helped the Army mitigate the effects of specific policy and resource constraints. If enough airlift capacity were available, the Army would prefer to use military personnel. If troop ceilings were higher, the Army would prefer to use military personnel. If the Army had enough active military personnel to handle all of its deployment responsibilities, it would prefer to use military personnel. In the presence of these and many other constraints, it has been necessary to use contractors to reduce the unnecessary risks that the Army faced in each deployment. Because, in all likelihood, such constraints will persist, the Army will continue to use contractors, even though its leaders might prefer to use military personnel in many cases.

We believe a deeper problem underlies the Army's dilemma about using contractors. Disagreement persists in the Army about specific uses of contractors on the battlefield. That is because people in different parts of the Army, with different priorities and different perspectives, lack a common structure and language they can use to present their concerns in comparable terms and reduce their disagreements. Without a common understanding of what affects the Army's use of contractors on the battlefield, many decisionmakers can continue to choose courses of action that increase the Army's dependence on contractors without even realizing it. Others who do understand their effects on the use of contractors have no Army-wide guidance to shape their decisions and so rely on their own priorities and assumptions about what mitigations will occur elsewhere to choose their own mitigations and sourcing decisions relevant to the use of contractors. When this occurs, people in one part of the Army can decry decisions being made elsewhere without having the power to improve those decisions from an Army-wide perspective.

This report offers a single, integrated model of how a large number of decisions affect the Army's use of contractors on the battlefield and of the principal factors relevant to these decisions. We hope this model and these factors can help shape a more constructive, precise, engaged discussion within the Army. As that discussion proceeds, it will become apparent which considerations are most important to differences in points of view. The Army can focus on collecting better empirical evidence about these considerations and use the evidence to improve its decisions about where, when, and how to use contractors on the battlefield.

Acknowledgments

The Assistant Deputy Assistant Secretary of the Army for Manpower Management, John C. Anderson, was the Army project officer for this work and took an active interest in its execution throughout. He provided useful ideas, references, and support, as did Eileen G. Ginsburg from his office. Thomas J. Edwards, Deputy to the Commanding General of the U.S. Army Combined Arms Support Command (CASCOM), and Gordon L. Campbell, Principal Deputy to the Commanding General for Acquisition of CASCOM, provided valuable input and support. Mike Noll and his staff in the Army Materiel Command Logistics Civil Augmentation Program (LOGCAP) Office helped us understand how LOGCAP supports deployed forces. Robert W. Gruber, Jr., A. Brian Brobson, and their staff at the U.S. Army Corps of Engineers Transatlantic Programs Center provided detailed information about the Balkans Support Contract (BSC) and, more generally, Army contracting in support of deployed forces. John Cowings, Kellogg Brown and Root (KBR) Program Manager for the BSC, and Mike Mulholland, KBR Program Manager, Houston Support Office, provided important insights from the contractor's perspective. Kevin S. Tomich of the Center for Army Analysis shared data from his historical review of the Army's use of contractors, as well as valuable insights.

We received helpful feedback during multiple presentations based on the material in this report in the Office of the Assistant Secretary of the Army for Manpower and Reserve Affairs; Headquarters, Department of the Army; Headquarters, Army Materiel Command;

Headquarters, Training and Doctrine Command; and CASCOM. Personnel in many other parts of the Army helped us understand better how the Army uses contractors to support deployed forces.

Bruce Orvis, director of the Arroyo Center Manpower and Training Program, supported and reviewed the work. John Bondanella, Brent Fulton, and Ellen Pint, who were studying minimum military-essential logistics capabilities in the Arroyo Center's Military Logistics Program, were generous with their data, contacts, and insights. Gail Kouril of RAND helped us find a wide variety of sources relevant to contracting on the battlefield. Discussions with John Ausink, Irv Blickstein, Roger Brown, Bob Clemence, Cynthia Cook, Carl Dahlman, John Dumond, Mike Hix, Dave Johnson, Leslie Lewis, Eric Peltz, and Mike Stollenwerk, all of RAND, provided useful insights. Susan Gates, Chip Leonard, and Ellen Pint of RAND and Frank A. Camm (LTG, USA, ret.) read earlier drafts closely and helped improve them.

We thank them all but retain responsibility for the accuracy of the findings reported and our conclusions.

Abbreviations

AAA	Army Audit Agency
ACO	Administrative contracting officer
ALO	Authorized Level of Organization
AMC	Army Materiel Command
AMSAA	U.S. Army Materiel Systems Analysis Agency
AO	Area of operations
AOR	Area of responsibility
AR	Army regulation
ASA (M&RA)	Assistant Secretary of the Army (Manpower and Reserve Affairs)
ASCC	Army Service Component Command
BIT	Built-in test
BRS	Brown and Root Services (now KBR)
BSC	Balkans Support Contract
CASCOM	(U.S. Army) Combined Arms Support Command
CINC	Commander in chief (now combatant commander)
CLS	Contractor logistics support
COCOM	Combatant commander
COR	Contracting officer representative

CSS	Combat service support
DCMA	Defense Contract Management Agency
DoD	Department of Defense
DODI	DoD instruction
DSB	Defense Science Board
FAR	Federal Acquisition Regulation
FM	Field manual
4 ID	4th Infantry Division
FYDP	Future Years Defense Program
GAO	General Accounting Office (now Government Accountability Office)
GSORTS	Global Status of Resources and Training System
ICS	Interim contractor support
ICT	Integrated concept team
IG	Inspector General
IGCA	Inherently Governmental/Commercial Activity (inventory)
JFC	Joint Forces Command
JSTARS	Joint Surveillance and Target Attack Radar System
KBR	Kellogg Brown and Root
LMI	Logistics Management Institute
LOGCAP	Logistics Civil Augmentation Program
LSE	Logistics support element
MACOM	Major command
MOS	Military occupational specialty
MTOE	Modified Table of Organization and Equipment
MWR	Morale, welfare, and recreation
NBC	Nuclear, biological, and chemical (warfare)

NSA	National Security Agency
O&M	Operations and maintenance
OMB	Office of Management and Budget
OPORD	Operational order
OPTEMPO	Operational tempo
OSA	Operational Support Agency
OSD	Office of the Secretary of Defense
POW	Prisoner of war
PPBES	Planning, Programming, Budgeting, and Execution System
QDR	Quadrennial Defense Review
SOFA	Status of forces agreement
TAA	Total Army Analysis
TO&E	Table of Organization and Equipment
TRADOC	(U.S. Army) Training and Doctrine Command
UAV	Unmanned aerial vehicle
UCMJ	Uniform Code of Military Justice
USACE	U.S. Army Corps of Engineers
USAREUR	U.S. Army Europe
USR	Unit status report

CHAPTER ONE

Introduction

> The most alarming trend is our seeming inability to learn from over two hundred years of experience with using contractors in support of military operations. . . . In each conflict, there is almost universal agreement that use of contractors versus military support forces was the necessary, but not preferred course of action. Our leaders stand before us today, grappling with the same issues their predecessors did when the nation was born.
>
> —Lieutenant Colonel Donald R. Curtis, Jr., USA (2001, p. 10)

Policy Motivation

For a variety of reasons, the Army is increasing its reliance on contractors to provide direct support for combat activities. With few exceptions, contractor support to Army operational forces in-theater has been satisfactory in the past.[1] For example, interviews with senior logisticians about the Army's use of contractors in the first Gulf War found that they were "almost unanimous in their belief contractors

---

[1] See, for example, Kaiser and Fabbro (1980); Mailander (2002, p. 14); Tomich (2001, p. 29); Zamparelli (1999, p. 15). The "tree-cutting incident" during the Korean War offers a widely repeated example of failure, even though a careful examination by the Defense Science Board (DSB) found that it did not really occur. Critical contractor employees supposedly abandoned their posts in a hazardous setting to ensure that their dependents were evacuated. The DSB found that they *wanted* to abandon their posts and asked for permission to see their dependents to safety, but in fact remained on station (DSB, 1982b). See also Buhler (2000, p. 12); Kaiser and Fabbro (1980, pp. 3–14). (Note that this incident differs from another serious "tree-cutting incident" that occurred in Korea during the 1970s. This second incident did not involve the role or behavior of contractors.)

played a vital role on the battlefield, especially in supporting high-tech weapon systems"(Dibble et al., 1993, p. 11). But as dependence on contractors has increased, Army officials have become increasingly concerned about a wide range of things that *might* go wrong in the future, putting American lives and potentially the outcomes of military engagements at risk.[2] One particularly forceful example states that "the future battlefield environment in which both soldier and civilian find themselves will most likely dictate the behavioral traits of future contractors on the battlefield. This leads us . . . to consider the changing face of the battlefield and understanding that the templates used in Vietnam, Saudi Arabia, Bosnia, or even Afghanistan will not be an adequate solution for tomorrow's conflicts"(Mailander, 2002, p. 10).[3]

Two recent surveys provide evidence that has concerned many Army leaders.[4] A survey of support for systems in active Army divisions and air cavalry regiments that would be deployed in a major theater war, for example, reported the following (McGauley, 2001):

- Forty-five systems relied on contractor logistics support (CLS) at the division level or below. An additional 27 aircraft systems used CLS at higher echelons.

---

[2] For example, it is likely for a variety of reasons that far fewer technicians with previous military experience will be available for contractors to hire. How might that affect the service contractors can provide to the Army, particularly in a hazardous setting? (Tolar, 1994, p. 14). See also Brooke (1998, p. 26); Zamparelli (1999, p. 15). Zamparelli (1999) is one of the most well-stated explorations of the challenges created when the Army uses contractors on the battlefield. It is widely cited and recognized.

[3] The flip side of this argument would state that unsatisfactory performance in the past need not imply poor performance in the future if we can learn from the past. That is, generating a list of things that have gone wrong when using contractors on the battlefield does not, by itself, build a case against using them in the future. It builds a case against using them *as we have* in the past and can help us understand where to seek change (Singer, 2003).

[4] Appendix A provides a more extensive review of the policy context for this report. It highlights major policy reviews and policy actions relevant to using contractors on the battlefield since about 1980. Policymakers and commentators repeatedly support the need for better risk assessment, but no one provides a specific way to assess the risks of using contractors on the battlefield.

- Sixty of these systems were scheduled to receive CLS over their whole lifetimes.
- Forty-two of these systems received more than 75 percent of their supply and maintenance services under CLS arrangements.
- In the 45 systems required to use CLS arrangements inside the divisions, about a third of the support occurred at the battalion or company level.

Because the survey was deliberately framed conservatively, the wartime role of contractors in-theater is likely to be even higher.

A similar survey of the 4th Infantry Division (4 ID), the most technologically sophisticated division in the Army and a potential harbinger of what is to come, revealed potential problems associated with the use of contractors (CASCOM, 2001, pp. 11–13).

- Support under 44 contracts, or half the contracts supporting 60 systems in the 4 ID, had a high probability of requiring extended deployments outside the United States during a contingency involving the 4 ID.
- Only 13 of these included "good" or "exceptional" planning guidance for operations during a deployment.
- Twenty-one included *no* planning guidance for operations during a deployment.
- Plans for contractor support during a deployment anticipated using only a quarter of the contract personnel that the 4 ID actually required to execute an exercise that closely simulated a deployment.

Why is the Army increasing its dependence on contractors on the battlefield? Is it doing the right thing? This report addresses these two questions. It identifies the arguments that Army personnel use to justify the use of contractors on the battlefield despite strong beliefs that military sources are often a preferred source of combat service support (CSS). And it outlines a framework that the Army could implement to place individual policy decisions relevant to sourcing outcomes in perspective and asks whether they in fact support the

Army's high-level goals. We believe that if the Army fully implemented the framework we propose, Army analysts could make the connections between policy decisions and sourcing outcomes more visible and support the development of more consistent policies across the Army that affect the use of contractors on the battlefield.

Approach

We asked first what processes in the Army were likely to affect the pattern of contract services observed on the battlefield. We then sought a simple analytic framework that would be compatible with operational planning on the battlefield used to develop support plans and could throw light on these broader processes that appeared to shape the constraints of support planning in ways that affected sourcing outcomes on the battlefield. We found the kernel of that framework in the Army's standard approach to risk assessment, which identifies hazards, identifies courses of action that can mitigate these hazards, and then measures the risks that remain following mitigation.

We then sought information we could use to apply this standard Army approach to the assessment of contracting on the battlefield. What types of hazards and risks were relevant? What kinds of mitigations? What might comprise a "course of action" in a sourcing assessment? We sought this information in Army and other DoD documents, field interviews, and the rapidly growing literature by Army personnel about their own experiences with contractors in deployments. We also studied the largest contract we could find that supported deployed Army forces, the Balkans Support Contract (BSC), and examined the hazards, mitigations, and risks associated with the Army's design and application of that contract.

This information showed how efforts to mitigate the effects on one hazard created other hazards whose effects the Army then had to mitigate in turn. Chains of effects could go through several rounds of such mitigations. To understand the root causes of any particular sourcing decision, we recognized that we needed a broad framework that could piece together many individual standard risk assessments until we could see all of the hazards and mitigations in play at one time. The need for such a framework ultimately led to the framework proposed here. It remains fairly conceptual in character. Additional work will be required to identify the detailed data the Army might use to implement it. That said, this conceptual framework helps explain current sourcing decisions and the risks associated with them more usefully than the alternatives the Army currently uses or might use in the near future.

For simplicity, the report emphasizes a choice between contract and military sources of support. A similar approach could include a broader set of alternatives—government civilians from different agencies; different types of military personnel; host-nation support; American, allied, and local contractor personnel; and so on. To keep this initial articulation of the approach proposed as clear as possible, we focus on what in many ways has become the most contentious sourcing decision on the battlefield. Future studies can expand the approach to other source types.

The report emphasizes that the pros and cons of using contractors on the battlefield depend heavily on how the Army chooses and manages its contractors. So decisions about when to prefer contract over organic military capability depend fundamentally on the Army's ability to manage, support, and protect contractors in a specific setting.

The Army's level of reliance on contractors ultimately depends on the decisions it makes in its design of systems to be deployed, design of the total force, design of arrangements to use contractor support in-theater, and plan for and execution during specific contingencies. To be effective, the Army must weigh the benefits and costs of using contractors on the battlefield in each of these organizational locations or "venues." Ideally, the Army should coordinate decisions relevant to sourcing in all of these venues to yield an effective outcome for the Army as a whole.

We largely completed the analysis underlying this report before data on Army use of contractors in the 2003 war in Iraq began to become readily available. We have not reviewed data from that war formally, but our strong impression is that the Army's experience in Iraq confirms the findings we report and draw on as empirical inputs in this report.

Roadmap

This report starts (Chapter Two) by arguing that the Army can use its standard approach to assessing risk to assess the pros and cons of using contractors on the battlefield. Chapter Three summarizes arguments that Army personnel have made recently about when, where, and how to use contractors on the battlefield.

The report next shows how to use the approach described in Chapter Two to place the arguments in Chapter Three in perspective in a way that should lead to better sourcing decisions. Chapter Four uses the basic approach outlined in Chapter Two to propose an analytical framework for assessing Army sourcing decisions on the battlefield. Chapter Five uses this framework to weigh the costs and benefits relevant to "traditional" sourcing decisions—decisions that hold nonsourcing policies and resource levels constant. It posits a checklist that Army analysts can use to parse the complexity of providing support on the battlefield and organize information relevant to the residual risk associated with mission success, employee safety, resource cost, and other effects outside a contingency when the Army uses military or contractor sources. Chapter Six uses the framework outlined in Chapter Four to examine how many nonsourcing policies influence sourcing decisions in the Army. It identifies relevant nonsourcing policies and provides a way to ask whether the effects of such policies on sourcing decisions can justify changing the policies.

The discussions in Chapters Five and Six reveal that decisions made in many different policy venues affect the Army's use of contractors on the battlefield, often without intending to. Chapter Seven examines the challenges of conducting risk assessments of decisions that affect Army battlefield sourcing in five venues: outside the Army, in the Army services acquisition community, in the Army force design and management community, in the Army community that designs new and modified systems, and in Army planning for and execution during specific contingencies. Chapter Eight concludes the report.

A number of appendices provide empirical detail that supports the arguments in the text. Appendix A summarizes developments that have framed the current policy context for choosing between military and contractor sources. Appendices B and C compile arguments about the use of contractors on the battlefield in Army and other DoD documents, literature on practitioner experience, and field interviews. Appendix D compares the approach proposed here with alternative approaches. Appendix E explains what the approach proposed here implies for the measurement of the readiness of contract services.

CHAPTER TWO

A Standard Way to Assess the Risks of Using Contractors on the Battlefield: An Overview

The Army has developed a standard way to assess and manage risk. This approach was originally designed to help commanders work quickly through the major hazards they faced on the battlefield and develop preferred "courses of action" that mitigated and balanced risks to achieve immediate mission goals. The approach can also be applied much more broadly in the Army. In particular, it offers a way to think of alternative sourcing decisions as different courses of action that offer different ways to manage current or potential future hazards on the battlefield, can present different hazards of their own that must be addressed, and result in different levels of risk. When the Army chooses among the courses of action considered, it makes a sourcing decision. In principle, those responsible for Army sourcing decisions could apply this approach as an integral part of broader force planning in a particular contingency or in anticipation of potential future contingencies that the Army might face. This chapter explains the standard Army approach to risk management and outlines a way to apply it to sourcing decisions between military and contract sources of support on the battlefield.

The Standard Army Approach to Risk Management

The Army's keystone doctrinal document for full spectrum operations addresses risk throughout the text. It runs the gamut of operations, from planning to preparation to execution. In the context of planning, it states:[1]

> Risk management is the process of identifying, assessing, and controlling risk arising from operational factors, and making aninformed decision that balances risk cost with mission benefit. . . . Commanders integrate risk management into all aspects of the operations process, from planning through execution. . . . Effective risk management results in mission accomplishment at least cost. (Field Manual [FM] 3-0, 2001, pp. 6–20.)

In the context of mission execution, it explains the necessity of risk-taking—"recognizing and acting on opportunity means taking risks"—and distinguishes between "intentionally accepting risk" and "gambling." Risk management helps a commander avoid *unnecessary* risk. It does *not* remove risk altogether or support a zero-defects mindset. On the battlefield, any effort to eliminate risk would be paralyzing and so self-defeating. Risk management explicitly seeks to preserve the commander's flexibility and initiative (FM 100-14, 1998, p. 1-4).

FM 3-0 later addresses risk in the context of sustaining operations and their protection. "Because threats [hazards] to sustaining operations can divert combat power from the decisive operation, commanders carefully weigh the need for such diversions against the possible consequences and decide where to accept risk" (FM 3-0, 2001, p. 8-71). "Adjusting CSS factors can entail risks. When necessary, commanders conduct a risk analysis to determine what CSS functions can be deferred, performed at reduced levels, or performed in alternative locations in the short term" (FM 3-0, 2001, p. 12-59).

FM 100-14 (1998, pp. ii, 1-3, 1-4) emphasizes a still broader applicability:

> Although the . . . prime focus [of FM 100-14] is the operational Army, the principles of risk management apply to *all Army*

---

[1] It states that risk management affects course of action development, the application of elements of operational design, task organization, control measures, and concepts of operations, fires, and CSS.

> *activities*. . . . Commanders compare and balance risks against mission expectations and accept risks only if the benefits outweigh the potential costs or losses. Commanders alone decide whether to accept the level of residual risk to accomplish the mission.[2]

Understanding the meaning of "risk" and "hazard" is central to applying the Army's approach to risk management to any issues, including the sourcing decisions at hand (FM 3-100.12, 2001, pp. Glossary-4–Glossary-6):[3]

- Hazard: A condition or activity with potential to cause damage, loss, or mission degradation and any actual or potential condition that can cause injury, illness, or death of personnel; damage to or loss of equipment and property; or mission degradation.
- Risk: The probability and severity of loss linked to hazards.
- Residual risk: The level of risk remaining after controls have been identified and selected for hazards that may result in loss of combat power.
- Acceptable risk: The portion of identified risk that is allowed to persist without further controls.

Given these definitions, the Army approach comprises a commonsense, continuous, five-step process that a commander can pursue at a level of detail and sophistication commensurate with the risks in play (see Figure 2.1). Hazards with more likely, severe, or complex risks warrant closer attention. Steps 1 and 2 constitute the risk *assessment*; steps 3 through 5 are intended to *mitigate* the risk (FM 3-100.12, 2001, pp. II-1).

---

[2] Emphasis added. FM 3-100.12 (2001) has replaced this document. Guidance in the two remains very close.

[3] FM 100-14 (1998, p. Glossary-1) refers to "hazards" instead of "threats" and defines them as "any actual or potential condition that can cause injury, illness, or death of personnel, damage to or loss of equipment [or] property or mission degradation; a condition or activity with potential to cause damage, loss, or mission degradation."

Figure 2.1
Simplified View of the Army's Risk Management Framework

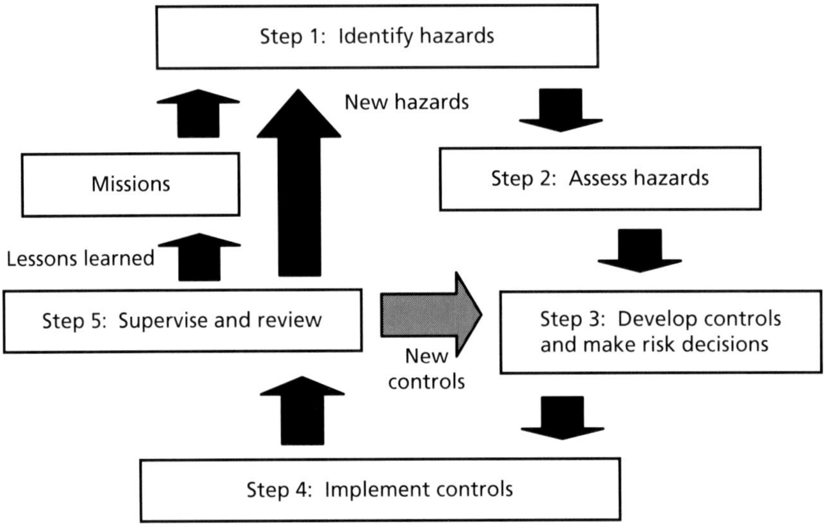

RAND *MG296-2.1*

Step 1—Identify Hazards. To identify the hazards so the commander can effectively mitigate and manage them, he should trace them to their root causes. The most obvious source of a problem is reflected in its *proximate* cause. For example, a contractor failure might occur because a task is not written into the original contract. Proximate causes can be traced back to *intermediate* causes. The clauses needed might be missing because no one had anticipated using this contract in a particular setting. Such intermediate causes can ultimately be traced back to *root* causes. For example, downsizing decisions and total force decisions may have removed key capabilities from the active Army. No one noticed the hole until a contingency arose and, unfortunately, the contractor chosen to fill the hole had planned to do something else because no integrated planning of basic changes in the shape of the force occurred.

Step 2—Assess Hazards to Determine Risk in Terms of a Combination of Probability, Severity, and Risk Level. The level of risk rises as the probability of a bad outcome increases and as the severity of that outcome increases. Tables 2.1 through 2.3 provide a simple, heuristic way to combine these factors to find their joint effects. Table 2.2 clarifies the definition of the four levels of severity used in Table 2.1 by relating its four levels to risks that a decisionmaker might encounter in the Army, on or off the battlefield. Similarly, Table 2.3 clarifies the definition of the five levels of probability used in Table 2.1. It does this by relating these four levels to four contexts in which a decisionmaker must consider risk.

Step 3—Develop Controls or Mitigations and Make Risk Decisions. Controls might seek to avoid a hazard, provide training or information about it, or take actions to reduce its effects. Given a set of proposed controls, the commander's staff can assess residual risk—the probability and severity of bad things happening, *given* the presence of all controls considered. The staff repeats this process for each decision option under review. The Army approach recommends comparing options and the residual risk associated with them in terms of feasibility, suitability, and the balance of benefit and cost. Based on the comparison, the commander makes a decision.

Step 4—Implement Controls. This step provides suitable support for the controls included in the option the commander chooses, assigns responsibility for the controls, and maintains accountability for their effective application.

Table 2.1
Risk Assessment Matrix

	Probability[b]				
Severity[a]	Frequent	Likely	Occasional	Seldom	Unlikely
Catastrophic	Extremely High Risk	Extremely High Risk	High Risk	High Risk	Moderate Risk
Critical	Extremely High Risk	High Risk	High Risk	Moderate Risk	Low Risk
Marginal	High Risk	Moderate Risk	Moderate Risk	Low Risk	Low Risk
Negligible	Moderate Risk	Low Risk	Low Risk	Low Risk	Low Risk

[a]See Table 2.2 for definition.
[b]See Table 2.3 for definition.
SOURCE: FM 3-100-12, 2001, p. A-D-1.

Table 2.2
Categories of Risk Severity

	Severity			
	Catastrophic	**Critical**	**Marginal**	**Negligible**
Mission capability, unit readiness	Unable to complete mission	Significantly degraded mission capability, readiness	Degraded mission capability, readiness	Little or no effect on mission capability
Personal disability	Death or permanent disability	Significantly degraded	Injury or illness	First aid, minor medical treatment
Equipment, systems	Loss of major or mission-critical items	Extensive damage	Minor damage	Slight damage; fully functional, serviceable
Property/ facilities	Major damage	Significant damage	Minor damage	Little or no damage
Environment	Severe damage	Significant damage	Minor damage	Little or no damage
Security	Mission-critical failure	Failure		
Collateral damage	Unacceptable damage	Significant damage		

NOTE: The contents of this table are illustrative and can be adjusted as appropriate to fit any particular setting. For example, a particular focus on security or collateral damage might call for a more complete scale that spanned all cells in each row.
SOURCE: FM 3-100.12, 2001, p. A-D-2.

Step 5—Supervise and Evaluate. This step "closes the loop" for the process, allowing continuing reassessment of hazards (Step 1), risks (Step 2), and the suitability of specific controls and decisions (Step 3).

As noted above, the Army has defined this approach most clearly for an operational setting, using "courses of action" as the options under review. However, a commander facing any decision can apply the approach. Because we will focus on using it to address policy questions, we will focus on Steps 1 through 3. Steps 4 and 5 would be relevant to any implementation and adjustment of the policies developed here.

Table 2.3
Definitions of Probability of Risk

Frequency	Definition	Single Item	Fleet or Inventory	Individual Person	All Personnel Exposed
Frequent	Occurs very often, continuously experienced	Expected to occur several times during a mission	Occurs continuously during a mission	Expected to occur several times during a mission	Occurs continuously during a mission
Likely	Occurs several times	Expected to occur during a mission	Occurs intermittently, often, at regular intervals	Expected to occur during a mission	Occurs intermittently
Occasional	Occurs sporadically	About 50% chance of occurring during a mission	Occurs several times in service life	May occur during a mission, but not often	Occurs sporadically (irregularly, sparsely, or sometimes)
Seldom	Remotely possible; could occur at some time	Not expected to occur during a mission	Could occur during service life, but rarely	Not expected to occur during a mission	Occurs rarely in exposed population
Unlikely	Can assume will not occur, but not impossible	Not impossible, but likely never to occur	Almost never occurs; improbable	Not impossible, but likely not to occur during a mission	Not impossible, but occurs very rarely

SOURCE: FM 3-100.12, 2001, p. A-D-3.

High-Level Risk Factors Relevant to Using Contractors on the Battlefield

What risks should the Army emphasize when making decisions about when, where, and how to use contractors on the battlefield? FM 3-100.12 (2001) focuses on risk factors relevant to mission success and losses on the battlefield. These are the factors of most direct importance to an operational commander. Even though the Army's sourcing decisions directly affect the resources available to an operational commander, the Army typically makes these decisions in a different setting, where other factors are also important. To understand this better, consider three different policy forums where the Army considers sourcing decisions: the Quadrennial Defense Review (QDR), the Total Army Analysis (TAA) process, and formal Army documents. Each highlights hazards and risks in different ways. After we review these alternatives, we will choose a set of risks that appear relevant across the venues in which policymakers make decisions that affect sourcing outcomes.

Quadrennial Defense Review

At a high level, the Quadrennial Defense Review (DoD, 2001, pp. 57–65) offers "a new, broad approach to risk management" that DoD can use to make decisions as it continues to transform itself. It promotes a strategy-driven balance across four related dimensions of risk:

- Force management—the ability to recruit, retain, and equip sufficient numbers of quality personnel and sustain the readiness of the force while accomplishing its many operational tasks. In our setting, for example, can the Army recruit and retain the personnel it needs to support the force on the battlefield? How does the use of contractors on the battlefield affect the Army's ability to train its personnel?
- Operational—the ability to achieve military objectives in a near-term conflict or other contingency. This factor is closest to those discussed above.
- Future challenges—the ability to invest in new capabilities and develop new operational concepts needed to dissuade or defeat mid- to long-term military challenges. Can the presence of contractors on the battlefield support ongoing efforts to develop and mature cutting-edge technology for the future force?
- Institutional—the ability to develop management practices and controls that use resources efficiently and promote the effective operation of the defense establishment. Institutional concerns,

by definition, address forces not present on the battlefield. But one might interpret this factor as asking how much the peacetime support of the force costs, how the use of contractors on the battlefield affects this peacetime cost, and, hence, how the use of contractors on the battlefield affects the availability of limited funds for other Army goals, such as modernizing the force.

These QDR "risks" are notable for the way they shadow DoD's high-level strategic goals. In effect, this definition views increased risk as a reduction in the likelihood of achieving any strategic goal. The approach we elaborate below adopts a similar view of risk.

Total Army Analysis

Within the Army, the TAA process asks how to structure the Army as a whole to get as much capability as possible from the military personnel available (Army Regulation [AR] 71-11, 1995).[4] It starts by identifying a set of missions given to the Army by higher-level guidance—from Congress and DoD. It ultimately links available military resources to these missions and identifies the level of risk associated with each mission, given the resources that the Army has placed against that mission.

Formal documentation of the TAA process contains very few explicit references to risk. In describing the third and penultimate phase of the TAA process, it states that this "qualitative analysis . . . provides the opportunity for the CINCs [now combatant commanders], [major commands (MACOMs)] or other staff agencies to present issues focusing on COMPO 4 (unresourced requirement), claimants versus bill-payers and priorities versus risks." AR 71-11 calls for participants to analyze and determine risk mitigation "through" or "in" the reduction of authorized levels of organization (ALOs). That is, it uses the fraction of required military force authorized for funding, captured in ALOs, to measure the level of risk associated with the

---

[4] This document prescribes objectives, procedures, and responsibilities for the TAA and associated force management activities.

force. By definition, the higher the ALOs in a portion of the force are, the lower the level of risk in that portion of the force.

This process currently gives no formal attention to risks specific to the use of contractors on the battlefield. Rather, in the TAA, the Army's assessment of "risk" depends on whether the Army can cover its assigned missions with its available active military, Reserve military, and National Guard military personnel. The TAA process always considers these components to be lower-risk than the alternatives. In effect, the TAA sees no need to compare the risks associated with military and other sources. It assumes them from the beginning without formal analysis. As currently structured, the TAA sourcing assessment process has no need for and cannot accommodate the Army's standard approach to assessing risk.

Formal Army Documents on Using Contractors on the Battlefield

Several Army documents specifically address contracting risks.[5] FM 100-21 offers the most complete discussion of risk assessment when it states that "the decision to use contractors in the area of operation requires an assessment of the risks posed to the contractor and his employees and the potential impacts on the operation itself" (FM 100-21, 2000, p. 2-4). A risk assessment should address four primary areas of concern (FM 100-21, 2000, pp. 2-4–2-6):

- Responsiveness of support. Commanders must evaluate the factors affecting performance that are not under the control of contractors, such as transportation and force protection. A contractor's responsiveness may depend, in part, on the structures in place to manage them on the battlefield.
- Transitioning from peace to war. First, the FM addresses the added requirement for force protection: "the commander must assess whether contractor support is vital enough to warrant the diversion of combat forces to contractor security duties." Sec-

[5] AR 700-137, 1985; Pamphlet 715-16, 1998; AR 100-10-2, 1999; AR 715-9, 1999; AMC Pamphlet 715-18, 1999; FM 100-21, 2000; DoD, 2001; FM 3-100.21, 2003.

ond, it addresses the preparedness of contractors to operate in a hostile environment and the need for training.

- Continuation of essential services. It calls for advance planning, leading to "the identification of the back-up source of support, the identification of resources necessary to enable the contractor to continue, or acceptance of the risk if the support is not provided."[6]
- Organic capacity, if it exists.

Looking across all of the pertinent documents, the policy relevance of a broader set of risks comes apparent. The four points above in effect capture elements of the risk summarized in the first point below:

- How much a contractor's performance contributes to mission success.
- How use of a contractor affects the safety of friendly personnel and loss of equipment, facilities, and property.
- How use of a contractor affects the consumption of funds that the Army needs to pursue other goals within its funding constraints.
- How use of a contractor affects the laws, regulations, and high-level policy guidance that an Army buyer must track and comply with.

The documents do not typically address the more mundane risk that a contract will simply cost more than expected. Nor do they tend to address broader risks, such as those relating to force management. The QDR guidance makes it clear that these elements of risk are

---

[6] As cited in FM 100-21 (2000), the Department of Defense (DODI 3020.37) requires plans and procedures to ensure the continuation of essential services, including the preparation of a contingency plan for obtaining services from alternative sources where a reasonable doubt exists that a contractor will continue to provide essential services.

important to broad Army decisions about where, when, and how to anticipate using contractors on the battlefield.

Risks to Consider in High-Level Assessments of Sourcing Options

These three brief descriptions tell us that the QDR, TAA, and formal Army documents on the use of contractors on the battlefield view risks in ways likely to yield very different recommendations about the use of contractors on the battlefield. The QDR puts such decisions in a broad policy setting. Formal Army documents emphasize the practical issues a commander in the field will likely face within the constraints in which he operates. The TAA view of risk always prefers military to contract sources on the battlefield. Which view of risk is most useful to the Army as a whole?

Our assessment of the documents above and other pertinent documents on recent Army use of contractors on the battlefield suggests that a high-level, Army-wide view should assess the risks associated with using contractors on the battlefield in terms of the effects of sourcing decisions on the following four factors:

- Current military performance, emphasizing responsiveness, transition from peace to war, and continuity of services.
- Safety of contractor personnel and loss of contractor material, facilities, and property in a contingency.[7]
- Dollar and manpower cost of resources used in a contingency.
- Other effects, of primary importance beyond military contingencies, including (among others) the following:
  - Future military performance, as reflected in the QDR.

---

[7] Discussions of the safety of personnel and other assets in-theater tend to focus on the safety of contractor personnel and other assets. These discussions include losses of military personnel and physical property as an integral part of military performance. Successful military performance achieves a specific goal against the enemy with an acceptable level of personnel and property losses, given the goal. Discussions that separate the safety of contractor personnel and property generally do not intend this separation to give contractor safety higher priority than the safety of military personnel and property. Some discussions do, however, argue that military and contractor organizations operate under qualitatively different rules and that the military rules tolerate higher losses than the civilian rules do. Our analytic approach takes no position on the relative importance of military and civilian losses.

— Force management issues raised by the QDR.
— Compliance issues raised in Army documents on the use of contractors on the battlefield.

We use these groups of risks to structure the analysis in the chapters that follow.

Note that, as in the QDR view of risk, each of these risks captures a particular high-level or strategic goal of the Army. The Army obviously seeks current military performance. However, for political and economic reasons unrelated to military performance, the Army also seeks to safeguard contractor personnel and other assets. It cares about dollar and manpower cost because the Army must decide which priorities to take care of with its limited resources, and reducing a source's cost increases what remains available to the Army to pursue other priorities. It also cares about a wide variety of other factors for a variety of reasons. In each case, the residual risk associated with a source tells the Army the likelihood that it can achieve each of its strategic goals if it uses that source. In this sense, a one-to-one mapping exists between the residual risks that the Army approach assesses and the Army's high-level, strategic goals.

Applying the Army Approach to Contractors on the Battlefield

To apply this standard Army approach to its use of contractors on the battlefield, we must define sourcing options as courses of action. In a sourcing setting, the definition of a course of action answers two types of questions:

- What particular CSS activity will the source provide, in what particular part of the battlefield, during what particular phase of the battle?
- How will the Army command structure its relationship with the source? This question addresses both details of how oversight

processes work together within the Army and how they ultimately relate to the source under review.

The two questions are related because the decision to use a contractor in a particular place, at a particular time, to do a particular thing, for example, will depend fundamentally on how the Army has structured its relationship with the contractor. The more risk of various kinds the Army can mitigate through an effective relationship, the more hazard the Army can expose the contractor to without experiencing unacceptable residual risks. Put another way, the harder it is for the Army to mitigate the effects of battlefield-related hazards through its oversight of a contractor, the more the Army will adjust placement, battle phase, and activity type on the battlefield to limit the residual risks associated with using a contractor.

The residual risks associated with any course of action depend on two very different sorts of considerations: the inherent quality of the source and the Army's arrangements to support the source and integrate it effectively with the rest of the force. Different courses of action might include the following:

- Sources from the Army active or reserve components, a sister service, host nation support, a long-term Army contractor, or a contractor identified in-theater as needed.
- Support concepts that place tasks in different parts of the theater or beyond it, with differing response times and levels of connectivity, reliability, and responsiveness.
- Contract administration concepts that maintain central visibility and oversight of contractors and other non-Army sources and integrate them with Army forces in different ways.
- Specific contractual terms that emphasize Army control of the contract process and inputs or focus on performance and measurement of output.
- Different levels of Army support for the contractor, beyond force protection, and different degrees of Army coordination of contractor access to local resources.

An Army risk analyst would evaluate these options in light of the military, political, and diplomatic challenges of the contingency in question; the past experience of the Army personnel expected to be engaged; and the sources available, with the terms of their existing contracts or other agreements with the Army.

Two observations become apparent immediately: First, in many ways, this defines the job of the staff preparing the logistics annex for the combatant commander's (COCOM's) operational plan. The logistics annex explains in some detail who will provide what, under what arrangements, to ensure that the commander's operational plan is feasible with acceptable risk. The discussion above simply gives special attention to one part of this broader problem—choosing when to use contractors and how to control them as an integral part of a broader campaign plan. From this perspective, the application of a standard Army risk assessment approach should simplify effective sourcing assessments as an integral part of broader Army planning efforts.

Second, the demands of such sourcing assessment would be overwhelming if a staff attempted to posit and evaluate all the alternative courses of action available. Rather, based on its experience and current capabilities, the staff must identify a small number of courses of action and apply risk management techniques to refine them quickly until a dominant solution emerges for the commander's final approval. The answers to the questions of where and when to use contractors and how to structure the Army's relationship with them during the contingency will drop out as integral parts of the overall support plan in the logistics annex.

In such a situation, it is easy to understand why a commander or command staff not familiar with the use of contractors on the battlefield would be reluctant to include them in the operational plan. If they do not know how to use contractors effectively, they probably make the right decision by relying on other alternatives, but learning to work with contractors can give them additional options. Risk management gives them a coherent and familiar way to think about these options.

The COCOM's planning activity is only one of many places where such sourcing assessment might occur. In fact, as we shall see, the COCOM's staff has very limited control over many Army sourcing decisions that dictate that contractors will appear on the battlefield. That said, a basic approach that works well in an operational setting is likely to have legitimacy elsewhere in the Army. Where sourcing assessment occurs, the Army's established approach to managing risk should be attractive because using it makes it easier to integrate the use of contractors into any overall support plan and helps Army planners less familiar with planning for the potential use of contractors assess the risks in a familiar way.

The next chapter summarizes recent arguments by Army personnel about what the Army's standard approach to risk assessment would call *hazards*, *risks*, and *mitigations* relevant to the use of contractors on the battlefield. These discussions highlight the factors that an Army risk assessor should address in Steps 1–3 of the risk management framework. By themselves, they do not give us all the information needed to determine the *residual risk* of a complete course of action, stated in terms of high-level goals relevant to the Army leadership. Chapter Four will refine these goals and offer a way to use them, in the standard Army approach presented here, to look across all the risks highlighted in the current debate.

CHAPTER THREE

How Army Use of Contractors Has Affected Risks on the Battlefield

When Army personnel discuss the use of contractors on the battlefield, a predictable set of arguments comes up again and again. Some of these arguments draw on direct personal experience with contractors in the past. Some draw on a broad lack of past institutional experience and a recognition that, without past experience, a commander will likely perform more effectively if supported by in-house capabilities, such as those she has experience with. Some simply imagine all the things that could go wrong with contract support. This chapter summarizes the arguments in the ongoing debate inside the Army. Appendices B and C provide a more detailed discussion of the arguments summarized here, with extensive annotation to the sources of these arguments. This chapter first examines the kinds of things that can go wrong when using contract support and then explains why Army commanders have almost always relied on some type of contract support despite these concerns.

Hazards and Risks Associated with Using Contractors on the Battlefield

Table 3.1 summarizes the arguments against using contractors on the battlefield and relates them to the risk management framework we proposed in Chapter Two.[1] The four columns display the strategic

[1] Appendix B provides a detailed, annotated discussion of each of these arguments.

goals relevant to Army use of contractors. Measures of risk and residual risk are ultimately relevant to the Army when they address the degree to which the Army can achieve mission success, keep contractor personnel and equipment safe, and limit resource costs in a particular contingency while also pursuing other high-level goals relevant outside any particular contingency. The rows display different hazards associated with using contractors on the battlefield. The table identifies these as "sources of concern" because, in plain English, that is how Army personnel think about them. They are legitimate "hazards" in the language of standard Army risk assessment. If the severity or the likelihood of any hazard increase, risks of the four types identified here can increase.

Although arguments in the Army are not always explicit about this, risks to the Army can increase despite its best efforts to mitigate the effects of these hazards. So the risks relevant to high-level decisionmaking are best thought of as *residual* risks—risks that remain despite the mitigation strategies the Army has applied to limit these effects. Similarly, arguments about risks are most meaningful if they speak of the *relative* residual risks that a hazard presents when a contract source is compared to a military source. In effect, Table 3.1 presents a summary of how various hazards are likely to affect residual risks relevant to the Army if the Army switches from using a military source to using a contractor source to provide a particular type of support.

When Army personnel speak of a "principal-agent" problem, they refer to the challenges that a principal faces when trying to induce its agent to do something the principal wants done. This source of hazard is inherent in any user-provider relationship, but key elements of government policy make the hazard larger with a contractor than with a military source. With a military source, a commander principal can use the standard command-and-control mechanisms of the Army to induce the military agent to perform. With a contract source, a commander principal faces many constraints in its control over the contract agent. The commander can only ask for things identified in a scope of work negotiated earlier, can only ask through

Table 3.1
Hazards and Risks Associated with Using Contractors on the Battlefield

	Residual Risks or Strategic Goals			
Source of Concern About Using Contractor	**Mission Success**	**Contractor Safety**	**Resource Cost**	**Effects Outside Contingency**
Principal-agent problems	Hurt user-provider alignment	Limited control of personnel off duty	Oversight mechanisms can be costly	Mitigation efforts face legal limitations
Chaotic battlefield	Allows more opportunistic behavior	Exposure to danger rises	Opportunistic behavior can raise cost	
Cannot force performance	Allows less control over performance		Maintaining alternatives costs money	Mitigation efforts face legal limitations
Status of employees under international law	Can discourage reliable participation		May require wage premium	
Burden on Army	Diverts military forces, leadership attention	Safety improves as Army commits more resources	Additional tactical reserves increase costs	
International agreements	May limit use of contractors		Tariffs, taxes, licenses on contractors raise cost	Mitigation efforts face treaty limitations
Organic to contract transition	Complicates continuity of support	Exposure rises during turbulent transition	Turbulence can raise cost	
Controls on contractors	Limit contract performance	Can reduce exposure to danger	Can raise labor, operating costs	Controls can be incompatible with acquisition reform
Catastrophic loss of government control	Contract sources are inherently vulnerable		Inescapable dependence can drive up costs	Dependence can wipe out training capability, career fields, expertise

NOTE: Hazards may also affect risks in the blank cells of the table, but such effects are likely to be smaller and of less interest to policymakers than those shown on the table.

a contract officer, and cannot compel a contract employee to do anything without going through this kind of chain of command. As a result, military decisionmakers worry that using a contract source rather than a military source is likely to increase the consequences, in magnitude and likelihood, of the principal-agent problems inherent in any user-provider relationship. The user-provider alignment is likely to fall, reducing the probability of mission success. Because a military commander has no direct control over what contract personnel do when not on duty, the commander has only a limited ability to protect their safety away from formal work sites. To avoid these problems, the commander may mitigate risk by imposing additional controls that cost money, but the commander is ultimately legally limited in what actions he can take to mitigate this risk. On balance, then, following mitigation actions taken when a contract source replaces a military source, that change is likely to have the effects on residual risk shown in the table.

When a battlefield becomes more chaotic or violent, Army personnel worry that residual risks are likely to rise if the Army switches from a military to a contract source. In effect, they argue that chaos intensifies the principal-agent problem by making it harder for a principal to hold an agent accountable for performance promised. It becomes harder for the principal to detect what the agent is actually doing. Because the goals and values of a military principal and contractor agent differ more than those of a military principal and military agent, a loss of accountability is likely to lead to more serious problems if the source is a contractor than if it is a military unit. That is, a contract source is likely to increase its opportunistic behavior more as chaos rises than a military source would.

As Table 3.1 indicates, increased opportunistic behavior is likely to reduce the probability of mission success and increase the resource cost of achieving success. As chaos rises, the danger to contractor employees and equipment is also likely to rise. The Army attempts to add controls in a more chaotic setting to limit these effects, but these controls themselves will divert the leadership from its primary military goals and add resource costs. So, even with an optimal mitigation strategy, residual risks rise as indicated.

In an undeclared war, contractor personnel are not subject to the Uniform Code of Military Justice (UCMJ). Army personnel consider a commander's inability to force contract performance in an undeclared war such a serious problem that we highlight this aspect of the principal-agent problem. Even if a commander could legally direct contract personnel to do something, the commander would have no immediate recourse if they refused to comply. The commander could only take the issue to court and/or terminate the contract for nonperformance. Neither option provides the immediate performance that can be critical on a battlefield. The commander faces no such problem with a military source. So, replacing a military source with a contract source adds a hazard of nonperformance on the battlefield. The Army can mitigate the effects of this hazard by maintaining alternatives—military or other contract sources—but such reserve capabilities are costly and the law limits the mitigation actions the Army can take. Following mitigation, shifting from a military source to a contractor source is likely to increase residual risks as shown in the table.

International law does not afford contract personnel the same protections that it affords military personnel, especially as the contract personnel perform tasks more and more like those performed by the combat personnel who actually employ weapons. International law calls for warring parties to treat civilian personnel accompanying an armed force as prisoners of war and not as unlawful combatants or criminals as long as the personnel do not present themselves in specific, stated ways as an organized military force and carry credentials that clearly identify their role and status on the battlefield. Unfortunately, the clearly stated language of the Hague and Geneva Conventions that defines these rules is hard to implement in an unambiguous way in any particular contingency. The ambiguity rises when a contract employee looks more and more like a warfighter. This ambiguity can limit contractor personnel's willingness to undertake specific tasks in specific parts and phases of a battle, complicating the military commander's principal-agent challenge. The commander can mitigate this problem by offering more money for service and by changing command-and-control arrangements to use contractors only where these issues do not arise. Such mitigation inherently reduces the likelihood of military success and increases the cost of control from the levels that the Army would associate with a military source.

Army personnel recognize that contractors are rarely self-sufficient in-theater. The Army often provides contractors with equipment, training services, theater entrance services, medical and mortuary services, and force protection. The Army provides the same services to military personnel entering a theater, but it is likely that contractors will require more incremental training and equipment and, especially, more force protection, than military personnel, who have already been trained to operate in combat circumstances and are equipped to protect themselves. This difference creates a differential burden that decisionmakers associate with the use of contractors on the battlefield. The differential support the Army provides to contractors diverts military resources and focus from more immediate mission concerns, reducing the likelihood of mission success, and may also force the Army to deploy additional tactical reserves to provide force protection for contractors when called on. The Army does these things to reduce the exposure of contractor personnel and equipment to danger. These actions generate the residual risks shown in Table 3.1. Note that the hazard that generates these risks flows directly from the Army's mitigation strategy to reduce the risks associated with other hazards.

Status of Forces Agreements (SOFAs) define the grounds on which the U.S. Army can enter other countries. Their conditions typically address what contractors the Army can bring or employ; what local laws the Army and its contractors are subject to; what taxes, tariffs, and other fees they most pay; and so on. The United States has comprehensive SOFAs with only a limited number of countries, typically where it already has a military presence. Elsewhere, SOFAs must be crafted quickly as contingency-specific military planning and operations begin unless the Army simply forcibly enters the country. The absence of SOFAs creates two problems relevant to Army use of contractors: It typically limits their use and raises their cost to the Army before a SOFA is completed, and it creates uncertainty about what any SOFA negotiated in the future will say about the treatment of contractors once it is complete. Neither problem is as severe for purely military support forces.

These problems create an inherent advantage for military over contractor sources. Army personnel worry that contractor sources are likely to be less capable of contributing to mission success and to cost more than military sources. Existing treaties limit the Army's ability to mitigate these disadvantages. Hence, the residual risks shown in Table 3.1.

One way to mitigate risks caused by chaos early in a campaign and by uncertainty about the status of contractors early in a campaign is to rely on military support personnel early and hand support tasks off to contractor personnel as the theater stabilizes and diplomatic agreements are finalized. Army personnel recognize that this mitigation strategy generates its own hazards, which flow from the difficulty of achieving continuity of support during a handoff. This becomes easier, less costly, and less critical to mission success as the Army force in question achieves more experience with using contractors, as a theater becomes more stable where the handoff occurs, and as contractor support affects services farther from the warfighter. The hazard of a handoff from one institutional form to another does not even present itself if military personnel retain a support mission without ever using contractors. Hence, the residual risks shown in Table 3.1.

Another way to mitigate risks associated with relying on a contractor is to impose controls on how the contractor performs its tasks. For example, the Army could require the presence of specific types of personnel, equipment, and information systems, in specific numbers. The Army could require the use of specific certified processes. The Army could even require use of personnel in an Army reserve component so that a contractor's operation could be mobilized and militarized in a contingency. Such mitigation actions create a hazard that Army personnel often overlook. By restricting how a contractor performs, they limit the contractor's ability to innovate and increase how much it can perform on the battlefield with a given set of resources. This hazard presents itself only when the Army chooses such mitigation actions. In effect, decisionmakers support actions that impose a penalty on the Army's ability to achieve mission success and increase its costs because these actions have positive effects elsewhere in the Army. These residual risks are differential relative to those of a military source because the Army does not employ such a mitigation strategy with military sources.

A final concern Army personnel raise is that, by relying on a contract source, the Army can experience a catastrophic loss of control that could not occur with a military source. In the short term, a monopoly contract provider could simply walk away or demand extortionate compensation to perform. Or the owners of a critical contractor source could withhold its availability for political, diplomatic, or other reasons. In the long run, the Army can lose the skills and processes it needs to perform tasks that it contracts for, potentially forcing it to settle for less desirable performance than it could have ensured in-house in the past. It may also lose functional skills relevant to contract oversight or to career fields that other parts of the Army have relied on. Once the Army loses such capabilities, the cost of recreating them may be so high that the Army accepts a long-term deficit in its capability level and operating costs. Hence, the residual risks shown in Table 3.1.

In sum, many good reasons exist to prefer military to contractor sources in the Army. More often than not, the arguments above point to things that *can* go wrong rather than things that *have* gone wrong or *will* go wrong if the Army relies on a contract. But the weight of the arguments all points in one direction. This raises the natural question of why the Army relies on any contract sources. In fact, Army personnel can identify many ways that the use of contractors on the battlefield actually reduces the residual risks that we have been discussing.

Reducing Risk by Using Contractors on the Battlefield

Table 3.2 summarizes the arguments in favor of using contractors on the battlefield and relates them to the risk management framework we proposed in Chapter Two.[2] It is analogous to Table 3.1 with one important difference. Table 3.1 focused on the relative residual risk associated with using a contract source rather than using a military source. Table 3.2 more often addresses the effects on residual risk of adding a contractor source to a contingency force while holding everything else constant. The difference is important, because the benefits of using contractors discussed below often stem from the constraints under which contingencies occur. These constraints typically do not allow a commander to choose between a military and contract source, but only between the presence and absence of a contract source. In this setting, the "hazards" presented in the rows of the table tend to be constraints that contractors can help the Army overcome. We refer to these hazards as "motivations for using contractors" because, in each row, the use of contractors mitigates the consequences of a hazard that the Army faces as a consequence of a constraint that it cannot or will not remove. This is not always true in Table 3.2. We will indicate where a commander has greater freedom to choose.

Over the last 15 years, the size of the active force has fallen even as deployment demands on the force have risen. Given the size of the force and the demands on it, both factors beyond the Army's own control, Army personnel believe that, by adding contract support to the force, the Army can increase its likelihood of mission success. This benefit can occur in two ways. It can occur if the Army either adds contract support to a deployed military force of given size or replaces deployed personnel with contractors so that a fixed force of military personnel need not deploy as often or as long. This second benefit accrues by helping the Army retain higher-quality active military personnel in the force over the longer term—perhaps beyond the planning horizon of any one contingency.

Adding contractor personnel and equipment exposes them to additional danger and increases the Army's dollar costs. But on net,

---

[2] Appendix C provides a detailed, annotated discussion of each of these arguments.

Table 3.2
Reducing Risk by Using Contractors on the Battlefield

	Residual Risks or Strategic Goals			
Motivation for Using Contractors	**Mission Success**	**Contractor Safety**	**Resource Cost**	**Effects Outside Contingency**
Smaller force, more missions	Supplements military force	Increases exposure to danger	Increases dollar cost	Mitigates retention problems
Low-density, high-demand skills	Enhances military capability	Increases exposure to danger	Increases dollar cost	
Need for high-technology skills	Enhances military capability	Increases exposure to danger	Increases dollar cost	
Spiral development	Enhances military capability	Increases exposure to danger	Increases dollar cost	Supports acquisition goals
Cost-effective commercial capabilities	Enhances military capability	Increases exposure to danger	Increases dollar cost	Increases political support from private sources
Dependence on reserves	Allows more CSS in mission	Increases exposure to danger	Increases dollar cost	Reduces political costs of mobilizing reserves
Limited airlift capacity	Supplements airlifted force	Increases exposure to danger	Increases dollar cost	
Troop ceilings	Supplements military force	Increases exposure to danger	Increases dollar cost	Supports political, diplomatic agreements
Lower military profile	Supplements military force	Increases exposure to danger	Increases dollar cost	Supports diplomatic agreements

NOTE: Hazards may also affect risks in the blank cells, but such effects are likely to be smaller and of less interest to policymakers than those shown in the table.

the Army chooses to add contractors because these increases in residual risk are less important than the increased likelihood of current and future mission success. This decision is easier to justify when contract personnel face smaller dangers in-theater and when the Army can control their costs more effectively and the net gain is large enough to offset the inherent risks, discussed above, of relying on contractors for support.

The Army cannot justify maintaining a large enough fleet of certain systems to justify sustaining a military career field that can support them. For example, the Army has relied on contractor support of the Guardrail surveillance aircraft for this reason, even though the aircraft was in high demand. Given the decision to limit the number of systems and in-house support for them, contractor support can enhance military capabilities, even though doing so increases the danger contractor personnel and equipment face and the monetary cost to the Army. The Army may also simply find itself with a smaller military capability that it needs at any time. Arabic interpreters are an example today; linguists in many languages are considered a critical shortage. Where such shortages exist, the Army can use contractor personnel to increase the likelihood of mission success in spite of the offsetting problems of exposure to danger and higher dollar costs.

Given its military personnel policies, the Army has difficulty retaining personnel with the skills and experience it increasingly requires to support increasingly sophisticated weapon and information systems. Given these policies, the Army benefits from adding contractor support because the likelihood of mission success, today and in the future, rises enough to offset additional dangers for contractor personnel and higher monetary costs for the Army. This is a case where the Army not only adds contractor personnel but also can and does actually replace military personnel with contractor personnel for the reasons above.

Defense acquisition policies that promote spiral development increase the need for highly skilled personnel in-theater for two reasons. First, spiral development fields systems before their support plans have stabilized enough to develop traditional technical orders. As a result, maintenance technicians need a broad enough understanding of the systems they support to proceed without detailed instructions on how to do so. Second, spiral development assumes ongoing collection of operational data to allow continuing system upgrades. Such data collection is more effective in a development regime without a stable design when the personnel collecting the data know enough to help development engineers who will receive the data understand the context in which they were collected. The first reason addresses immediate mission success; the second addresses broader acquisition goals in the Army as a whole. Contract personnel can offer attractive alternatives to military personnel on both scores, even if they face dangerous circumstances in-theater.

More broadly, Army support activities with close commercial analogs often simply cannot keep up with the rapid pace of innovation in the much larger, dynamically competitive commercial sector. Here, the Army may replace military personnel with contractor personnel simply because contractor personnel perform better at a lower cost, despite the principal-agent and other problems inherent in using a contract source. Army personnel recognize that government contractors are a politically potent constituency that tends to overstate such advantages in political channels to get access to government contracts. The Army can often resist such pressure to ensure that a contract source really can enhance the Army's likelihood of achieving mission success, today and in the future, more than an organic source can.

Since the mid-1970s, the Army has relied heavily on its reserve components to provide CSS when the Army deployed. As long as the pace of deployment was moderate, the Army could mobilize reserve forces as needed without endangering its ability to sustain its reserve components. High deployment rates make the continuing use of reserve CSS capabilities more problematic, both politically and from the perspective of reserve personnel retention. If political and retention concerns limit the Army's access to reserve CSS capabilities, contractor personnel offer an available alternative that enhances the likelihood of mission success enough to offset higher exposure to danger for contract personnel and higher dollar costs to the Army. An alternative way to frame this sourcing decision is to suggest that, when the Army substitutes a contract source for a reserve military source, it can benefit from lower residual risks associated with reserve component goals that transcend the goals in the theater.

The Army does not control the level of military and contract airlift available in any contingency. Given the airlift the Army is allocated in any contingency, it can focus its use of airlift on the activities most important to its mission success by relying on either local or regional contract support that does not require airlift support or global contract support that arranges its own strategic airlift. Given the conditions the Army faces, contract support can enhance its likelihood of mission success enough to offset the additional danger contractor personnel face and the additional cost to the Army. This is particularly true when policymakers worry less about the safety of non-American contract personnel than about American lives.

Similarly, the Army does not control troop ceilings that political leaders impose on deployments for a variety of diplomatic and political reasons. Given these ceilings and the portion of a ceiling allocated to the Army in any contingency, the Army can focus its use of its portion on the activities most important to its mission success by relying on contractor support, which is typically not covered by such ceilings. Given the conditions the Army faces, contract support can enhance its likelihood of mission success enough to offset the additional danger contractor personnel face and the additional cost to the Army. Again, this is particularly true when policymakers worry less about the safety of non-American contract personnel than about American lives.

Even in the absence of a formal troop ceiling, the combatant commander may decide to maintain a low military presence in-theater to achieve certain diplomatic or local political goals. Such an approach may become increasingly important in security and stabilization operations where a low military profile may support effective nation building. Use of local or American contractor personnel offers the Army the same benefits here that it does in the presence of a formal troop ceiling.

Summary

Army personnel have a great deal to say about the pros and cons of using contractors on the battlefield. On the one hand, they can identify many things that inherently favor the use of military personnel over contractor personnel in many support activities. The principal-agent problem and a military commander's inherent inability to control contractor sources as well as he can control military sources lie at the heart of many of these arguments. On the other, they can explain why it is completely rational for the Army to use contract support, as it has always done, in specific circumstances. For the most part, these explanations turn on an argument that contract support allows the Army to offset the negative effects of resource constraints imposed on it by outside actors or by history.

To integrate these arguments, we need a system view of the forces that influence Army sourcing decisions that can place each of these arguments in a broader, internally consistent perspective. In particular, this system view should help us understand how the Army's efforts to mitigate risks in one place create hazards elsewhere with consequences that the Army must also mitigate and, ideally, should weigh against the initial risks that induced the Army to create these hazards in the first place. The residual risks of ultimate importance to the Army should be the risks that remain after all these mitigations relevant to a source decision have been accounted for and examined. We turn to the construction of such a system view in the next chapter.

CHAPTER FOUR

Using Risk Considerations to Frame a Sourcing Decision: Analytic Preliminaries

The information presented in the last chapter is characteristic of what Army personnel know today about risks associated with using contractors on the battlefield. We can summarize the character of this information as follows:

- It is rich but not quantitative or even systematically based on the Army's extensive experience with contractors. Rather, it captures the wisdom of many knowledgeable practitioners about specific hazards and risks associated with using contractors.
- It contains important insights into many causal relationships, but it does not map these to show how all of these hazards and risks relate to one another or to the higher-level strategic goals relevant to Army sourcing policy.

As a result, the information presented, by itself, is difficult to apply to support specific sourcing decisions. If anything, the form of most discussions of the use of contractors on the battlefield tends to select a number of the points discussed above and use them in an informal way to develop specific recommendations on when and how to use contractors on the battlefield. Many of these discussions are useful and may be adequate for the specific issues they address, but none points to a systematic way for the Army to approach the general challenge to deciding where, when, and how to use contractors on the battlefield. Without such an approach, the Army cannot ensure that its policy decisions relevant to sourcing outcomes are internally consistent and work together toward common strategic goals.

This and the next two chapters seek an approach that can yield such strategic coherence in Army sourcing policy. This chapter highlights the strategic goals relevant to such analysis. It highlights the basic considerations that will likely condition sourcing decisions about specific activities. It then suggests that sourcing decisions should proceed in two steps.

The first step identifies a series of key assumptions that the policymaker responsible for a specific sourcing decision cannot control. They concern such factors as the nature of contingencies to be faced, the size of the Army, the amount of airlift likely to be available to the Army, the relevance of spiral development, the type of compensation policy the Army will use for military personnel, and so on. The first step asks how to choose between a contract and military source when all of these assumptions continue to hold. Chapter Five proposes a checklist to gather the information relevant to such a decision.

The second step then reviews the assumptions held constant in the first step and asks which might be revisited in light of concerns about the use of contractors on the battlefield. It asks how sourcing decisions between a contract and military source could change if specific assumptions changed. Chapter Six explores the issues that arise when we consider relaxing "nonsourcing" constraints that often appear to drive sourcing decisions today.

This chapter summarizes the basic analytic perspective we use to pursue these two steps. To inform sourcing decisions on the battlefield, this analysis uses a comparative approach, emphasizing the *relative residual risk* associated with contractor and military sources for CSS activities on the battlefield. It emphasizes four aspects of risk and highlights five considerations likely to heavily influence sourcing decisions on the battlefield. It posits three perspectives for such analysis and chooses two for closer attention. This approach leads to a form of risk assessment that can support sourcing decisions relevant to the force as a whole. That is, the ultimate intent of the assessment described here is, for any particular activity, to ask what mix of contractor and military capability is likely to be appropriate for the Army as a whole to seek to meet the contingencies it anticipates over an appropriate planning horizon.

Comparing Specific Alternatives

The approach proposed here is comparative throughout. Even when the text does not state this explicitly, it intends to compare a contract and military source. For each alternative type of source, the analysis identifies risks and mitigations that can ameliorate these risks. Mitigations can generate risks of their own, which the analyst must track. That is, as analysis proceeds, the analyst attempts to offer and then assume mitigations that drive down the *unnecessary* risk associated with each sourcing alternative under review. The final choice will compare the *residual* risks associated with each option and so will be between, not just two sources, but also two sets of mitigations that yield the best outcomes for each source. The final decision compares the residual risk associated with each alternative and chooses the alternative with the lowest residual risk.[1]

Four Aspects of Risk

We cannot summarize the residual risk of a sourcing alternative in a single measure that can be used to compare all sourcing alternatives. Based on the discussion in Chapter Two, we choose to highlight four different aspects of risk to sourcing decisions on the battlefield:

- Current military performance or readiness. What is the probability of a shortfall in military performance and, if it occurs, how severe is the shortfall?

---

[1] The Army, of course, has many potential sources for relevant CSS. As noted above, this report focuses on only two, characterized at a high level—military and contract. Although we do not attempt it here, we see no serious barriers to extending the analysis offered here to consider a broader set of sources in the future.

- Safety of personnel and equipment in the contractor organization. What is the probability of captivity, injury, death, or damage and, if it occurs, how severe are the consequences?[2]
- Cost of resources used to support a contingency. What is the probability of high costs and, if they occur, how high will they be?
- Other effects, relevant to such factors as future military performance, force management, and compliance with the law. What is the probability that these effects will be worse than planned and, if so, how much worse will they be?

Different decisionmakers will have different priorities among these aspects of risk, and priorities are likely to vary in different circumstances. The main goal is to clarify how source decisions are likely to affect risk in these four dimensions in a way that will help decisionmakers make choices about sourcing that are more nearly compatible with their high-level goals.

To assess the comparative risks of contractor and military sources, a risk analyst must make assumptions about all the mitigations that accompany a sourcing decision. The assumptions about mitigations will depend in turn on assumptions, if only implicit, about the relative importance of the four dimensions above. If the analyst assumes that cost has high relative importance, she will choose mitigations for each alternative source relevant to the decision that limit the probability of experiencing high costs and, if they occur, the level of costs. This will yield a different set of mitigations than an assumption that cost is unimportant compared to current military capability. It could also very well yield a different sourcing decision.

In sum, although we do not formalize the relative importance of the four dimensions relevant to a sourcing decision, an analyst using the approach proposed here must apply assumptions about relative importance. They should reflect the likely priorities of the decisionmakers whom the analysis supports. If the analyst does not know

---

[2] Again, this approach captures the safety of military personnel as an integral part of military performance.

those preferences, it may be appropriate to apply sensitivity analysis to show how different priorities can drive the final sourcing decision.

Five Considerations Likely to Affect Sourcing Decisions

The arguments of Army personnel summarized in Chapter Three (and annotated in Appendices B and C) suggest that the four aspects of risk associated with any alternative are likely to depend on the following five factors:

Type of Support Activity. Some activities are far more important to mission success that others. As a result, some pose far larger risks to mission success than others. Support of the network that links the personnel in a Stryker combat team poses far higher risks than support of accounting for bills of lading in a port of entry.

Type or Identity of Source. Sources using American citizens pose different issues from those using host nation support employees. Host nation support employees can present hazards to the Army that American employees do not; the Army may treat the safety of American employees as more important than the safety of host nation support employees. Some specific sources have unique capabilities or have reputations as partners with DoD. For example, the Windows operating system has unique capabilities different from those of Macintosh or Linux. For many years, because it viewed General Electric as a more cooperative and responsive provider than Pratt and Whitney, the Air Force applied much more detailed oversight to Pratt than to General Electric contracts (Crocker and Reynolds, 1993). For some activities, government and private rights and responsibilities differ in ways that complicate using a contractor to provide service equivalent to what the government can provide. For example, government duties with respect to civil rights, labor standards, and regulatory compliance inherently differ from the duties of a private firm performing exactly the same service, even if the private firm performs the service for a government buyer. Such differences can create risks for a contract source that are inherently not present with a government source.

Nature of the Contingency. An enemy with effective heavy armor and missiles poses a set of hazards to plan against different from that of an enemy who uses primarily light infantry and nonconventional forces. A campaign expected to be fought primarily from fixed bases poses sets of hazards to plan against different from those of a campaign that envisions high mobility and long, lightly defended supply lines.

Location and Battle Phase Within a Contingency for a Source. The hazards to plan against are far higher if a source of support services accompanies a highly mobile, fairly self-sufficient force than if the source provides CSS remote from the fighting and the warfighter reaches back for this support. The hazards are higher if the source is in the theater during heavy combat rather than waiting for hostilities to subside to support stabilization activities.

Quality of Government Oversight for the Source. The hazards relevant to a sourcing decision are lower if the government activities that oversee a source have solid experience with such oversight and the know-how to design and administer a control plan during a contingency than if they do not.

These considerations by themselves can govern many sourcing decisions. For example, consider the two courses of action portrayed in Table 4.1 and defined in terms of the five considerations above.[3] Course of action one represents an extreme case in which every consideration favors the use of a contractor. Course of action two represents the other extreme. Every consideration favors using an Army unit. Such cases require little analysis. More often, the considerations relevant to a course of action will give mixed findings and require additional assessment. Chapter Five explains how to identify where these five considerations affect factors relevant to a sourcing decision and how to compare their effects on the relative residual risk of using a contract source.

---

[3] The first consideration appears in the first row. The second appears in rows two and three. The third appears in row four. The fourth appears in rows five and six. The fifth appears in row seven.

Table 4.1
Simple Comparison of Two Extreme Courses of Action

Attribute of Course of Action	Course of Action One	Course of Action Two
Type of activity	Administrative office support	Hands-on repair of combat damage in the field
Relative quality of contract product	Unique, proprietary process with demand for high-tech skills	Standard process manned by lower-skilled retired military personnel
Relative responsiveness of contract source	Highly regarded as a cooperative partner seeking long-term mutual gain	Known to look for government weaknesses to exploit
Nature of contingency	Stable, low-intensity peacekeeping	Unstable, high-intensity, with uncertain outcome
Location of source	Short flight from the theater in another country	In the personnel carriers with the troops
Battle phase for source	After the fighting is over and stabilization is secure	In the heat of combat, before resolution
Relative quality of oversight	Highly experienced, well trained, well resourced	Little experience with contractors or support to oversee them
Sourcing decision	Use a contractor	Use an Army unit

Decision Perspective

Any sourcing decision depends on assumptions about what can change as part of the sourcing decision. Consider three different perspectives.

Short-Term. The Army deploys on short notice in a come-as-you-are contingency. It does not have time to craft anything special for the contingency and must decide immediately what portions of the support plan contractors will provide.

Midterm Constrained. The Army takes as given a set of policies that transcend sourcing decisions and then seeks to determine where contract support should occur within a force that pursues these policies. In effect, sourcing outcomes are not considered important enough to revisit and adjust any of these policies, despite their effects on sourcing decisions. The policies held constant are the following:

- Downsized force, despite a continuing high demand for deployment
- Total-force policy that continues to hold a large share of the Army's military CSS capability in its reserve components
- Persistent limits on airlift capacity
- Persistent requirement for high-level skills to support new systems on the battlefield
- Persistent application of spiral development to new systems on the battlefield
- Persistent application of troop ceilings and diplomatic preference for low military profile
- Stable military personnel management and compensation policies.

Long-Term Unconstrained. The Army concludes that it would be worth adjusting the policies in midterm point described above to reduce its use of contractors on the battlefield. When this occurs, changes in policies unrelated to sourcing can yield outcomes that in effect change sourcing decisions in their own right. The key here is ensuring that the Army weighs the gains from a sourcing outcome against the losses it experiences when it adjusts a policy that it has supported in the past for unrelated reasons.

The first perspective is very important in the moment that sourcing decisions are made, but it is too restrictive to give much attention here. In effect, it assumes that the factors that drive many sourcing outcomes in the Army today are simply not open to examination. Chapter Five focuses on the more traditional sourcing decisions that arise in the second perspective. Chapter Six then asks what to expect when priorities associated with sourcing decisions compete with the priorities that drive other, apparently unrelated policies.

Planning Horizon and Relevant Contingencies

The most attractive thing about the first perspective above is that it has a clear planning horizon and associated contingency—the next contingency up, starting immediately and continuing through the end of the contingency. The second and third perspectives are more interesting because they have a broader purview. This breadth poses the serious challenge of asking which contingencies are relevant to a sourcing decision and how differences in contingencies should affect sourcing decisions.

The TAA faces exactly the same challenge, in part because it is a sourcing decision process itself, asking how to commit different kinds of military units against contingencies to make the force as capable as possible. The analysis proposed here would benefit from a similar perspective (AR-71-11, 1995). Following the lead of the TAA, at least conceptually, this sourcing analysis would consider a "simultaneity stack" of contingencies that captures the Army's mission as stated in defense planning guidance documents. The simultaneity stack is a list of missions that the Army could reasonably be expected to execute simultaneously at the end of the Future Years Defense Program (FYDP) relevant to a particular TAA cycle. Examples relevant to the use of contractors on the battlefield currently include a specific set of contingencies that range from low-demand peacekeeping operations to high-risk major combat operations.[4]

Given a list of missions that might reasonably arise simultaneously, a risk assessment of the use of contractors would then ask how many of these missions pose relative risks of using contractors that favor plans to rely on contractors. Because relative risks will depend on the five considerations above (type of activity, type or identity of contract, nature of contingency, location and battle phase for source within a contingency, and quality of government oversight), an assessment of sourcing for any particular activity will often suggest that a portion of the required force could be filled by military organizations and another portion by contractor organizations. Together, when facing the complete list of simultaneous contingencies relevant to Army planning, these organizations could place military personnel in situations where the relative risk of using contractors favors mili-

[4] Details on these contingencies are classified. They are included in the rules of engagement for the current round of TAA, TAA-11.

tary personnel and contractor personnel in situations where the relative risk of using contractors favors contractors.

Summary

Table 4.2 summarizes the proposed approach.[5] The next two chapters apply this approach to compare courses of action for alternative sources of activities on the battlefield. They explore the effects of

Table 4.2
Summary of the Proposed Approach

No.	Proposed Step
1.	Choose "simultaneous" contingencies relevant to the appropriate planning horizon.
2.	For each contingency, develop a course of action that places each CSS activity, in time and location, on the battlefield. Do this for a contract source and a military source.
3.	For each source of an activity in each contingency, assess the residual risk relevant to mission success, employee safety, resource cost, and effects outside individual contingencies. Compare these to determine the relative residual risk of using a contract rather than a military source to provide a particular activity on the battlefield.
4.	In the course of this assessment, consider the importance of activity, type or identity of contractor, type of contingency, location and battle phase on the battlefield, and oversight arrangements.
5.	Drawing on the assessments above, determine the most appropriate mix of military and contractor sources, in the Army as a whole, for each CSS activity.

[5] This approach so nearly parallels the standard approach that TAA uses that it could be appropriate to conduct such assessments in the context of the TAA process itself. To do this, TAA would have to accommodate a very different view of risk than it uses today. Alternatively, this analysis could simply draw on the simultaneity stack developed by the TAA to identify the specific missions that the Army associates with any particular CSS activity. Contractors on the battlefield either accompany military units as manufacturers' field technicians for the systems that the units own or substitute for military units to provide specific CSS support at echelons above corps. For any particular activity, data from the TAA process should be able to identify how large the activity needs to be to support a particular mission and, for major combat operations, where that activity occurs on the battlefield through the course of a contingency.

these courses of action on the four aspects of risk discussed above. In doing so, they give close attention to the five considerations likely to affect sourcing decisions. Chapter Five looks at traditional sourcing decisions. Chapter Six looks at broader policy decisions that can affect sourcing outcomes on the battlefield.

CHAPTER FIVE

Using Risk Considerations to Frame a Traditional Sourcing Decision

The discussion of Army personnel perspectives in Chapter Three argues that sourcing decisions in the Army are driven by perceived risks and constraints relevant to the activities sourced. The analysis of "traditional" sourcing decisions here maintains a large number of constraints that, by themselves, may drive sourcing outcomes. It leaves room for considerable exploration of mitigations. The exact time horizon used to frame this approach depends on how much time the Army takes to implement mitigations. To accommodate a range of options, the analysis refers to "current" capabilities, which look very much like what the Army has today, and "future" capabilities, which might apply, for example, in the last year of the FYDP relevant to current planning. In the end, sourcing decisions depend heavily on how much mitigation exists today and how much more is plausible over the relevant planning horizon.

This chapter opens with a brief summary of the sequence of reasoning we have distilled from the material on the perspectives of Army personnel in Chapter Three. It then walks through a checklist that elaborates on this sequence of reasoning and applies it to identify the information most relevant to traditional sourcing decisions. The checklist also helps organize this information for application to a final sourcing decision. The chapter closes with a discussion of several points that become apparent as we walk through the checklist.

A Brief Summary of the Sequence of Reasoning Used Here

The analysis uses the perspectives of Army personnel discussed in Chapter Three to structure a checklist of questions about how contract and military sources are likely to compare in particular situations. Figure 5.1 summarizes the sequence of reasoning distilled from the perspectives in Chapter Three that underlies this checklist. Despite its apparent complexity, it is fairly easy for an analyst to walk through the relationships identified in Figure 5.1, weighing mitigation options as he or she goes.

The basic sequence of reasoning behind the figure is discussed in the following paragraphs.

The boxes in the column in the upper left identify reasons for the Army to use contractors on the battlefield. Unless such reasons exist, a sourcing decision is not interesting, so this is the first logical place to look. The boxes in the column in the upper right capture factors relevant to the ease of using contractors effectively in-theater. This is where the primary opportunities for mitigating risk exist. These opportunities explain why the right column looks more complicated than the left column. The three heavily outlined boxes at the bottom—labeled *mission success*, *resource cost*, and *effects outside contingency*—represent the final aspects of risk that have no necessary intermediate effects on other aspects of risk.

Sourcing decisions depend on the *relative residual risk* of contractor and military sources, defined in terms of *mission success*, *employee safety*, *resource cost*, and *effects outside contingency*.[1] The figure highlights these four aspects of risk in heavily outlined boxes. A number of boxes appear within the heavily outlined box for *effects outside contingency* to highlight the diverse nature of considerations that the Army needs to track here.

---

[1] For simplicity in the figure the discussion of the checklist, we summarize the safety of all contractor assets in terms of "employee safety." Where contractor assets other than employees are relevant to a sourcing decision, the checklist accommodates them wherever it mentions employee safety.

Figure 5.1
How Major Risks Associated with Using Contractors on the Battlefield Relate to Higher-Level Goals

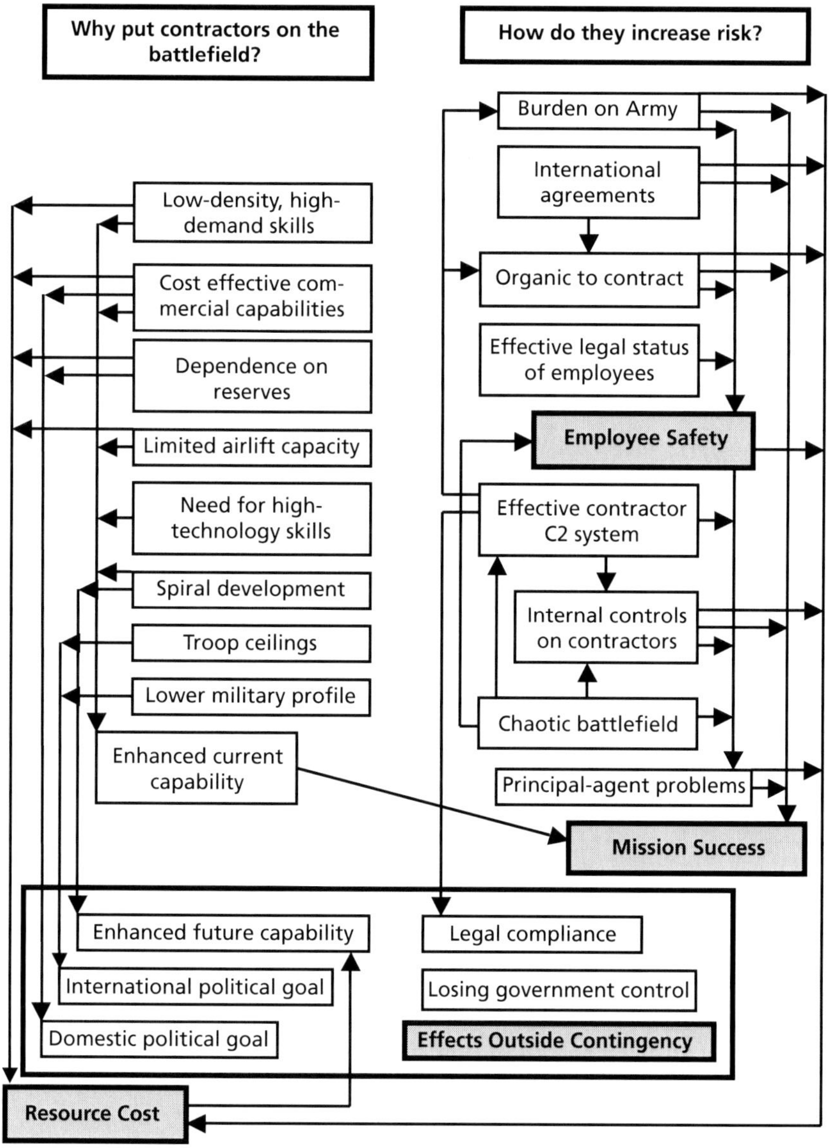

RAND *MG296-5.1*

The attributes relevant to any particular sourcing decision affect the residual risk relevant to these four aspects of risk through *channels of influence* illustrated by the arrows in the figure. These channels of influence are complex, because risks can beget mitigations, which beget further risks, and so on. But the channels in Figure 5.1 have been drawn to avoid recursion. This requires some simplification but does not appear to neglect any major channels of influence. Such simplification allows us to walk from each of the basic attributes in this map to their final effects on the four aspects of relative residual risk without having to backtrack. This supports the analyst's ability to walk systematically through a checklist. The map provides the basis for choosing an order of questions that allows such a walk-through.

The five considerations explained in Chapter Four and detailed in Table 4.1—type of activity, type or identity of source, nature of the contingency, location and battle phase for a source within a contingency, and quality of government oversight for the source—underlie the level of risk associated with the channels of influence in Figure 5.1. Each of the steps in the checklist below identifies which of these considerations deserves attention in each step. In effect, the checklist identifies how these five considerations ultimately affect the relative residual risk of using a contract source in each part of the model illustrated in Figure 5.1.

In this arrangement, employee safety is both an interim and a final outcome. It is an aspect of risk of interest in its own right. It is also a factor likely to affect the degree of difficulty with principal-agent alignment, which in turn directly affects the level of risk associated with mission success and resource cost.

Employee safety differs from the other aspects of risk in another subtle but important way. The employee safety aspect of risk associated with a military source is always zero, making the relative residual risk associated with employee safety positive at all times.[2] Circumstances can change the magnitude of this risk but never suggest that a

---

[2] Again, this does not imply that the Army is not concerned with the safety of military personnel. But discussions of the use of contractors typically, implicitly or explicitly, include this as a part of mission success, which directly addresses personnel losses as a criterion.

contract source is preferred to a military source. Relative residual risks for the other three aspects of risk can be negative or positive. In the end, the other aspects of risk must give contractors enough of a relative advantage to overcome the basic, unavoidable relative risk associated with contractor employee safety.

A Walk Through the Checklist

The checklist provides an orderly way to compile information—judgments, assumptions, qualitative or quantitative data from historical experience, whatever is available—about a particular activity that is relevant to the relative residual risk associated with each aspect of risk associated with that activity. When assessing risks associated with any particular activity, an analyst walks through the checklist compiling information about the levels of risk and mitigations relevant to each aspect of risk and compiles this information in one "account" each for mission success, employee safety, cost, and other effects.

Ideally, an "account" would tabulate objective, auditable, quantitative data that an analyst could then place in a formula to compute a defensible relative residual risk. Such an approach is not feasible today and is unlikely to be feasible in the foreseeable future. Rather, the accounts proposed here systematically "account for" all the factors relevant to assessing a relative residual effect and provide the information an analyst needs to develop a defensible, auditable "account" of how each assessment of relative residual risk is derived.

An auditable account is possible only if relevant observers can agree on the structure underlying the account and the language used to compose it. The checklist proposed here is a first attempt to define a structure for assessing risk that is manageable but still subtle and complete enough to capture most effects of using contractors on the battlefield that come up in Army discussions of the topic. The checklist and the four aspects of risk, the five considerations that affect them, the planning horizon, and the TAA concept of simultaneous contingencies offer a first attempt to provide a vocabulary in which to compare different points of view about specific issues and understand where they fit in the broader set of issues relevant to Army sourcing decisions on the battlefield.

The checklist consists of 15 questions, summarized in Table 5.1. These provide an initial attempt to articulate, simplify, compare, and contrast the basic issues that drive the debate today on where and how to use contractors on the battlefield. We intend the language below to offer more of an explanation of the approach than an explicit set of instructions ready for immediate implementation. They will surely evolve when applied, as experience reveals more expeditious ways to collect and organize the information sought here.[3]

Table 5.1
15 Steps of the Checklist

No.	Proposed Step
1.	Why put contractors on the battlefield?
2.	How do international agreements allow contractors to operate on the battlefield?
3.	How chaotic is the battlefield expected to be where and when a support activity operates there?
4.	What is the effective status of contractors performing an activity on the battlefield under the international law of war?
5.	How well does the contract oversight system deal with the principal-agent difficulties associated with using a contractor?
6.	Can the Army transfer an activity smoothly from military to contract provision on the battlefield?
7.	Can the Army control internal contract processes to reduce relative risks?
8.	Can the Army provide effective force protection for contractors on the battlefield?
9.	Can the Army provide other effective support for contractors on the battlefield?
10.	What is the relative residual risk associated with employee safety?
11.	How well can the Army limit principal-agent problems associated with using a contractor?
12.	What is the relative residual risk associated with mission success?
13.	What is the relative residual risk associated with resource cost?
14.	What is the relative residual risk associated with other effects?
15.	Would a decision to outsource an activity lead to any unacceptable loss of Army control not considered above?

[3] See also sequence of analytic steps for strategic sourcing in Camm (2002, pp. 412–426).

1. Why Put Contractors on the Battlefield?

The Army perspectives discussed in Chapter Three explain the possible reasons. Figure 5.1 captures these reasons and links them with aspects of risks compatible with those identified in Table 3.1. If any of these reasons applies for a particular activity, a potential opening exists to explore the use of contractors on the battlefield. The level of value, in lower residual risks, of using a contractor, assuming no difficulty in getting this value from a contractor, depends on the activity, contractor, nature of contingency, and location and battle phase on the battlefield.

The more of these reasons that apply and the higher the value of each one, the lower the residual risk to mission success, resource cost, and other effects. Setting aside concerns about the relative ability to control contract and military sources on the battlefield and the Army's role in supporting a source, identify the specific ways a contract source can offer an advantage relative to a military source. Enter relevant information in the appropriate account:

- Mission success account (Entry M1)[4]: Relative advantages by source, contingency, and location and battle phase on the battlefield.
- Resource cost account (Entry C1): Relative advantages by source, contingency, and location and battle phase on the battlefield.
- Other effects account (Entry X1): Relative advantage to future capability by contractor and contingency. Relative advantage for international political goals by contingency. Relative advantage for domestic goals by contractor.

In the absence of a mention here, an activity remains military. A mention here opens a need for information relevant to employee safety:

---

[4] To keep track of entries, we assign each a letter (M for mission success, C for resource cost, S for employee safety, and X for other effects) and a number.

- Employee safety account (Entry S1): Information on sources, type of contingency, and location and battle phase on the battlefield relevant to the activity under review.

2. How Do International Agreements Allow Contractors to Operate on the Battlefield?

As noted in Appendix B, only five SOFAs in place today address this question. Looking to the future, the Army's use of contractors will depend fundamentally on the answer to this question. Where the Army wants to expand opportunities to use contractors, it has two options. Either it can develop standard language and work to include it now in SOFAs in parts of the world where future engagements appear likely, or it can develop a support plan that assumes only limited early reliance on contractors, accepts higher costs for their early use, and assumes that the U.S. government will negotiate more favorable SOFAs as a contingency unfolds. This second approach points to a mixed strategy in which the Army might retain enough in-house capability to work without contractors until SOFA problems are resolved. In effect, such military capabilities would arrive early in-theater, leave as soon as contractors replaced them, and prepare for deployment early in another contingency elsewhere.

If the Army makes no progress improving SOFAs relevant to an activity, the use of contractors appears to pose high risks to mission success and resource cost. Note these effects relative to a military source in the relevant account:

- M2.0. Ability to use contract support today, by contractor type (host nation or not), contingency, and location on the battlefield.
- C2.0. Cost implications of using contract support today, by contractor, contingency, and location on the battlefield.

Given improvements that could be made in standard language, changes in existing SOFAs and support plans that incorporate SOFA changes early in a contingency, moderate these risks. Adjust these assessments to reflect expectations of progress over the relevant planning horizon:

- M2.1. Ability to use contract support in the future, by contractor type, contingency, and location on the battlefield.
- C2.1. Cost implications of using contract support in the future, by contractor, contingency, and location on the battlefield.

3. How Chaotic Is the Battlefield Expected to Be Where and When a Support Activity Operates There?

"Chaos" is primarily a function of how predictable the situation is and how dangerous it could become without warning. Unpredictability supports opportunistic behavior, which, as explained by the Army perspectives discussed in Chapter Three, we expect to be more of a problem with contract sources than with military sources. Unexpected danger is similarly likely to provoke a more opportunistic response from a contract source than from a military source.

Using today's standard oversight arrangements on a chaotic battlefield, the use of contractors appears to pose significant risks to mission success and employee safety. Note issues relevant to the activity in the account for each aspect of risk:

- M3. Nature of concern about mission success by contractor type, type of contingency, and location and battle phase on the battlefield.
- S3. Nature of concern about employee safety by contractor type, type of contingency, and location and battle phase on the battlefield.

4. What Is the Effective Status of Contractors Performing an Activity on the Battlefield Under the International Law of War?

Effective status under international law is important to the assessment of employee safety on the battlefield. The level of risk differs across activities, types of contingencies, and location on the battlefield. It depends on how well contractors obey the guidelines in place today, how much their tasks look like traditional warfighting tasks, and whether the enemy can be expected to respect international law regarding contractors on the battlefield.

Although considerable disagreement exists, the use of contractors appears to pose a wide range of risk levels depending on the considerations above. Note concerns in the account for employee safety:

- S4. Effective status of contractors on the battlefield under the international law of war, by activity type, contractor type, contingency, and location on the battlefield.

5. How Well Does the Contract Oversight System Deal with the Principal-Agent Difficulties Associated with Using a Contractor?

The effectiveness of overseeing contractors depends on the nature of the task being performed and the degree to which inherent differences exist between government and contractor provision. The larger the inherent differences, the harder it will be to achieve effective oversight. Given any inherent differences, the effectiveness of overseeing contractors depends on the quality of competition used to choose a contractor, the quality of their contracts, the quality of the contract administration process in-theater, the integration of contract administration with operations, and the experience and skill of the commander and command staff when using these arrangements. The effectiveness of oversight also depends on how well it is matched to the contractors present in particular contingencies at particular locations and times.

Given today's contract oversight system, the use of contractors appears to pose risks that vary with circumstances. The effectiveness of an oversight system depends both on what problems it must overcome and how well it is designed to manage these problems. We are interested in the risk consequences of both factors. Note the effects for the activity in question in the relevant accounts:

- M5.0. Current Army capability to induce performance relevant to mission success from contract sources, by contingency and location and battle phase on the battlefield.

- C5.0. Current Army capability to control the cost of contract sources, by contingency and location and battle phase on the battlefield.
- X5.0. Level of confidence that the Army can ensure compliance today with applicable laws and regulations, by contingency and location and battle phase on the battlefield.

Given improvements that could be made in contracts, contract administration, integration with operations, and command staff capability over the planning horizon, moderate these risks. Note the effects for the activity in question in the relevant accounts:

- M5.1. Future Army capability to induce performance relevant to mission success from contract sources, by contingency and location and battle phase on the battlefield.
- C5.1. Future Army capability to control the cost of contract sources, by contingency and location and battle phase on the battlefield.
- X5.1. Level of confidence that the Army can ensure compliance in the future with applicable laws and regulations, by contingency and location and battle phase on the battlefield.

6. Can the Army Transfer an Activity Smoothly from Military to Contract Provision on the Battlefield?

The Army can wait for contractor entry into a theater only if it has an ability to transfer control smoothly from a military to a contract source. The Army must prepare a standard approach to a support plan that includes this transfer of control and train its command staffs and contractors in its use.

Given statements by observers about current arrangements, the use of contractors appears to pose modest risks to mission success and resource cost. Note these effects in an account for each aspect of risk:

- M6.0. Current Army capability to control operationally a smooth transition from a military to a contract source, by contingency and location and battle phase on the battlefield.

- C6.0. Current Army capability to control the cost during a transition from a military to a contract source, by contingency and location and battle phase on the battlefield.

Adjust these assessments to reflect expectations of progress over the relevant planning horizon. Note these relative effects in the relevant accounts:

- M6.1. Future Army capability to control operationally a smooth transition from a military to a contract source, by contingency and location and battle phase on the battlefield.
- C6.1. Future Army capability to control the cost during a transition from a military to a contract source, by contingency and location and battle phase on the battlefield.

Delaying the entry of contractors reduces the risks that contract employees face, both because they are in-theater for a shorter time and because they reach the theater when it is less dangerous. Note this relative effect in the account for employee safety:

- S6. Reduction in risk to employee safety, when a contractor enters a theater later, by contingency and location on the battlefield.

7. Can the Army Control Internal Contractor Processes to Reduce Relative Risks?

The Army can specify the types of employees a contractor uses, the organization of the contractor's process, the information systems it uses, and so on. Such changes give the Army greater real-time control on the battlefield but can reduce the effectiveness and increase the cost of a contractor.

In CSS activities that resemble combat and are close to combat on the battlefield, with today's controls, the use of contractors appears to pose a risk to mission success. Note this effect in the account for mission success:

- M7.0. Factors that increase risk in mission success today because of limited control over internal contractor processes, by contractor, contingency, location and battle phase on the battlefield, and oversight arrangements.

Changes that could be made over the relevant planning horizon could tighten controls, reducing principal-agent concerns and concerns about the status of contractors under international law, while aggravating other risks to mission success and cost. Note these aggravating effects in the relevant accounts:

- M7.1. Increase in risk of mission success induced by expanded internal controls, by contractor, contingency, location and battle phase on the battlefield, and oversight arrangements. (The checklist captures offsetting benefits of reduced principal-agent risks elsewhere.)
- S7. Reduction in risk associated with effective status on the battlefield under international law, when contractor employees are members of the reserve components and mobilized for deployment, by contractor, contingency, and location on the battlefield.
- C7. Increase in risk of high cost induced by expanded internal controls, by contractor, contingency, location and battle phase on the battlefield, and oversight arrangements. (The checklist captures offsetting benefits of reduced principal-agent risks elsewhere.)

8. Can the Army Provide Effective Force Protection for Contractors on the Battlefield?

The Army plans to have combat forces available to protect contractors if necessary. A military source would need less force protection or might provide its own. It also provides nuclear, biological, and chemical (NBC) gear; medical support; training; and other goods and services relevant to contractor security. The protection needed by contractors depends on the activity, type of contingency, location and battle phase on the battlefield, and oversight arrangements.

Given current Army capabilities, the use of contractors appears to raise large issues relevant to risks to mission success, employee safety, and cost. Force protection dramatically reduces risks relevant to employee safety, increases relative risks relevant to costs, and may increase relative risks relevant to mission success (before the value of higher employee safety is considered). Note these effects in the relevant accounts:

- M8.0. Increased risk to mission success today, caused by a contract source that requires external military support and cannot contribute military capability when called on, by contractor, contingency, location, and battle phase on the battlefield, and oversight arrangements. (The checklist captures offsetting benefits of reduced principal-agent risks elsewhere.)
- S8.0. Reduction in risk to employee safety today attributable to force protection, by contractor, contingency, location and battle phase on the battlefield, and oversight arrangements.
- C8.0. Increased risk to resource cost today, caused by a contract source that requires external military support and cannot contribute military capability when called on, by contractor, contingency, location and battle phase on the battlefield, and oversight arrangements. (The checklist captures offsetting benefits of reduced principal-agent risks elsewhere.)

Changes that could be made during the relevant planning horizon could provide better NBC support, improve oversight arrangements that coordinate protection with operational planning, and so on. Note these effects in the relevant accounts:

- M8.1. Increased risk to mission success in the future, caused by a contract source that requires external military support and cannot contribute military capability when called on, by contractor, contingency, location and battle phase on the battlefield, and oversight arrangements. (The checklist captures offsetting benefits of reduced principal-agent risks elsewhere.)

- S8.1. Reduction in risk to employee safety in the future attributable to force protection, by contractor, contingency, location and battle phase on the battlefield, and oversight arrangements.
- C8.1. Increased risk to resource cost in the future, caused by a contract source that requires external military support and cannot contribute military capability when called on, by contractor, contingency, location and battle phase on the battlefield, and oversight arrangements. (The checklist captures offsetting benefits of reduced principal-agent risks elsewhere.)

9. Can the Army Provide Other Effective Support for Contractors on the Battlefield?

The Army provides a wide range of support to contractors to ensure that they provide effective support to the Army. The Army plans military and contractor CSS resources to provide logistics support, life support, facilities, and so on for other contractors. It can coordinate access to local resources to limit cost inflation. The effects of these activities depend on activity, contractor, type of contingency, location on the battlefield, and oversight arrangements.

Given current Army capabilities, the use of contractors appears to raise large issues relevant to risks to mission success and cost. Using contractors absorbs resources that could directly support the fight, increasing risk to mission success, but also supports contractors whose products help reduce risks to mission success. Army support for contractors creates direct increases in risk to cost but may help avoid other risks to cost. Note these effects in the relevant accounts:

- M9.0. Net effect on risk to mission success today when the Army supports a contractor on the battlefield, reducing risk to mission success, but to do so commits resources that could reduce risk to mission success more directly. The effect depends on contractor, contingency, location and battle phase on the battlefield, and oversight arrangements.
- C9.0. Net effect on risk to resource cost today when the Army supports a contractor on the battlefield rather than requiring the contractor to support itself. The effect depends on contractor,

contingency, location and battle phase on the battlefield, and oversight arrangements.

Changes that could be made during the relevant planning horizon could improve oversight arrangements by, for example, standardizing contract requirements, improving contractor-military integration, and limiting cost inflation in-theater. Note these effects in the relevant accounts:

- M9.1. Net effect on risk to mission success in the future when the Army supports a contractor on the battlefield, reducing risk to mission success, but to do so commits resources that could reduce risk to mission success more directly. The effect depends on contractor, contingency, location and battle phase on the battlefield, and oversight arrangements.
- C9.1. Net effect on risk to resource cost in the future when the Army supports a contractor on the battlefield rather than requiring the contractor to support itself. The effect depends on contractor, contingency, location and battle phase on the battlefield, and oversight arrangements.

10. What Is the Relative Residual Risk Associated with Employee Safety?

As Figure 5.1 indicated, employee safety depends on the level of chaos on the battlefield, when and where contractors are used on that battlefield, the effective status of employees on the battlefield under international law, the Army's efforts to protect contractors, and the quality of contractor oversight and the Army's ability to make the transition from organic to contract sources on the battlefield. At this point in the checklist, the employee safety account includes information about all of these factors, summarized for convenience in Table 5.2. This information provides the basis for the following assessments, which conclude the employee safety account:

- S10.0. Relative residual risk for employee safety today, by contractor, contingency, location and battle phase on the battlefield, and oversight arrangements.
- S10.1. Relative residual risk for employee safety in the future, by contractor, contingency, location and battle phase on the battlefield, and oversight arrangements.

11. How Well Can the Army Limit Principal-Agent Problems Associated with Using a Contractor?

As Figure 5.1 indicated, the level of difficulty attending principal-agent problems depends on the degree of chaos on the battlefield,

Table 5.2
Data Contents of the Employee Safety Account

No.	Data
S1.	Information on contractors, type of contingency, and location and battle phase on the battlefield relevant to the activity under review.
S3.	Nature of concern about employee safety, by contractor type, type of contingency, and location and battle phase on the battlefield.
S4.	Effective status of contractors on the battlefield under the international law of war, by contractor type, contingency, and location on the battlefield.
S6.	Reduction in risk to employee safety, when a contractor enters a theater later, associated with the Army's ability to manage the military to contractor transition well, by contingency and location on the battlefield.
S7.	Reduction in risk associated with effective status on the battlefield under international law, when contractor employees are members of the reserve and mobilized for deployment, by contractor, contingency, and location on the battlefield.
S8.0.	Reduction in risk to employee safety today attributable to force protection, by contractor, contingency, and location and battle phase on the battlefield.
S8.1.	Reduction in risk to employee safety in the future attributable to force protection, by contractor, contingency, location and battle phase on the battlefield, and oversight arrangements.
	Entries above provide the information needed to assess
S10.0.	Relative residual risk for employee safety today, by contractor, contingency, location and battle phase on the battlefield, and oversight arrangements.
S.10.1.	Relative residual risk for employee safety in the future, by contractor, contingency, location and battle phase on the battlefield, and oversight arrangements.

the quality of Army oversight of contractor sources on the battlefield, the effects of Army controls on internal contractor processes, and the level of employee safety on the battlefield.

At this point in the checklist, the data needed on each of these points is now available, as shown in Table 5.3. These data provide the basis for the following assessments of the principal-agent problem:

Table 5.3
Factors Relevant to Control over Principal-Agent Problems

No.	Data
M3.	Nature of concern about mission success, by contractor type, type of contingency, and location and battle phase on the battlefield.
M5.0.	Current Army capability to induce performance relevant to mission success from contract sources, by contingency and location and battle phase on the battlefield.
C5.0.	Current Army capability to control the cost of contract sources, by contingency and location and battle phase on the battlefield.
M5.1.	Future Army capability to induce performance relevant to mission success from contract sources, by contingency and location and battle phase on the battlefield.
C5.1.	Future Army capability to control the cost of contract sources, by contingency and location and battle phase on the battlefield.
S10.0.	Relative residual risk for employee safety today, by contractor, contingency, location and battle phase on the battlefield, and oversight arrangements.
S10.1.	Relative residual risk for employee safety in the future, by contractor, contingency, location and battle phase on the battlefield, and oversight arrangements.
	Entries above provide the information needed to assess
M11.0.	Level of principal-agent problems relevant to mission success today, by contractor, contingency, location and battle phase on the battlefield, and oversight arrangements.
C11.0.	Level of principal-agent problems relevant to resource costs today, by contractor, contingency, location and battle phase on the battlefield, and oversight arrangements.
M11.1.	Level of principal-agent problems relevant to mission success in the future, by contractor, contingency, location and battle phase on the battlefield, and oversight arrangements.
C11.1.	Level of principal-agent problems relevant to resource costs in the future, by contractor, contingency, location and battle phase on the battlefield, and oversight arrangements.

- M11.0. Level of principal-agent problems relevant to mission success today, by contractor, contingency, location and battle phase on the battlefield, and oversight arrangements.
- C11.0. Level of principal-agent problems relevant to resource costs today, by contractor, contingency, location and battle phase on the battlefield, and oversight arrangements.
- M11.1. Level of principal-agent problems relevant to mission success in the future, by contractor, contingency, location and battle phase on the battlefield, and oversight arrangements.
- C11.1. Level of principal-agent problems relevant to resource costs in the future, by contractor, contingency, location and battle phase on the battlefield, and oversight arrangements.

12. What Is the Relative Residual Risk Associated with Mission Success?

As Figure 5.1 indicated, the relative residual risk associated with mission success depends on the relative advantages available from a contractor absent governance and support issues, the availability of contractors under international agreements, the combat capability absorbed to support contractors, the negative performance effect of imposing controls on internal contractor processes, and the level of principal-agent problems.

At this point in the checklist, the data needed on each of these points are now available, as shown in Table 5.4 (current risk) and 5.5 (future risk). This information provides the basis for the following assessments of the relative residual risk associated with mission success:

- M12.0. Relative residual risk for mission success today, by contractor, type of contingency, location, and battle phase on the battlefield, and oversight arrangements.
- M12.1. Relative residual risk for mission success in the future, by contractor, type of contingency, location, and battle phase on the battlefield, and oversight arrangements.

Table 5.4
Data Contents of the Mission Success Account Relevant to Current Relative Residual Risk

No.	Data
M1.	Relative advantages in mission success, by contractor, contingency, and location and battle phase on the battlefield.
M2.0.	Ability to use contract support today, by contractor type (host nation or not), contingency, and location on the battlefield.
M6.0.	Current Army capability to operationally control a smooth transition from a military to a contract source, by contingency and location, and battle phase on the battlefield.
M7.0.	Factors that increase risk in mission success today because of limited control over internal contractor processes, by contractor, contingency, location, and battle phase on the battlefield, and oversight arrangements.
M8.0.	Increased risk to mission success today, caused by a contract source that requires external military support and cannot contribute military capability when called on, by contractor, contingency, location, and battle phase on the battlefield, and oversight arrangements. (The checklist captures offsetting benefits of reduced principal-agent risks elsewhere.)
M9.0.	Net effect on risk to mission success today when the Army supports a contractor on the battlefield, reducing risk to mission success, but to do so commits resources that could reduce risk to mission success more directly. The effect depends on contractor, contingency, location and battle phase on the battlefield, and oversight arrangements.
M11.0.	Level of principal-agent problems relevant to mission success today, by contractor, contingency, location and battle phase on the battlefield, and oversight arrangements.
	Entries above provide the information needed to assess
M12.0.	Relative residual risk for mission success today, by contractor, type of contingency, location and battle phase on the battlefield, and oversight arrangements.

13. What Is the Relative Residual Risk Associated with Resource Cost?

As Figure 5.1 indicated, the relative residual risk associated with resource cost depends on the relative advantages available from a contractor absent governance and support issues, the availability of contractors and terms that define how they work under international agreements, the combat capability absorbed to support contractors, the negative cost effect on imposing controls on internal contractor processes, and the level of principal-agent problems. That is, the factors relevant to cost closely parallel those relevant to mission success.

Table 5.5
Data Contents of the Mission Success Account Relevant to Future Relative Residual Risk

No.	Data
M1.	Relative advantages in mission success by contractor, contingency, and location and battle phase on the battlefield.
M2.1.	Ability to use contract support in the future, by contractor type, contingency, and location on the battlefield.
M6.1.	Future Army capability to operationally control a smooth transition from a military to a contract source, by contingency and location and battle phase on the battlefield.
M7.1.	Increase in risk of mission success induced by expanded internal controls, by contractor, contingency, location and battle phase on the battlefield, and oversight arrangements. (The checklist captures offsetting benefits of reduced principal-agent risks elsewhere.)
M8.1.	Increased risk to mission success in the future caused by a contract source that requires external military support and cannot contribute military capability when called on, by contractor, contingency, location and battle phase on the battlefield, and oversight arrangements. (The checklist captures offsetting benefits of reduced principal-agent risks elsewhere.)
M9.1.	Net effect on risk to mission success in the future when the Army supports a contractor on the battlefield, reducing risk to mission success, but to do so commits resources that could reduce risk to mission success more directly. The effect depends on contractor, contingency, location and battle phase on the battlefield, and oversight arrangements.
M11.1.	Level of principal-agent problems relevant to mission success in the future, by contractor, contingency, location and battle phase on the battlefield, and oversight arrangements.
X1.	Effects of spiral development that reduce future relative risks of using contractors in terms of mission success, by contingency and location and battle phase on the battlefield.
	Entries above provide the information needed to assess
M12.1.	Relative residual risk for mission success in the future, by contractor, type of contingency, location and battle phase on the battlefield, and oversight arrangements.

At this point in the checklist, the data needed on each of these points are all available, as shown in Tables 5.6 (current risk) and 5.7 (future risk). These data provide the basis for the following assessments of the relative residual risk associated with mission success:

- C13.0. Relative residual risk for resource cost today, by contractor, type of contingency, location and battle phase on the battlefield, and oversight arrangements.

Table 5.6
Data Contents of the Resource Cost Account Relevant to Current Relative Residual Risk

No.	Data
C1.	Relative cost advantages, by contractor, contingency, and location and battle phase on the battlefield.
C2.0.	Cost implications of using contract support today, by contractor, contingency, and location on the battlefield.
C6.0.	Current Army capability to control the cost during a transition from a military to a contract source, by contingency and location and battle phase on the battlefield.
C7.	Increase in risk of high cost induced by expanded internal controls, by contractor, contingency, location and battle phase on the battlefield, and oversight arrangements. (The checklist captures offsetting benefits of reduced principal-agent risks elsewhere.)
C8.0.	Increased risk to resource cost today caused by a contract source that requires external military support and cannot contribute military capability when called on, by contractor, contingency, location and battle phase on the battlefield, and oversight arrangements. (The checklist captures offsetting benefits of reduced principal-agent risks elsewhere.)
C9.0.	Net effect on risk to resource cost today when the Army supports a contractor on the battlefield rather than requiring the contractor to support itself. The effect depends on contractor, contingency, location and battle phase on the battlefield, and oversight arrangements.
S10.0.	Relative residual risk to employee safety today, by contractor, contingency, location and battle phase on the battlefield, and oversight arrangements.
C11.0.	Level of principal-agent problems relevant to resource costs today, by contractor, contingency, location and battle phase on the battlefield, and oversight arrangements.
	Entries above provide the information needed to assess
C13.0.	Relative residual risk for resource cost today, by contractor, type of contingency, location and battle phase on the battlefield, and oversight arrangements.

- C13.1. Relative residual risk for resource cost in the future, by contractor, type of contingency, location and battle phase on the battlefield, and oversight arrangements.

14. What Is the Relative Residual Risk Associated with Other Effects?

As Figure 5.1 indicated, the relative residual risk associated with other effects outside contingencies differs qualitatively from the relative residual risks we have discussed above. In a sense, this is a catch-all

Table 5.7
Data Contents of the Resource Cost Account Relevant to Future Relative Residual Risk

No.	Data
C1.	Relative cost advantages, by contractor, contingency, and location and battle phase on the battlefield.
C2.1.	Cost implications of using contract support in the future, by contractor, contingency, and location on the battlefield.
C6.1.	Future Army capability to control the cost during a transition from a military to a contract source, by contingency and location and battle phase on the battlefield.
C8.1.	Increased risk to resource cost in the future caused by a contract source that requires external military support and cannot contribute military capability when called on, by contractor, contingency, location and battle phase on the battlefield, and oversight arrangements. (The checklist captures offsetting benefits of reduced principal-agent risks elsewhere.)
C9.1.	Net effect on risk to resource cost in the future when the Army supports a contractor on the battlefield rather than requiring the contractor to support itself. The effect depends on contractor, contingency, location and battle phase on the battlefield, and oversight arrangements.
S10.1.	Relative residual risk to employee safety in the future, by contractor, contingency, location and battle phase on the battlefield, and oversight arrangements.
C11.1.	Level of principal-agent problems relevant to resource costs in the future, by contractor, contingency, location and battle phase on the battlefield, and oversight arrangements.
X1.	Effects of spiral development that reduce future relative risks of using contractors in terms of resource cost, by contingency and location and battle phase on the battlefield.
	Entries above provide the information needed to assess
C13.1.	Relative residual risk for resource cost in the future, by contractor, type of contingency, location and battle phase on the battlefield, and oversight arrangements.

category for important risks not associated with the primary points of focus with regard to using contractors on the battlefield—mission success, employee safety, and cost. It summarizes the following significant relative residual risks:

- Relative value of using contractors in support of international political and diplomatic goals that lead to troop ceilings in-theater and a preference for a low military profile in-theater (captured in Entry X1).

- Relative value of using contractors in support of domestic political goals related to the mobilization of the reserve force and the welfare of contractors associated with the defense industrial base (captured in Entry X1).
- Relative value of using contractors as part of spiral development that reduces future Army risks, by contingency and location and battle phase on the battlefield (captured in Entry X1).
- Level of confidence that the Army can ensure compliance today with applicable laws and regulations, by contingency and location and battle phase on the battlefield (captured in Entry X5.0).
- Level of confidence that the Army can ensure compliance in the future with applicable laws and regulations, by contingency and location and battle phase on the battlefield (captured in Entry X5.1).

No further aggregation of these risks is necessary, as each is somewhat sui generis. Decisionmakers must consider these side by side with those discussed above in support of any sourcing decision.

15. Would a Decision to Outsource an Activity Lead to Any Unacceptable Loss of Army Control Not Considered Above?

The sequence of reasoning portrayed in Figure 5.1 does not naturally highlight a number of important risks because, even though sourcing decisions on the battlefield affect them, such effects do not manifest themselves immediately on the battlefield. If the analysis above suggests that an activity should be outsourced, the Army should review the following factors before doing so:[5]

- X15.1. Will outsourcing an activity compromise the Army's ability to sustain a career field needed to develop and sustain skills still required in the military force?

---

[5] These derive from issues raised in Chapter Three and in Camm (2002).

- X15.2. Will outsourcing an activity degrade training the Army needs to develop and sustain skills still required in the military force?
- X15.3. Will the Army lose its ability to provide effective oversight to the contractors providing outsourced activities in-theater?
- X15.4. Will the Army lose its ability to restore a military capability that experience demonstrates should not have been outsourced?
- X15.5. Will outsourcing an activity subject it to enemy attack or influence that could degrade its availability when required in a contingency?

Discussion

Is This Approach Too Complex?

The number of questions in the checklist and the number of factors in the accounts developed for each aspect of risk may seem daunting. There are a number of ways to react to this apparent complexity.

The complexity is real. The battlefield is a complex place, with many sources of risks and many demands on risk mitigation. The complexity above is simply a reflection of this reality. A quick review of discussions of risk management on the battlefield in FM 3-0 (2001) and FM 3-100.12 (2001) makes this apparent. As in these manuals, the intent of the checklist above is to begin parsing that complexity to help practitioners understand it and ultimately overcome it. Understanding should help practitioners internalize the points raised here more systematically, helping them move quickly through the sequences above. Experience will reveal that a few factors are likely to dominate a sourcing decision. These factors deserve the most serious attention in the checklist.[6]

---

[6] It could be argued that rules of thumb used to support sourcing decisions today do this now. We expect this framework to support the development of more meaningful rules of

A common reaction to using contractors on the battlefield has been that it was simply too complicated, and so it simply added risk in an already risky environment, making the presence of contractors undesirable. New weapons or tactics also add risks to the battlefield, risks that the Army seeks to overcome to exploit the opportunities that innovation offers. As the discussion above highlights, the Army has discovered repeatedly that contractors can offer new opportunities worth exploiting on the battlefield but impose risks as well. The checklist offered above lays out a framework for asking where the risk lies and how it might be mitigated to give the Army access to worthwhile contractor opportunities.

The framework offers a common language that practitioners can use to discuss such risks. It offers a fairly simple way to pose some questions that are important to force design:

- Which aspect of risk is really important? What is the relative importance of the four aspects of risk in different settings?
- Employee safety is an end in itself, but it is also connected to mission support. Army protection of contract employees enhances their safety and hence the likelihood of mission success, but it also degrades the forces that the commander can apply directly to the fight. How high a priority should the commander give force protection for contractors with the limited resources available?
- Imposing controls on a contractor's internal processes enhances the Army's control, but it is likely to degrade the contractor's contribution to mission success and increase its cost. Which effect dominates in various parts of the battlefield over time?

Honest disagreement exists on each of these questions. This framework seeks to parse the complexities of the battlefield to help Army personnel better understand why they disagree and look for ways to resolve their differences productively.

---

thumb that reflect more effectively what the hazards of the battlefield mean for the Army as a whole when the Army uses contractors there.

Where a few dominant factors stand out as an analyst walks through the checklist, as is likely, a natural question will arise. If, for example, the Army's inability to ensure the reliability of host-nation contract employees in military posts comes up repeatedly, perhaps the Army should seek to improve that capability over the longer term. If the Army repeatedly rejects contract provision of services because planners do not think that Army commanders and their staffs have demonstrated the ability to use contractors effectively on the battlefield, perhaps the Army should seek to improve the capabilities of its commanders and staffs by changing their experience with contractors between contingencies and changing the training they receive.

In sum, in specific cases, the apparent complexity of this framework is likely to resolve itself into a few major issues that can open the door to improved use of contractors on the battlefield over time.

Does Resource Cost Get Too Much Attention Here?

The current key Army documents on the use of contractors on the battlefield give little attention to risks associated with resource costs.[7] In contrast, the checklist above gives resource cost extensive attention. In fact, it gives resource cost as much attention as mission success gets, even though the keystone documents focus most their attention on mission success. Is this difference appropriate?

An easy answer would be that, as stated above, the checklist makes no assumptions about the relative importance of the four aspects of risk explored. Analysts could apply it giving only modest attention to resource cost to implement the priorities apparently highlighted in the keystone documents. If resource cost, broadly writ, were clearly not a real concern, however, the Army could simply buy its way out of many of the problems it faces when it struggles to make contract sources reliable and effective on the battlefield. In fact, most of the apparent relative advantages that contractors appear to offer on

---

[7] As noted above, these include AR 700-137 (1985); Pamphlet 715-16 (1998); AR 100-10-2 (1999); AR 715-9 (1999); AMC Pamphlet 715-18 (2000); FM 100-21 (2000); and FM 3-100.21 (2003). See also DoD (2001).

the battlefield result from their availability to help the Army deal with resource constraints of various kinds.

What is probably happening here is the following. The key Army documents on the use of contractors on the battlefield focus on how to plan and execute the next contingency. In effect, they take many basic sourcing decisions as given and ask how the Army can get the highest level of mission success possible, within mandatory legal and regulatory constraints, from the contract and military resources currently available to it to execute a contingency. Resource concerns actually dominate such a setting, but, because the levels of so many resources are set, their *dollar* and *manpower* costs are not important to the analysis. The level of mission success the Army can legally achieve is the main concern of the analysis.

As important as this challenge is, it is not the challenge faced here. By deliberately choosing a perspective in which the Army has more control over the contract-military mix on the battlefield and the arrangements the Army uses to ensure the reliability and effectiveness of contract sources there, this analysis heightens the relative importance of dollar costs. Preparing for potential future contingencies, the Army must repeatedly ask whether it wants to cover the cost of training and sustaining a military capability when, for example, the money required to do this could also be used to develop or purchase new weapons. Resource cost is an integral part of the approach offered here and receives as much attention as mission success because the Army can still make choices about where to place its resources as it reviews the sourcing decisions and criteria raised here.

Should the Mission Success and Resource Cost Aspects of Risk Address Future as Well as Current Circumstances?

The answer depends on the context of the analysis. The QDR, for example, clearly enumerates risks associated with both current and future capabilities among the four risks it highlights. An assessment evaluating capabilities over the next year, as a traditional readiness assessment does, would tend to focus only on current capabilities to ensure that anyone considering the use of the force over the next year had a good sense of the relative readiness of contract and military alternatives.

Even when assessing readiness, however, current and future readiness can be important. High levels of deployment in recent years, relative to the size of the force, have focused attention on the use of existing defense capabilities. Because this deployment has disrupted training, it has tended to reduce future capability, in effect drawing down future capability to sustain current capabilities in a hazardous environment. A more balanced view of readiness would consider the effects of current decisions and actions on current *and* future capabilities (Dahlman and Thaler, 2002). In the context of the current discussion, for example, such a balanced view could allow use of contractors in some activities to induce a shortfall in mission success today, if using contractors today gave commanders and their staffs the experience they needed to use contractors to increase mission success in the future. Even if current capability is the focus of a risk assessment, highlighting current and future risks helps ensure that the decisionmaker understands the nature of this trade-off between current and future capabilities.

More broadly, it is likely that much of the disagreement within the Army today about using contractors results from the focus of some observers on current risks and capabilities while others are focusing on the future. Those who highlight shortcomings in current Army sourcing and contract oversight policy caution against too high a dependence on contractors on the battlefield. Those who highlight likely solutions to such shortcomings, such as the authors of the key Army documents on the use of contractors on the battlefield today, point to the potential available to the Army from using contractors. In general, opponents are likely to focus more on the present; advocates, more on the future. They may both find that they agree on many issues if they see the issues presented in the right light. Clearly distinguishing current and future risks to mission success and resource cost is a step toward helping them see that distinction. Perhaps current opponents can agree that contractors can be used in the future for particular activities if specific changes occur. If so, they can focus on the more important issue for the future of whether the Army should use its scarce resources and leadership focus to make such changes.

Summary

The approach to assessing "traditional" sourcing decisions offered here focuses on four aspects of the relative residual risk—mission success, employee safety, resource cost, and other effects—associated with choosing between military and contractor sources. It draws on recent discussion about the use of contractors on the battlefield to map the risks and mitigations relevant to such use. This map gets complicated because providing support on a battlefield is complicated. To consider how the Army sources any particular CSS activity, the approach offered here uses a 15-step checklist to develop information relevant to each of the aspects of risk above. Analysts can then give decisionmakers the information developed regarding relative residual risk to help them make the final sourcing decision. Analysts can also use the structure of the approach to help parse the complexity inherent in operations on the battlefield and thereby better understand how risks and mitigations relevant to sourcing affect one another in a combat setting.

This approach to traditional sourcing decisions basically weighs the benefits and costs of using alternative sources on the battlefield. The benefits associated with using contractors often flow from constraints on Army decisions. The approach in this chapter has taken these constraints as given. The next chapter considers removing these constraints. This "nontraditional" approach looks beyond sourcing as an issue in its own right to ask what nonsourcing policies shape the Army's sourcing decisions on the battlefield and how changes in these policies might easily change Army use of contractors on the battlefield. Analysts cannot determine whether such policy changes are desirable without looking well beyond sourcing issues alone.

CHAPTER SIX

Using Risk Considerations to Examine Changes in Nonsourcing Policies with Sourcing Implications

The discussion of Army perspectives in Chapter Three offers a list of constraints that help account for the Army's use of contractors on the battlefield. None of these constraints exists primarily to affect the source of CSS activities in a contingency. But in the presence of these constraints, the Army benefits from adding contractors to the support plan for the contingency. This chapter examines the policy implications of loosening these constraints as a strategy for reducing the relative value of using contractors on the battlefield and, therefore, the Army's need to use them.

The chapter starts by noting that three different types of constraints are important in the discussion of Army perspectives in Chapter Three: resource constraints, policy constraints, and a mix of the two. The issues differ for each type of constraint. The chapter then addresses each type in turn. It concludes with a discussion of general issues raised here.

Three Types of Constraints

It is straightforward to classify the constraints in Chapter Three as follows:

Resource constraints result from decisions that limit the total level of resources available to the Army or limit how the resources available will be used:

- A *smaller force*, with *more missions*, limits the level of military end strength available in the face of higher than expected or growing operational tempo. The Army can spend fungible dollars on contractors to increase the likelihood of mission success. A larger military force or fewer missions could allow the Army to rely less on contractors.
- Dollar constraints may discourage the Army from accepting the low utilization rates for high-cost military personnel that would result if the Army used them to staff *low-density, high-demand skills* in the force. With looser dollar constraints, the Army could potentially use additional dollars to substitute military personnel for contractors.
- Similarly, dollar constraints may discourage the Army from accepting the higher costs and lower quality levels that would result from using military personnel instead of *cost-effective commercial capabilities*. With looser dollar constraints, the Army could potentially use additional dollars to substitute military personnel for contractors.
- Constraints on dollars and the size of the active-duty force encourage the Army to *depend on the reserve components* for CSS capability. More dollars and a shift in end-strength constraints could potentially allow the Army to substitute active personnel for the contractors it currently uses to mitigate political risks associated with mobilizing reserve components.
- Constraints on dollars and bureaucratic politics may discourage the Air Force and Transportation Command from investing resources in capabilities, such as *airlift capacity*, that will tend to benefit other services.[1] With more dollars and higher end strength, the Air Force could buy more airlift capacity to benefit the Army. This would allow the Army to substitute more military personnel for contractors in-theater.

---

[1] The Army must rely on these outside parties to get access to military and contractor aircraft. In any particular contingency, the combatant commander allocates the Army a portion of the airlift assets of all kinds available in-theater.

Policy constraints result from acquisition policies that limit support options on the battlefield as an unintended consequence of seeking the development of high-performance systems:

- Emphasis on the military performance of systems rather than on their supportability on the battlefield has yielded systems that require the presence of *high-technology skills* on the battlefield. Given military personnel policies, the Army must rely on contractors to provide these high-technology skills. Greater emphasis on supportability relative to performance or increased development funding for supportability improvements could reduce the Army's need for contractors.
- *Spiral development*, which attempts to make new capabilities available to the warfighter faster and use operational experience to mature new systems faster, tends to require the presence of high-technology skills on the battlefield to support systems with incomplete support concepts and limited reliability. Given military personnel policies, the Army must rely on contractors to provide these high-technology skills. Keeping immature systems off the battlefield could reduce the Army's need for contractors.

Constraints on the presence of military personnel in-theater result from policy decisions motivated by domestic and international politics. They yield constraints on military end strength allowed in the theater, which motivate the Army to rely more on contractors. Policy constraints yield resource constraints. These *mixed* constraints then drive behavior on the battlefield:

- Formal *troop ceilings* result directly from such constraints. Less attention to the political goals that drive troop ceilings could raise the ceilings and thereby reduce the Army's demand for contractors on the battlefield.
- Political or diplomatic demand for a *low military profile* in-theater results from the same kind of constraints and may have similar effects even in the absence of a formal troop ceiling. Less attention to the political goals that drive a demand for a lower

military profile could reduce the Army's demand for contractors on the battlefield.

Consider the effects of loosening constraints for each type in turn.

Resource Constraints

The sourcing effects of having a small force with high operational tempo provide a good place to open the discussion of resource constraints. Consider first how changes in constraints relevant to this case are likely to affect Army use of contractors on the battlefield. Then look at the other cases of resource constraints as variations on this one.

When considering the effects of a *smaller force*, with *more missions* on sourcing decisions, the most relevant constraint is on military manpower, which is used to define the "size" of the force. Money is available to fund this manpower as well as other resources, including contract services. With a constraint on military manpower, the Army naturally turns to other resources to expand its ability to deal with expanded workload. In effect, military manpower is sized for a lower level of workload than the one that prevails in the world today.

Figure 6.1 illustrates this situation. It shows military resources (M_i) on the horizontal axis, nonmilitary resources (N_i) on the vertical axis, the maximum combinations of these that the Army can buy with different budgets (B_i), and the maximum levels of military capability (C_i) that the Army can achieve with different combinations of these resources.[2] The military manpower ceiling is set at M_0, a level compatible with a budget of B_0 (at e_0). With a higher budget, B_1, but

[2] Figure 6.1 uses basic microeconomic tools explained in any introductory text (Varian [2002] is widely used today). C_i are isoquants from the production function that links military and nonmilitary resources to the Army leadership's perception of military capability. Because this discussion is about behavior and not optimal outcomes, it does not matter if the production function underlying the C_i reflects fundamental service biases. To the extent that such biases shape the decisions discussed, the reader should be cautious about drawing inferences about optimality from the discussion.

Figure 6.1
"Substitution" and "Income" Effects of Resource Constraints

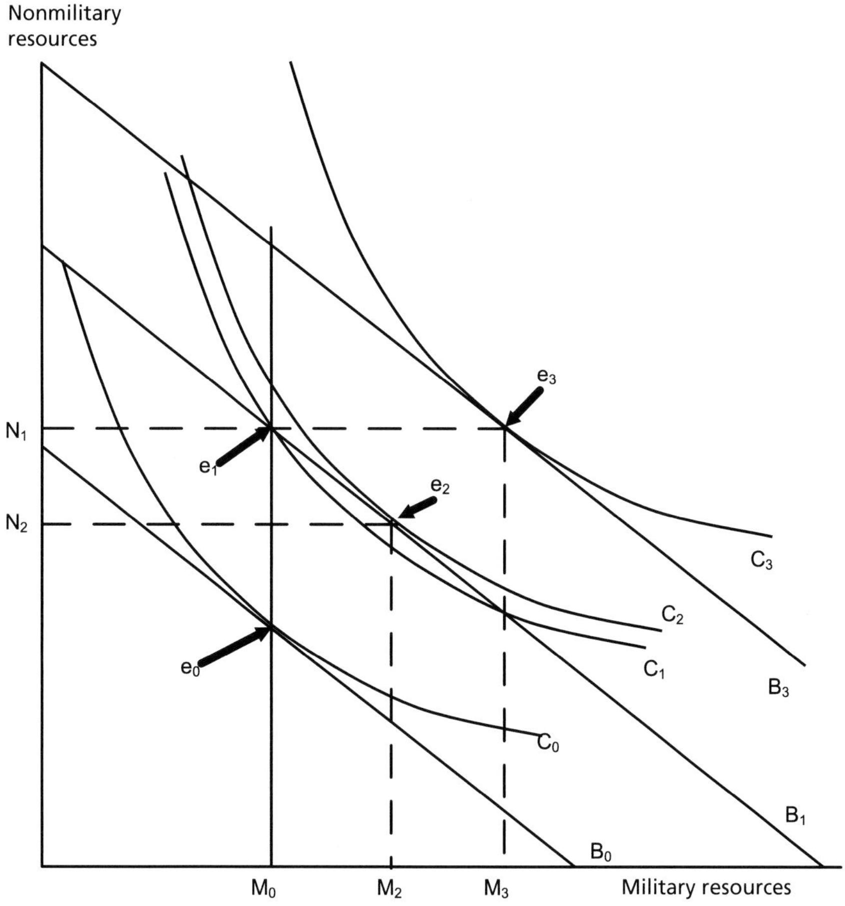

RAND *MG296-6.1*

the same manpower ceiling, the Army can only improve its capability by buying more nonmilitary resources. With a level of nonmilitary resources, N_1, the Army can achieve capability C_1 (at e_1). If the manpower ceiling were raised, the Army would increase its use of military resources from M_0 to M_2 and decrease its use of nonmilitary resources, including contract services, from N_1 to N_2 (at e_2). Removing the constraint on military manpower would reduce the Army's use of contractors on the battlefield and allow a higher level of capability, C_2.

Suppose constraints were eased on manpower and dollars at the same time. Suppose, for example, that the budget were raised from B_1 to B_3 and the Army were left free to choose whatever level of military resources it preferred. It could achieve a level of capacity C_3 by using M_3 military resources and N_1 nonmilitary resources (at e_3). In this case, removing constraints has no effect on the demand for nonmilitary resources and by inference, on the use of contractors. Loosening the budget constraint still farther would actually encourage the Army to *increase* its use of contractors.

At an admittedly high level of abstraction, this discussion illustrates the two ways that resource constraints can affect rational behavior.

- Relieving the constraint on military manpower induces a "substitution" effect; within a fixed budget, it encourages the Army to substitute military for nonmilitary resources because the level of military resources has been artificially constrained in the past.
- Letting the Army choose any combination of military and nonmilitary resources it wants within a budget, relieving the constraint on dollars induces an offsetting "income" effect. In any production setting resembling the Army's use of contractor support services, such an income effect almost always encourages the producer to expand its demand for all resources when its budget increases.[3, 4]

[3] This is not required. An organization can reduce its demand for an "inferior" good when its budget rises. This is rarely observed in major production activities using resources as broadly defined as military and nonmilitary or contract support resources.

[4] One way to think about the substitution and income effects is to use a vector from e_1 to e_2 to measure the substitution effect and a vector from e_2 to e_3 to measure the income effect. The vector $e_1e_3 = e_1e_2 + e_2e_3$ captures both the substitution and income effects. Note that these effects are closely related to but defined slightly differently from the familiar income and substitution components of an uncompensated price elasticity.

It could be argued that, if the Army had a larger budget and no manpower constraint, it could hold its combat force structure constant and spend the additional dollars to reduce risks associated with supporting that structure by substituting military units for contractor CSS organizations on the battlefield. Alternatively, the Army could hold the risk of supporting any size combat force constant and increases the size of the combat force structure available to field. Looking farther afield, the Army could leave its current combat force structure and the risk associated with supporting it fixed and invest the additional funds in new systems that improve future performance. Historically, the Army has tended to preserve and expand combat force structure when it could and worry about the resources to support it later (Lewis and Brown, 2001). Today, the Army is struggling to find funds to support its Future Combat Systems, even as the demands for readiness with increased operational tempo tie resources to the operational force. In this setting of high-level, competing priorities and constraints, it appears unlikely that the Army would use additional dollars to substitute military billets for contractor positions on the battlefield. Put another way, it is reasonable to ask those who propose such a use of additional dollars to defend that use in the face of competing high-level demands for dollars within the Army.

In sum, if the military manpower ceilings in the Army are too low for the budget that the Army now has, loosening these ceilings might well encourage the Army to reduce its reliance on contractors on the battlefield. If, however, the Army is free to allocate any resources it receives, it is more likely that it will spend additional dollars on buying more of a variety of resources than on more military manpower to reduce its need for contractors. As important as the risk associated with the presence of contractors on the battlefield is to those who have studied it carefully, it would have to be very important indeed to compete with current Army demands for new systems and, potentially, additional combat force structure.

This discussion of a smaller force with more missions sets the stage for addressing the other examples of resource constraints presented here.

The importance of *low-density, high-demand skills* affects sourcing primarily because military billets cost more than commercial billets do in peacetime, especially when we take availability and training and recruiting costs into account. Raising military manpower ceilings will not change this cost difference. With many priorities competing for any additional military manpower billets made available, it is highly unlikely that all additional billets would replace contractor positions. Rather, loosening a manpower constraint is likely to allow some military billets to replace the most risky contractor billets, but many new billets will go elsewhere.

Releasing budget constraints can be expected to have an even smaller effect on Army use of contractors because there are so many competing demands for additional dollars. As noted above, organizations tend to expand their demand for all resources when their budgets rise. Even if the Army chose to use some additional money to replace contractor positions with military billets, it has many other competing demands for any additional dollars that become available.

These arguments also apply, point for point, to the effect that *cost-effective commercial capabilities* have on the use of contractors on the battlefield. Added manpower billets will not change the cost and performance advantage of specific capabilities. Many priorities will compete for added dollars.

The effect of the Army's *dependence on reserves* on its use of contractors on the battlefield is a bit more complicated because constraints can be relaxed in more complex ways. For example, if the active force is undersized relative to the Army budget today, increasing the active military manpower ceiling could well allow the Army to move some deployment responsibilities from the reserve components to the active force and substitute active military billets for the contractor positions that the Army has used to limit its reliance on the reserve components. This is a straight substitution effect as described in Figure 6.1.

The Army is more likely to change its manpower constraints in a different way, however. Today, in direct response to its high operational tempo, the Army is actively discussing moving responsibilities between the active and reserve components, even while it holds the end-strength constraints constant for those components. Current discussions envision moving CSS activities from the reserve components to the active force and moving heavy combat capabilities, likely only to be employed in a major combat operation, from the active force to the reserve components. The United States appears to have increasing control over large military campaigns today, allowing the reserve components time to achieve the readiness level required for combat. Also, the political constraints on mobilizing the reserve components will likely be lower for large, infrequent contingencies than for smaller, fairly common or persistent contingencies.

If the current use of the Army reserve components encourages use of contractors on the battlefield, such a change would reduce the Army's reliance on contractors. It is noteworthy that the current high-level discussion of such a change does not currently reflect such a sourcing effect. If the risks of contractors on the battlefield are large enough to warrant restricting their use, they must be large enough to become part of this ongoing discussion. In fact, this ongoing discussion is precisely where an important policy decision that could affect the use of contractors on the battlefield will be made. In effect, if risks associated with the use of contractors are high enough, they should dictate a larger transfer of deployment responsibilities from the reserve components to the active force than decisionmakers would choose without thinking about sourcing issues.

Beyond this total force discussion, increasing the Army budget, coupled with a raised active military manpower ceiling, might open the door for the Army to substitute additional active billets for contractor positions. For the same reasons explained above, adding dollars in this way will likely have only a limited effect on using contractors as substitutes for reserve billets.

The effect of *limited airlift capacity* on the Army's use of contractors on the battlefield offers its own complications. First, note that the relevant constraints may occur outside the Army (or not, as we shall see). The easiest way to relieve them would be to give the Air Force the dollars and/or manpower ceiling it requires to provide additional airlift capacity. Despite decades of concern that airlift capacity was too small, DoD and Congress have never done this. The budget shares of the armed services have been stable for 50 years and have varied systematically only a few times, in response to strategic concerns of the very highest order, such as concern about the adequacy of the country's nuclear deterrent. New sourcing arguments are not likely to change that record.

If airlift capacity is to expand, it probably must do so within the dollar and manpower constraints of the Air Force. Within the Air Force, senior leaders have systematically preferred Air Force–centric capabilities to airlift capabilities. Even with the successful introduction and ongoing expansion of the C-17 fleet, the Air Force can lift only a fraction of the Army—far less than the Army needs to achieve its current goals to deploy effective combat force globally on short notice (Peltz, Halliday, and Bower, 2003; Vick et al., 2002).[5] As efforts to reconcile Army and Air Force resource decisions relevant to airlift capacity continue, the effects of expanded airlift on sourcing decisions have not been raised as an issue in this discussion. If the Army could make a case that the risks of using contractors on the battlefield are important enough to be reflected in this debate, they should help drive the Air Force to buy more C-17s and drive the Army to lighten its demands on airlift still further. This ongoing debate is the most likely place to affect sourcing decisions today by changing the Army's effective constraint on access to airlift.

Airlift capability could expand in another way. Because the Army is the principal beneficiary of expanding airlift beyond the goals set by the Air Force, the Army could cede budget and manpower billets to the Air Force to achieve this change. Such an action is not being discussed and is highly unlikely. If the Army were given the choice of doing this, however, the current debate about airlift capacity strongly suggests that concerns other than the Army's dependence on contractors on the battlefield would drive the decision. When asked where it wishes to place its scarce manpower and dollar resources, the Army has many concerns to compete with concerns about the presence of contractors on the battlefield.

---

[5] These papers identify a number of constraints on deploying Army units, only one of which is airlift capacity.

Policy-Induced Constraints

Constraints associated with system development and personnel policies currently induce requirements for highly skilled personnel on the battlefield, personnel that only a contractor can provide today.

DoD system development policy shapes the Army's *need for high-technology skills* on the battlefield. Once those needs exist, DoD personnel policy forces the requirement for contractors on the battlefield. Both of these policies offer opportunities to change nonsourcing policies to affect sourcing decisions.

The first policy is one reflection of two much broader phenomena that have been observed throughout DoD acquisition for decades. First, when requirements developers identify the priorities relevant to new systems, they routinely give mission capability much more attention than they give to supportability in the field. Even when supportability in the field is a stated goal, when development programs must make trade-offs over the course of a development (as they typically do), they routinely give up supportability to preserve military capability. As a result, support concepts, including the continuing need for contractors on the battlefield, have almost always received less attention than operational concepts. This suggests that, even if a development program began with the goal of designing a weapon system to allow its maintenance by low-skilled personnel on the battlefield, it would be challenging to sustain and realize this goal through the multiyear life of the program (Glennan et al., 1993).

Second, despite repeated efforts to use total life-cycle costs of ownership to discipline the development of new systems, DoD has routinely valued dollars spent today much more, relative to dollars saved ten years from now, than the Office of Management and Budget's (OMB's) prescribed discount rates would justify. That is, in practice, DoD routinely spends less than a dollar during development to save a dollar in net present value of support costs over a system's lifetime. For similar reasons, DoD has proven reluctant to spend a dollar during development to achieve a dollar's worth in net present value of supportability over a system's lifetime. Because DoD tends to think of all of the support-related "ilities"[6] as different from mission capability, this preference for the present over the future aggravates the general tendency to deemphasize support issues during development (Samaniego, 2002, pp. 65–68).

These concerns normally have nothing to do with sourcing, but they tend, more or less by default, to deemphasize the importance of contractor-related risks during system development. A recent memorandum from the Assistant Secretary of the Army (Acquisition, Logistics, and Technology) has stated that this neglect must end (Bolton, 2002a). Ending this neglect will be challenging for reasons that have nothing to do with sourcing policy.

Once a system is designed to require high-technology skills to support on the battlefield, it is challenging to change the design (Resetar, Camm, and Drezner, 1998). The remaining decision is to choose a source for the high-technology skill. The Army has used personnel policies to attract and retain highly skilled medical personnel. Similar policies could be used to do the same thing for the equipment support skills required on the battlefield. This would require an increase in compensation for the relevant personnel and perhaps changes in their personnel management to help them stay up to date with relevant skills. A contractor source must do the same thing, and, when the Army relies on such contractor support, it pays for such arrangements. Loosening the personnel management constraint is particularly attractive because it allows the Army to address risks associated with contractors on the battlefield immediately, without waiting to change the support concepts of the primary systems on which it relies on the battlefield.

Application of *spiral development* affects the Army's need for high-technology skills on the battlefield in a different way. Even if the final product of system development is a support concept that requires only low skills on the battlefield, under spiral development, some development activities almost surely must occur on the battlefield itself. This occurs because, under spiral development, the Army

---

[6] For example, reliability, availability, and maintainability.

fields a system still in development. Simply to operate the system and make its capabilities available to the warfighter, development personnel must be present until operating procedures become standard enough to hand off to a normal operator. And it is highly likely that development personnel will want to be present on the battlefield to collect operational data to help mature and refine the system as real-world operations offer rigorous, realistic testing. Such maturation may occur on the run as the developer-operators encounter problems that must be resolved to keep the system operating and worth having on the battlefield. In sum, a battlefield presence is an integral part of spiral development.

To date, policy has constrained development personnel to be contractor personnel. In principle, the Army could train and sustain highly skilled in-house personnel who specialized in spiral development on the battlefield as part of an Army-contractor integrated team. In all likelihood, such personnel would have to be even more skilled than the personnel discussed above, but, with appropriate compensation and personnel management arrangements, the Army could groom such personnel. Even if they proved to be somewhat less productive than the contractor personnel they replaced, the higher level of reliability they offer on the battlefield might be worthwhile.

A much larger change in policy would end or limit spiral development of systems that pose unacceptably high risks on the battlefield. The risks that such systems pose must be kept in perspective. For the most part, systems in development bring capabilities to the battlefield that would not exist in their absence. For example, the use of the Joint Surveillance and Target Attack Radar System (JSTARS) in the first Gulf War and of unmanned aerial vehicles (UAVs)—armed and unarmed—in Afghanistan and elsewhere has given the United States capabilities that simply did not exist before. Even if these capabilities failed entirely, their effect on mission success—relative to the alternative of not having them in-theater at all—could not be negative. The risk of failure is far more likely to come from the immature technology involved than from the type of personnel providing support or even operating the systems. Nonetheless, if the risks of failure, or risks to the support personnel themselves, were too high, the Army could avoid spiral development of systems on the battlefield. To some extent, the Army already makes such decisions, because it brings weapons to the battlefield only when they are mature enough to offer some prospect of success there. A heightened awareness of the risks of using contractor personnel on the battlefield could encourage the Army to demand a higher likelihood of success before fielding a system still in development.

Mixed Constraints

Constraints on the number of military personnel on the battlefield mix the resource and policy considerations discussed above. The constraint with the most immediate effect on sourcing is a resource constraint—the number set as a ceiling for military personnel in-theater. The Army cannot relieve that constraint, as it can the resource constraints discussed above, without immediately encountering the policy constraint behind the resource constraint—the political consideration that motivates a limit on military personnel. In effect, although such a constraint induces behavior as a resource constraint does, the Army must address a specific policy constraint to loosen the resource constraint.

Troop ceilings are perfect examples of the situation portrayed in Figure 6.1. The Army faces a tight constraint on military end strength but is free to add other resources. Given M_0 in the figure, the Army is free to push its budget for the contingency from B_0 to B_1 or beyond and to use the budget to pay for N_1 nonmilitary resources or more. In this setting, raising the troop ceiling would very likely increase use of military billets and reduce use of contractor positions immediately.[7] Raising the troop ceiling and easing the dollar constraint together—for example, by paying for the contingency using only supplemental congressional funds—might actually increase the Army's use of contractors in-theater as it sought to dominate the situation to limit risk to the force.

---

[7] This assumes that another constraint, such as political reluctance to mobilize the reserve, does not become constraining and continue to limit the military manpower level in-theater.

In this situation, the Army can release a resource constraint only by releasing a policy constraint. In effect, the Army would have to convince the relevant high-level policymakers that the domestic or international political benefit of applying a troop ceiling was not worth its costs. If a ceiling induces greater use of contractors in-theater and their presence increases risk enough, the Army could argue that the policymakers who set the ceiling had not considered the cost of this risk. If they had, they would have allowed a higher ceiling. In this setting, as above, risks associated with contractors on the battlefield must compete with many other concerns to affect such a decision. But to the extent that the Army were going to ask for a change in a troop ceiling to limit risks attending contractors on the battlefield, this is where the Army would have to sell the argument.

Policies designed to keep a *low military profile* in-theater are less formal than specific troop ceilings, but the effects relevant to sourcing decisions mirror those for troop ceilings exactly.

Summary

The discussion above raises a number of points.

First, policies that appear to have nothing to do with sourcing decisions on the battlefields do in fact affect such decisions.

Second, changing these policies effectively amounts to changing specific resource constraints, policy constraints, or a combination of the two. The effect of changing such constraints depends heavily on how the change occurs. Changes that give the Army more freedom to choose between military and contract sources on the battlefield will likely induce the Army to substitute military for contractor sources. Changes that give the Army additional resources to spend on whatever activities it prefers, on the other hand, are likely to have a much smaller effect on the use of contractors and could easily increase their use on the battlefield in particular cases.[8]

---

[8] Put another way, it is far more likely for a specific constraint on the use of military personnel to induce increased dependence on contractors than a constraint on dollar funds.

Third, even where a change in a nonsourcing policy was likely to reduce the Army's dependence on contractors on the battlefield, the Army can effect that change only by placing its concerns about the risks of using contractors on the battlefield in a nonsourcing setting. How large do the risks associated with using contractors on the battlefield have to be to induce policymakers elsewhere in the Army or DoD to change how they use the resources available to them? For example, in response to risks associated with using contractors on the battlefield, how many more CSS billets should move from the reserve components to the active force than is now contemplated? How many more heavy armored billets should move from the active force to the reserve components to make this possible? How much more should the Air Force spend on airlift capacity and less on the F/A-22 than it has planned? How much more emphasis should new Army system developments give to ensuring low-skill support requirements on the battlefield than is currently planned? How much less emphasis should be given to the military capability of new Army systems to make this possible? And so on. Those concerned about the risks of using contractors on the battlefield must develop answers to such questions to affect the nonsourcing policies that force contractors onto the battlefield.

This discussion drives home the fact that the Army has many priorities. Reducing the risk associated with using contractors on the battlefield is one of them. As all of these priorities compete for access to the limited resources available to the Army, all will experience some frustration. With another dollar or another military billet, it will always be possible, at least in principle, to reduce risk on the battlefield to some degree, today or in the future. Using that dollar or billet to reduce the risks caused by the presence of contractors on the battlefield is only one option. By definition, requirements will always

Although some argue that cost considerations have forced the Army to use contractors when it would prefer to use military personnel, this argument is not as compelling as it might first sound. Cost considerations ultimately govern everything that the Army does. They force the Army to make choices. Where a dollar constraint induces the Army to use a contract source on the battlefield, it is likely because the alternative is simply less desirable to the decision-maker vested with this responsibility.

exceed authorizations, requiring the Army to bear risk in one form or another. This is most apparent when the Army considers changing nonsourcing policies to satisfy its concerns about risks associated with sourcing decisions on the battlefield.

CHAPTER SEVEN

Where to Address the Risks of Using Contractors on the Battlefield

As so often happens when the Army faces a challenging resource management issue, it must be prepared to address it in several organizational locations or venues. The discussions in Chapter Five and Six indicate that the Army should be prepared to assess the risks associated with using contractors on the battlefield in five distinctly different venues:

1. Decision venues *outside the Army*. OSD, the Joint Staff, the Executive Branch, and Congress can all affect decisions throughout the Army in various ways, but these players dominate decisions about the *end strength of Army components* and their *operational tempo* (OPTEMPO), *airlift capacity* available, *flexibility of using government civilians*, and the level of *troop ceilings and military presence* more generally in individual deployments. Each of these decisions occurs in a separate venue. These decisions frame major constraints that in turn shape Army sourcing decisions.
2. Decision venues associated with the *services acquisition community*. Army decisionmakers, often in close coordination with counterparts from the rest of DoD, develop policies on the selection of contractors, administration of contractors in-theater, developing habitual relationships with contractors, and design of individual contracts. Working with operators, they implement this policy in specific contractual vehicles and peacetime arrangements to train military and contractor personnel to work

together when they deploy. These decisions directly affect the level and types of risks associated with using contractors.

3. Decision venues associated with *force design and management.* These develop the shape and content of the total operational force. In the TAA, force developers determine what portion of total requirements to resource from active, Guard, and reserve military end strength. The Planning, Programming, Budgeting, and Execution System (PPBES) process and combatant commanders' application of operations and maintenance (O&M) funds determine which additional requirements to cover with contractors. These decisions determine what military and contractor organizations are available at any time to provide support assets to COCOMs in deployments.
4. Decision venues associated with *system design.* Developers of new and modified systems and their support concepts determine the primary supportability characteristics of the systems as well as the skills required to support them on the battlefield. Developers applying spiral development help support and gather detailed operational data on new systems. Developers in both roles affect the skills that the Army needs on the battlefield and hence the need for contractors on the battlefield.
5. Decision venues relevant to planning and executing *specific contingencies.* Given past decisions made in the venues above, when a COCOM and his staff plan the forces and support needed in a new contingency, they make a large number of specific sourcing decisions. In effect, the COCOM is the final gatekeeper that must assess the relative residual risks of using contractor and military sources in a specific setting and make the sourcing decisions that determine where and how the Army actually uses contractors on the battlefield.

This chapter reviews each of these venues in turn. In each venue, it starts with the decisions that affect the Army's use of contractors on the battlefield and asks what *benefits* contractors offer on the battlefield, what *risks* they pose, and what *mitigations* the Army can use to limit these risks.

Sourcing decisions in each venue are integrally linked to decisions about mitigations, but no venue has control over all the mitigations relevant to its sourcing decision. The discussion of these venues will be easier if we review the mitigations relevant to all of them first and then focus in each venue discussion on those under the control of that venue. The discussion reveals the importance of coordinating the decisions that the Army makes in these different venues.

Mitigations Relevant to All Venues

A common set of potential mitigations is relevant to all of the venues above. Without information about which of these the Army will implement, decisionmakers cannot make fully informed decisions under their control and relevant to the Army's use of contractors. The arguments of Army personnel summarized in Chapter Three suggests the following list of mitigations to consider:

- Implement the "standard contracting improvement package" itemized in the discussion of service acquisition below to improve preparation to use contractors. To the full extent possible in the period leading up to a deployment, upgrade this package for the deployment force being assembled.
- Release major policy and resource constraints that govern the level and OPTEMPO of military end strength, airlift capacity, and so on discussed in Chapter Six. The discussion of each venue below identifies those under the control of that venue.
- Change Army personnel compensation and career management to make it easier to attract and retain the high-level skills that contractors currently provide and keep these skills in military units to reduce the relative benefit of contractor support.
- Require that contractors operating on the battlefield use only employees in the Army reserve components. Mobilize them before deploying them and place relevant contractor operations under military control.

- Design simplified field support into new systems to eliminate the need for highly skilled contractor personnel in the forward part of the battlefield.
- Stop planning on contractor logistics support (CLS) over a system's lifetime. Or if the Army pursues this, seek ownership of enough technical data to support development of a second source.
- In connection with system fielding, pay extra to speed stabilization of the support concept in the field and training of military support personnel to take over from interim contractor support (ICS) personnel in the field.
- Limit contractor personnel to safer parts of the battlefield that do not require the Army to divert much capability to protect them. Commensurate with the level of hazard and unpredictability in-theater, the terms of existing SOFAs, military resources available, contractors to be used, the contracting oversight skills of the COCOM staff, and so on, wait to deploy contractors until the theater stabilizes and place them in a secure portion of the battlefield.
- To keep contractor personnel away from danger on the battlefield, develop technologies that allow remote sensing and data collection.
- Ensure that the resources required to protect and support contractors in-theater are included in the operational and support plans.
- Limit reliance in the field on the performance of new systems early in their lives before risks are fully understood and under reasonable control.
- Delay introduction of a system for spiral development on the battlefield until the likelihood that it will work and the magnitude of the benefit it can yield are high enough to justify the risks to contractor personnel and the diversion of military resources required to protect and support these personnel.

The relevance of these mitigations will vary across support activities and contingencies, but information about their potential use is relevant to almost every sourcing decision discussed below.

Outside the Army

Standard, standing processes do not exist to determine the end strength and OPTEMPO of the components of the Army, the level of airlift available for COCOMs to employ in specific contingencies, the level of flexibility to use government civilians, or the levels of troop ceilings or, more generally, military presence chosen for specific contingencies. The government revisits these decisions as needed. The Army can shape these decisions, but only as one member of a broader coalition with goals that transcend the Army's immediate concerns about using contractors on the battlefield.

When these decisions are reopened for discussion, the Army must address all of the benefits, risks, mitigations, and residual risks that it associates with any specific decision. The benefits, risks, mitigations, and residual risks that it associates with using contractors are among these. If contractor-related issues are important to the Army, relative to the other issues under discussion and the general level of uncertainty that inherently surrounds such high-level discussions, the Army should capture these contractor-related issues in its broader deliberations. To do this, it must then be prepared to translate the residual risks associated with using contractors into terms relevant to the other participants in each venue—broader mission success, resource costs, and other goals that could easily change from one reopening to the next. The discussion here does not attempt to wrestle with the details of the decision spaces relevant to each of these venues. It focuses on the portion of these spaces occupied by the effects of the decisions at hand on the Army's use of contractors.

Decisions

Although we could address a number of high-level decisions, we focus on the following five:

- Should the military end strength for a component of the Army increase?
- Should the Army's ability to use government civilians flexibly in-theater increase?[1]
- Should the portion of the Army deployed beyond its permanent station at any point in time decrease?
- Should the level of ready, available airlift that DoD maintains to support deployments increase?
- In a deployment, should the level of military force allowed to deploy increase?

An affirmative response to each of these decisions would release a resource constraint relevant to the Army and its use of contractors. In each case, we assume that *dollar resources available to the Army do not change.*

Benefits

In each case, we saw in Chapter Six that tightening a constraint could plausibly increase the Army's demand for contractors on the battlefield. Relaxing the same constraint should have the opposite effect, reducing Army demand for contractors. The Army demands fewer contractors because, with a lower constraint, the contractor resources offer smaller benefits at the margin than military or government civilian resources would. So, in each decision, the net benefits to the Army from using a fixed number of contractors fall.

Figure 7.1 illustrates how this occurs.[2] The horizontal axis shows the Army's budget, from O_M to O_N. The vertical axis shows

---

[1] OSD has recently claimed that DoD could use more government civilians to displace contractors in Iraq and Afghanistan stabilization efforts if federal personnel management policy were more flexible. Our review of the Army discussion on the use of contractors on the battlefield never raised this issue. We have no evidence from Army operators about its relevance or importance to Army sourcing decisions. We address the issue here solely because it has become such a prominent issue in recent OSD statements about sourcing policy in-theater.

[2] Figures 7.1 and 7.2 use basic microeconomic tools explained in any introductory textbook. They simplify the problem to facilitate graphical presentation. To begin, Figure 7.2 focuses

how much the Army is willing to pay, given its budget, for marginal military resources on the left axis and marginal nonmilitary resources on the right axis. V_M shows the marginal value of military resources, which falls as the Army adds them from the left. V_N shows the marginal value of nonmilitary resources falling as the Army adds them from the right. With total resources of O_MO_N, the Army prefers to use O_MP military resources and O_NP nonmilitary resources, because P is the point at which military and nonmilitary resources yield the same marginal value per dollar. An end-strength constraint may limit the military resources to a size of O_MM. At this point, the Army would prefer to substitute military resources for nonmilitary or contractor resources because V_M is higher than V_N at this constraint.

Figure 7.1
Effects of Releasing a Constraint on Military Resources

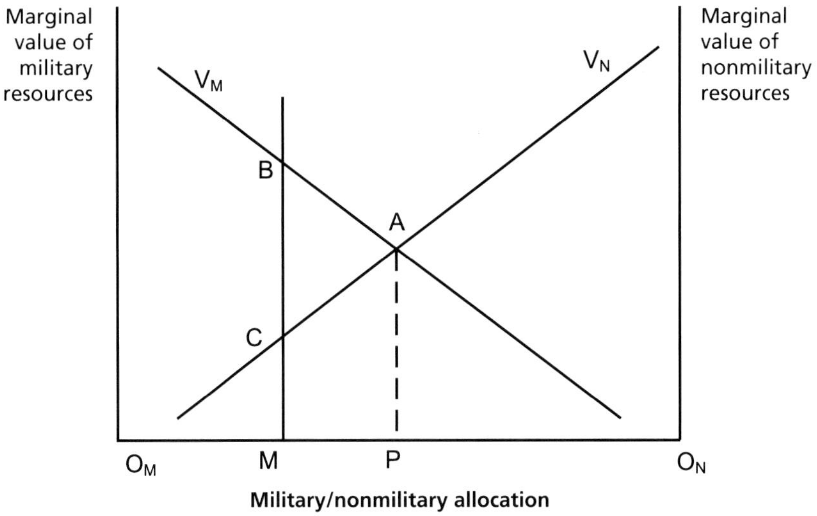

RAND *MG296-7.1*

on one military component and assumes that effects on contractor resources can be inferred directly from effects on nonmilitary resources. These simplifications are comparable to those made in the discussion of Figure 7.1.

Given that it can buy only nonmilitary resources and that they still have a positive marginal value, the Army buys O_NM nonmilitary resources. Additional nonmilitary resources give the Army additional value equal to the area of the trapezoid APMC.

Following an affirmative decision to increase military end strength for a component, at the margin, the Army is now allowed to choose the military alternative and will do so as long as V_M is higher than V_N for the level of military end strength chosen. Loosening the constraint until the Army chooses O_MP military resources brings the Army to its preferred allocation. Substituting military for nonmilitary or contractor resources gives the Army net value equal to the area of the triangle ABC. Loosening the constraint on military end strength any further would make it nonbinding; doing so would not encourage the Army to continue replacing nonmilitary or contractor with military resources.

Loosening constraints on airlift capacity or a troop ceiling works in essentially the same way if we apply the analysis to the resources that the Army deploys to deal with a contingency. In each case, the Army substitutes military capability for nonmilitary or contractor capability until the constraint is no longer binding. If the change is large enough to remove the constraint completely, the Army will not eliminate all the nonmilitary or contractor capability that it could. It will continue to buy contractors rather than buying its full military end strength or deploying all the military allowed in-theater. If airlift capacity increases enough, it will give contractors some space on military assets rather than giving all the space to military capability.

A reduction in the portion of the force deployed has a slightly more subtle effect. Figure 7.2 illustrates this case. The axes and curves have the same meaning here as in Figure 7.1, if we focus on deployed resources. Consider a base period in which the Army did not have to worry about the effects of excessive rotation. It would choose to deploy O_MP military resources and O_NP nonmilitary or contractor resources with a fixed deployment budget, for the reasons explained before in Figure 7.1. Now suppose the military end strength of the Army shrinks relative to its deployment obligations, increasing the

Figure 7.2
Effects of Reducing Military Deployment Responsibilities

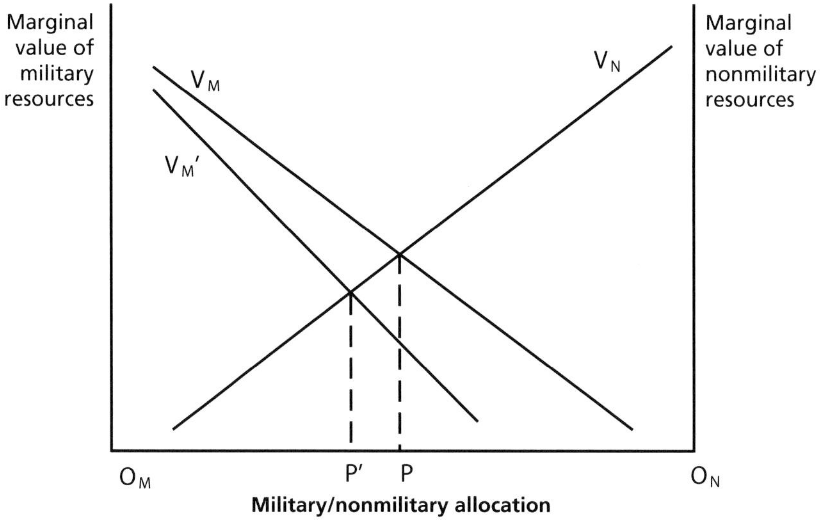

RAND *MG296-7.2*

relevance of overdeployment. In effect, the marginal value of military resources falls somewhat and falls more, the more military resources are deployed because more deployment aggravates rotation problems at an increasing rate. Marginal value falls from V_M to V_M', shifting the preferred allocation point from P to P′. In this case, the rotation concern actually makes nonmilitary (contractor) resources more valuable at the margin than military resources are, encouraging the shift. If the Army can relieve this rotation concern, this process is exactly reversed. Marginal value returns from V_M' to V_M. Military resources can once again assert their superiority and displace nonmilitary (contractor) resources. The Army will substitute military for nonmilitary resources to move from P′ to P.

Increasing the Army's ability to use government civilians flexibly affects use of contractors in a way very similar to that shown in Figure 7.2. Let the horizontal access now represent O&M funds, so that the figure allocates a fixed O&M budget between government civilians and contractor sources. V_M and V_M' now reflect the marginal value of using government civilians. Increasing the flexibility with which DoD can use them presumably shifts their marginal value from V_M' to V_M, effectively shifting the preferred allocation point from P′ to P.

In sum, an affirmative decision for any of the five questions above reduces the benefits of using contractors relative to those of using military assets, encouraging the Army to substitute military for contractor assets. This substitution creates benefits for the Army that the higher-level decision process may not consider. This is the benefit that must be highlighted here.

Risks

Answering any of the five questions above in the affirmative does not directly affect the risk associated with using a given level of contractor support. To the extent that an affirmative decision leads to a reduction in the Army's use of contractors, it reduces the risks imposed by such use. In particular:

- It reduces the risk to *mission success* associated with concerns about lack of control and diverting military resources to protect contractor personnel.
- It increases the likely level of *safety of contractor personnel.*
- It reduces the risk of *resource cost* from protecting and supporting contractor personnel. (Note, of course, that it increases the cost of protecting and supporting military personnel who replace the contractor personnel.) It also reduces the risk of *resource cost* from losing control over contractor costs (and replaces it with an analogous risk of using military assets).
- It reduces concerns about *compliance* with services acquisition laws and policies, including the risk of corruption and public scandal.

Potential Mitigations

Because affirmative decisions do not increase risks associated with using contractors, mitigations are not required to limit these risks. But any assessment should keep in mind the extent that the Army currently mitigates the risks above, limiting the danger associated with them. These decisions get credit only for removing the *residual* risk that remains following mitigation. Analysts making such assessments must make assumptions about these mitigations, even though none of the venues in which these analysts operate has any control over these mitigations.

Summary

As explained in Chapter Six, decisions made outside the Army to change its size, its deployment obligations, the level of airlift capacity, the flexibility of government civilians, or troop ceilings in specific contingencies have their own benefits, risks, and mitigations not considered here. If the residual risks associated with using contractors, relative to using military assets, are large enough, however, they could affect the higher-level decisions. The discussion here asks how these decisions might affect the relative residual risk of using contractors. Affirmative decisions reduce the relative benefits of using contractors and have no direct effect on the relative risks of using contractors at a given level. This change encourages the Army to substitute military for contractor billets. As it does so, both the benefits and the risks to the Army of using contractors fall. If this effect is large enough, it can offer additional support to an affirmative decision. The sequence of reasoning above simply applies the perspective presented in Chapter Six to several specific constraints related to Army use of contractors.

Services Acquisition Community

The risks of using contractors on the battlefield that the Army can do the most to mitigate involve how the Army chooses contractors, writes contracts, administers contracts, and trains Army and contractor personnel to use these contracts in deployments. All but the last concern are the responsibility of the Army's services acquisition community, and that community has an important role to play in promoting and providing training. The Army logistics community, which contracts for the majority of the services used on the battlefield, has been most active is identifying relevant risks and seeking mitigations. It has led the way to developing the formal doctrine that exists today.

In effect, what this community advocates is a consistent package of services acquisition policy, which it has been refining over the last five years. Each iteration brings more detail, but the essence of the argument might be summed up in a "standard contracting improvement package":[3]

- Choose contractors likely to cooperate in-theater. Develop habitual relationships with them to create the basis for such cooperation at the personal, process, and data interface level. Balance habitual relationships with competition to maintain long-term leverage.
- Write contracts properly to cover relevant workscope, accommodate flexibility likely to be needed in a deployment, cover all topics relevant to deployment, motivate effective performance during a deployment, and so on.
- Train Army, contractor, and other relevant personnel together in peacetime to prepare to execute relevant tasks together in a contingency. Complete relevant levels of training for all personnel, from the commander to the contracting officer's representative, before a deployment.
- Negotiate favorable SOFA terms with relevant countries as soon as international risks suggest that the Army may need to use them.
- Fully fund the contract workscope before a contingency so that funding is not a surprise constraint on the battlefield.
- Ensure that COCOM staff understands relevant contract contents in any contingency. Create a point of central visibility over all contracts to provide a single point of contact on all contrac-

[3] This summary attempts to capture the major points offered in AR 700-137 (1985); Pamphlet 715-16 (1998); AR 100-10-2 (1999); AR 715-9 (1999); AMC Pamphlet 715-18 (2000); FM 100-21 (2000); DoD (2001); and FM 3-100.21 (2003). See Appendix A for more detail on FM 3-100.21, the most recent reference included here.

tor obligations to the Army and all Army obligations to its contractors.

- Administer contracts as an integral part of the COCOM's support plan. Include contractors in planning to allow quick, effective exchanges with regard to needs and capabilities. Give contractors access to the operational planning data they need to prepare the support that operations will require.
- Ensure that contractors receive the Army support they require to perform.

Opportunities exist to tweak current Army doctrine. As data accumulate from ongoing deployments, larger opportunities for improvement will inevitably become evident. The major challenge to the Army today is implementing the doctrine that its logistics services acquisition community has already developed. The doctrine already in place provides a comprehensive set of mitigations for many of the risks associated with using contractors on the battlefield. These mitigations cannot eliminate that risk. However, the commander's primary responsibility is to manage risk well enough to ensure mission success, not to eliminate risk. Commanders need only implement existing doctrine to mitigate many of the risks they must manage.

In the remainder of this chapter, the issue of how far the Army has gone toward implementing the package above arises repeatedly. In each case, decisions about the use of contractors depend directly on how much of this package has been implemented. In most cases, the decisionmakers who want to know the answer have little control over how much of the package is in place. They will require standard guidance on what to assume about this package as they pursue their own concerns relevant to sourcing. To make that point, we will refer repeatedly to the "standard contracting improvement package" above. The contents of the package may differ from one support activity or contingency to another in any given setting, but its general structure will remain constant.

Force Design and Management Community

Decisions

Four types of decisions are important here:

- What tasks in the operating force active, Reserve, and Guard military units will provide (TAA resourcing process).
- Relative to their requirements, what levels of military resources each active, Reserve, and Guard military unit in the operating force will receive (TAA resourcing process).
- What O&M resources the operating force will receive through the PPBES process.
- How relevant commanders ultimately commit O&M resources to Army civilian, contractor, and other sources (major command execution, as shaped by PPBES outcomes).

These are the natural venues in which to raise issues relevant to the use of contractors on the battlefield. Assignment of tasks that support deployed forces between the active and reserve components currently appears to affect use of contractors on the battlefield because it is politically easier to deploy active than reserve personnel. So shifting tasks that support deployed forces from the reserve to the active component can reduce use of contractors. Assignment of tasks between those resourced from military end strength and those resourced through O&M funds affects demand for contractors even more directly. The TAA resourcing process is the natural place to raise these issues.

More specific and direct decisions about using contractors occur in the PPBES and MACOM decision processes and should be addressed there. By this point, the benefits and risks relevant to using contractors become the dominant factors in a decision and can be addressed directly.

Benefits

Moving tasks that support deployed forces from the reserve to the active component and, to compensate, moving other tasks from the active to the reserve components should reduce reliance on contractors by relieving a constraint. The discussion above about how to measure benefits relevant to using contractors in processes outside the Army, based on the perspective in Chapter Six, applies here as well.

Contractors create benefits on the battlefield more directly when they help the Army support high-demand, low-density systems and when they provide superior performance, achieve lower cost, or help the military commander focus on combat activities. The Army can state these benefits directly in the venues where they are most relevant, using the approach explained in Chapter Five.

Risks

Using contractor support imposes the risks, identified above, related to the following:

- *Mission success* associated with concerns about lack of control and diverting military resources to protect contractor personnel.
- *Safety of contractor personnel.*
- *Resource cost* from protecting and supporting contractor personnel. (Note, of course, that it reduces the cost of protecting and supporting military personnel who replace the contractor personnel.) It also increases the risk of *resource cost* from losing control over contractor costs (and replaces an analogous risk of using military assets).
- *Compliance* with services acquisition laws and policies, including the risk of corruption and public scandal.

Note that, where the Army reduces its use of contractors by moving activities between active and reserve components, these risks (as mitigated) fall. Hence, risks rise when applying the constrained sourcing perspective in Chapter Five. They fall when applying the broader sourcing perspective in Chapter Six.

Potential Mitigations Controlled Here

The Army force design community can mitigate risks that rise in several ways:

- Move tasks that support deployed forces from the reserve to the active component. Compensate by moving tasks relevant only to infrequent deployments with significant lead time from the active to the reserve components. These mitigations impose risks of their own, which the Army must identify and balance. The TAA resourcing process presumably already attempts to capture these risks.
- Require that contractors operating on the battlefield use only employees in the Army Reserve. Mobilize them before deploying them and place relevant contractor operations under military control. This community must coordinate this mitigation with the services acquisition community to specify the terms of such arrangements and the system design community to ensure that such arrangements fit the system to be supported.
- Ensure that the Army funds, from military end strength, all capabilities that would be inappropriate for a nonmilitary organization to provide under international law.
- Ensure that the Army maintains, from military end strength, enough reliable military capability to back up high-risk, critical contractor sources. This would presumably entail providing a portion of a capability, such as life support or facility support, from both contract and military sources and ensuring that enough military capability is available quickly to replace contractors whose reliability is uncertain, but whom the Army will choose as the first source in critical situations.

Community That Designs New and Modified Systems

This community addresses two sets of decisions that can affect Army demand for contractors on the battlefield: those associated with spiral development and those associated with more traditional support concept design. This subsection addresses each set separately.

Spiral Development

Decision. For any particular program and contingency, the Army must decide whether and how to pursue spiral development of the program in that contingency. The desirability of spiral development and how the Army pursues it are likely to differ from one program to the next and from one contingency to the next. Presumably the program manager and COCOM's staff must discuss the relevant costs and benefits of using spiral development and reach agreement for how and when to bring each new capability onto the battlefield under these circumstances. The analytic approach suggested in Chapter Five should support their discussion. It points in the following direction.

Benefits. The Army gains two kinds of benefits. The first is accelerated access to a new, presumably superior but not fully tested and thus risky, capability in the contingency where the Army first introduces a new system. The second is faster and more thorough operational testing of a new capability. This might easily yield no immediate benefits but could increase the capabilities available to the Army in the future. This increase comes from faster maturation. It may also come from collection and use of information not normally observed—information that can create new capabilities that would never exist without direct observation on the battlefield.[4]

Risks. Using contractor support imposes the risks, identified above, related to the following:

- *Mission success* associated with concerns about lack of control and diverting military resources to protect contractor personnel. Lack of control is of limited importance so long as the Army does not depend heavily on an experimental capability under development. If it works, the Army benefits. If it does not, the

---

[4] Arguments in favor of maturation, for example, favor getting thorough information from users to determine what capabilities they really use in the field and so what capabilities should be refined and to provide as much contextual information as possible to help improve diagnosis of operational problems. For more detail, see Gebman, McIver, and Shulman (1989).

Army is no worse off, for lack of control, than if it had not been present.

- *Safety of contractor personnel.*
- *Resource cost* from protecting and supporting contractor personnel. (Note, of course, that it reduces the cost of protecting and supporting military personnel who replace the contractor personnel.) It also increases the risk of resource cost from losing control over contractor costs (and replaces an analogous risk of using military assets).
- *Compliance* with services acquisition laws and policies, including the risk of corruption and public scandal.

Potential Mitigations Controlled Here. The Army can mitigate these risks in a wide variety of ways. They include the following:

- Prohibit spiral development to dispose of the problem altogether.
- Support force designers in identifying contractor activities to militarize by requiring that their employees be reservists whom the Army can mobilize to support a deployment.
- Assume the systems being introduced will not work and design any campaign in which they are deployed based on that premise. Do not require information feeds from the systems.
- Limit civilian personnel involved in spiral development to safer parts of the battlefield that do not require the Army to divert much capability to protect them.
- Devise methods for such personnel to be "present" to advise on the use of a new system and observe its performance without being physically present. For example, use telecommunications to link these personnel to the user in dangerous parts of the battlefield. Use built-in test (BIT) technology to collect data during an operation and send those data to contractor personnel in a safer place. Prepare and train joint teams of military and contractor personnel so that the military can conduct simpler tasks and collect information in dangerous areas and interact with more highly skilled contractor personnel in less dangerous areas.

- Delay introduction of a system for spiral development on the battlefield until the likelihood that it will work and the magnitude of the benefit it can yield are high enough to justify the risks to contractor personnel and the diversion of military resources after the Army has completed the mitigations suggested above. Work with COCOMs to make decisions about this for individual contingencies.

As noted above, each situation will likely differ. It may be appropriate to use a capability in one contingency but not another. It may be appropriate to wait longer to introduce a new system if the hazards contractor personnel face are high than if they are not.

Support Concept Design

Decisions. Every new system depends on contractor support during the interim between its introduction to the force and the beginning of organic support for the system. This ICS is always required to stabilize the support plan, with specific technical orders, and to train military personnel to provide the support. Over the longer term, the Army has the choice of whether to continue CLS, potentially for the life of the weapon. U.S. Army Training and Doctrine Command (TRADOC) and Army Materiel Command (AMC) work together to make decisions about ICS and CLS policies as part of a broader set of decisions about the support concept for each new system. In all likelihood, support in the field will have to be easier to provide if the Army plans to use military personnel than if it plans to use contractor personnel over the longer term.

Several interrelated decisions are important here:

- What contractor support (as opposed to maturation) capabilities should it decide to retain on the battlefield over the life of a deployable system?
- How quickly should the Army make the transition from contractor to military support for a new system or modification? How much should it be willing to spend to accelerate that transition?

- How much should the Army invest in research, development, test, and evaluation (RDT&E) activities to simplify support activities in the field?

The Army will want to make these decisions in an integrated way, using such an approach as the one presented in Chapter Five, and it is likely to make different decisions for different systems.

Benefits. The benefits of a contractor presence are the likelihood of high-quality support and avoidance of the need to develop a military career field, with training, other infrastructure, and a rotation base to provide in-house support, at least as long as contractor support remains viable. These risks exist on and off the battlefield, inside and outside the operating force.

Risks. Using contractor support imposes the risks, identified above, related to the following:

- *Mission success* associated with concerns about lack of control and diverting military resources to protect contractor personnel.
- *Safety of contractor personnel.*
- *Resource cost* from protecting and supporting contractor personnel. (Note, of course, that it reduces the cost of protecting and supporting military personnel who replace the contractor personnel.) It also increases the risk of resource cost from losing control over contractor costs (and replaces an analogous risk of using military assets).
- *Compliance* with services acquisition laws and policies, including the risk of corruption and public scandal.

Potential Mitigations Controlled Here. The Army can mitigate these risks in a wide variety of ways. They include the following:

- Stop planning on CLS over a system's lifetime. Or if it persists in such planning, seek ownership of enough technical data to support development of a second source.

- Pay extra to speed stabilization of the support concept in the field and training of military support personnel to take over from contractor personnel in the field.
- Make simplified support in the field and remote support to the field from a distance (see above) key performance parameters during development. Provide the funding needed to do this. Protect that funding when compromises on development goals are required.
- Limit reliance in the field on the performance of new systems early in their lives before risks are fully understood and in hand.

Discussion. The Army is likely to combine these in different ways for different systems. As it does, two points will be important.

First, the Assistant Secretary of the Army (Acquisitions, Logistics, and Technology) memorandum on avoiding the use of contractors to support new systems in the division area or equivalent suggests that these decisions and mitigations are important, but it gives little guidance on how to make these decisions and mitigations.

Second, key elements of these decisions about the support concept depend on assumptions about the Army's readiness—in contract terms and contracting readiness—to integrate contractor support into a deployed force. For example, they depend on how the Army pursues training during peacetime to integrate these contractors with the Army force and to train both Army and contractor personnel. TRADOC and the program manager do not control such factors, however.

The organizations making the decisions suggested above need guidance about what to assume about the Army's general ability to use contractor support for new systems once they are fielded. This guidance should presumably come from a source in the Army that can see all efforts to address issues associated with the use of contractors on the battlefield and attempt to align them with one another. That alignment could take the form of an integrated plan to seek coordinated changes in all four settings addressed here over a specified timeline in the future.

Specific Contingencies

Decision. The primary decision here is an integral part of developing the operational and support plans for a specific contingency. What capabilities are required and who exactly should provide them at particular places and times during the contingency? Answers to these questions yield the ultimate sourcing decisions that determine how the Army will use contractors on the battlefields. Answers may change as the contingency unfolds and the COCOM accumulates additional information on his needs in the theater.

Benefits. The benefits include the following:

- Contractors help the COCOM add capability while accommodating constraints on airlift, military resources allowed in-theater, and mobilization of reserve components. The Army can measure the benefits such contractors can provide using the approach based on Chapter Six and described above for decisions made outside the Army.
- Given the decisions made in the venues above, contractors provide capabilities not available in the military force. This may occur because they have some inherent advantage or because the COCOM simply needs more of a capability than is available from the military force. Either way, these capabilities depend integrally on the readiness of available contractors. The Army can measure this in a variety of ways, discussed in Appendix E.

Risks. Using contractor support imposes the risks, identified above, related to the following:

- *Mission success* associated with concerns about lack of control and diverting military resources to protect contractor personnel.
- *Safety of contractor personnel.*
- *Resource cost* of protecting and supporting contractor personnel. (Note, of course, that it reduces the cost of protecting and supporting military personnel who replace the contractors.) It also adds to the risk of resource cost of losing control over contractor costs (and replaces an analogous risk of using military assets).

- *Compliance* with services acquisition laws and policies, including the risk of corruption and public scandal.

Potential Mitigations Controlled Here. As the final gatekeeper before actual use of contractors on the battlefield, the COCOM has many mitigations to consider. The COCOM has the most complete understanding of all relevant Army mitigations because he can see what the Army has already done and knows more about the circumstances in which contractors will work on the battlefield in his deployment than anyone else. That said, the COCOM has to work within the constraints of decisions made before he entered the picture, and he has only a limited ability to mitigate the effects of these decisions.

- To the full extent possible in the period leading up to deployment, use the "standard contracting improvement package" described above to improve preparation to use contractors.
- If arrangements have been made to do this, mobilize contractor employees whom the Army plans to use in their existing positions as reservists in-theater.
- Delay introduction of a system for spiral development on the battlefield until the likelihood that the system will work and the magnitude of the benefit it can yield are high enough to justify the risks to contractor personnel and the diversion of military resources after the Army has completed the mitigations suggested above. Work with system developers to make decisions about this for individual contingencies.
- Ensure that the resources required to protect and support contractors in-theater are included in the operational and support plans.
- Commensurate with the level of hazard and unpredictability in-theater, the terms of existing SOFAs, military resources available, contractors to be used, the contracting oversight skills of the COCOM staff, and so on, wait to deploy contractors until the theater stabilizes and place them in a secure portion of the battlefield.

- Limit reliance in the field on the performance of new systems early in their lives before risks are fully understood and in hand.

Where a COCOM can choose between military and contractor sources, this sourcing decision should depend on the extent to which the COCOM can implement these mitigations. That is, the COCOM's mitigations are an integral part of the sourcing decision. Existing Army doctrine identifies all of these mitigations, but it does not emphasize enough how they should shape sourcing decisions in specific contingencies.

Discussion. This review of decisions relevant to sourcing and the diversity of venues in which they occur emphasizes how fragmented decisionmaking relevant to the Army's use of contractors on the battlefield is. Many relevant decisions occur outside the Army itself. The decisions that occur in all of these venues are important to many activities that contractors provide on the battlefield. Table 7.1 summarizes where effective decisions about the mitigations relevant to sourcing decisions can occur throughout the Army and beyond.

Without central guidance from the Army about what to expect from other venues, decisionmakers can react to this fragmented authority in two ways. One is to neglect the effects of their actions on the use of contractors altogether. It is unlikely that decisionmakers responsible for choosing the level of airlift capacity ever even think about how their decisions affect the Army's use of contractors. In most cases where this is likely to apply and that we have reviewed, that neglect has probably led to Army overuse of contractors. Evidence is not available to say how serious that overuse is.

When a decisionmaker chooses a course of action that clearly does affect Army use of contractors, she must make assumptions, if only implicit, about all the relevant mitigations, made elsewhere, that she does not control. In the absence of evidence or guidance, it is natural for her to act conservatively, assuming that where risks do exist, they will not be adequately mitigated by decisionmakers elsewhere. To the extent that this occurs, we should expect Army underuse of contractors. Evidence is not available to say how serious that underuse is.

Table 7.1
Where Effective Decisions About Relevant Mitigations Can Occur

	Venue				
Mitigation	**Outside Army**	**Services Acquisition**	**Force Design**	**System Design**	**Specific Contingencies**
Use standard contracting improvement package		Primary control			Secondary control
Release a constraint under a venue's own control	Control		Control	Control	
Change compensation, career management for highly skilled technical military personnel	Control				
Militarize contract workforce		Secondary control	Primary control	Secondary control	
Delay introduction of system or spiral development				Control	Control
Plan for lifetime CLS support only if second source exists				Control	
Speed transition from ICS to military field support				Control	
Locate, time contract employees to protect them				Share control	Share control
Protect and support contractors					Control
Keep contractors out of inappropriate combat-type activities			Primary control	Secondary control	Secondary control
Maintain backup source for high-risk, critical support			Control		Control
Do not let the operation plan depend critically on experimental support					Control

In the absence of evidence, we can only predict that, where use of contractors is justified by their ability to relieve a constraint, the Army probably uses them too often. Where use of contractors is justified only by their ability to provide inherently higher quality or lower cost than military sources, the Army probably uses them too little. Where the information about the status of decisions in all venues is the best, which exists when a COCOM assembles a deployable force, the Army is likely to make the best decisions that it can make today. This ability to make good decisions here is enhanced by the recent focus of the Army's doctrine about using contractors on the battlefield on precisely this venue, refining the framework available to Army decisionmakers assembling a force for a contingency. Combat has traditionally offered strong incentives to craft arrangements well suited to the circumstances, even if they are unconventional. Decisionmakers working with the COCOM may be able to compensate for less-informed decisionmaking earlier. That is, they should be better able to identify cases of overdependence and improve mitigations in the deployment support plan where they are forced by decisions made earlier and elsewhere to take contractors they would not have chosen to use. They should also be better able to choose contract sources disproportionately from among those available to perform tasks where contractors do have an inherent advantage.

Such a supposition is a useful place to start improving the assessment of risk in these various venues. As the final gatekeeper, the COCOM's venue is critical but probably assesses risks more effectively than the other venues reviewed here. Risk assessment can probably be improved a great deal more in the other venues. Doing so will give the COCOM a better set of options to draw from as he stands by his gate.

More generally, this view of diverse venues emphasizes the value of developing and maintaining more complete and clear Army guidance on where to mitigate risk in the use of contractors on the battlefield so that decisionmakers in all of these venues have a better understanding that their decisions do affect Army use of contractors and of what mitigations they should expect to occur elsewhere as they make their own decisions over various planning horizons.

CHAPTER EIGHT

Summary and Conclusions

Everyone agrees that using contractors on the battlefield is risky. What should the Army do about that? It is hard to reach agreement, because those who worry about these risks do not describe the risks in terms that help them understand one another's concerns and work toward a common understanding of the risks and their implications.

The Standard Army Approach to Assessing Risk

The Army has a standard method for dealing with risk (Chapter Two). FM 3-100.12 clearly explains how a decisionmaker can

- identify the hazards relevant to a decision,
- identify the risks associated with each hazard,
- mitigate these risks, and
- assess the residual risk associated with any decision—the risk that remains after the decisionmaker has implemented appropriate mitigating controls.

The manual explains this approach in the context of operations, starting from the premise that a commander does not seek to eliminate risk but to avoid unnecessary risks. A great deal of the commander's operational art is embedded in identifying what risks are unnecessary, but the basic framework provides a clear way to apply that complex art to specific decisions on the battlefield.

As FM 3-100.12 explains, the approach described can be applied to any decision that a commander faces. It is well suited to the decisions of where, when, and how to use contractors on the battlefield precisely because these decisions are integral parts of any field commander's support plan. These sourcing decisions are most appropriately made as an integral part of the commander's development of a basic course of action on the field.

This report proposes using this standard Army approach to structure risk assessment that compares the residual risks of contractor and military sources of combat service support on the battlefield. It refers to the *relative residual risk* of using a contractor as the risk of using a contractor, relative to the risk of using a military source, after the commander has applied all appropriate mitigations for each source. That is, the report compares two courses of action. Each course of action includes the choice of a contractor or military source and the choice of the mitigations that accompany the use of that source. Mitigations remove unnecessary risks associated with each course of action. The approach prefers the source with the lower residual risk and recognizes that the commander's job is not to eliminate the risk associated with choosing a source but to manage it appropriately within the constraints that the commander faces.

A Disciplined Way to Assess Risks Associated with Using Contractors

This report applies this approach through the following sequence of reasoning.

- Commanders use contractors only if doing so offers some advantage (Chapter Three, Appendix C). If no apparent advantage exists, the issue of using contractors on the battlefield never arises. We need to understand what advantage a contractor offers. The report identifies two classes of advantages: inherent advantages relative to a military source and relief from policy and resource constraints that the commander faces.

- The use of contractors on the battlefield presents specific risks (Chapters Two and Four). We need to understand what risks the commander should worry about. The report identifies four relevant risks: shortfalls in mission success, the safety of contractor employees and their equipment, resource costs, and other specific but broader goals typically outside a field commander's immediate military concerns, such as total force management or compliance with administrative law.
- The risks relevant to any specific sourcing decision in this context stem from key hazards associated with the intensity and predictability of military action during a contingency, status of international agreements on the status of forces, the status of contractor employees under international law, the Army's ability to control a contractor, the Army's responsibilities to protect and support a contractor, and a number of other factors (Chapter Three, Appendix B). These hazards are interrelated; some may be influenced by efforts to mitigate the risks associated with other hazards.
- The Army has extensive opportunities to mitigate the effects of hazards associated with using contractors to provide CSS (Chapter Three, Appendix B). The risks the Army faces when using contractors in any particular circumstance ultimately depend on the extent to which the Army takes advantage of the mitigations available. A sourcing decision is as likely to depend on the mitigations anticipated as on the severity or probability of the initial hazards themselves.
- Even if the Army takes advantage of all the mitigation strategies available when it uses a contractor source, some risks will remain (Chapter Five, Appendix B). Inherent differences between doing work in-house and depending on an outside source create unavoidable risks. These risks are well known. The Federal Acquisition Regulation (FAR) is designed explicitly to help manage them. But in the end, the Army must compare such remaining risks with the benefits it gets from using a contract source and with the risks and benefits of using an in-house military or government civilian source.

- When the Army applies appropriate mitigations, the relative residual risks associated with using contractors will likely vary across CSS activities and contingencies (Chapter Four). Their levels are likely to depend on five basic considerations: the type of activity, the type or identity of the contractor, the nature of the contingency, the location and battle phase of the contractor on the battlefield, and the quality of government oversight of the contractor.
- An analyst conducting a standard Army risk assessment can weigh the factors above in a systematic way to determine whether a contractor or military source is preferable for a particular activity under particular circumstances (Chapter Four). Using a "simultaneity stack" of missions—a set of missions that defense planning guidance suggests the Army should be able to execute simultaneously—such as the one used in each TAA, an Army analyst can use a standard assessment to determine what mix of contractor and military sources is appropriate for any CSS activity in the Army force as a whole.
- It is very likely that this sequence of reasoning will yield a mix of contractor and military CSS sources, in part because contractors have inherent advantages in some circumstances and in part because contractors help the Army overcome constraints imposed for reasons unrelated to sourcing policy in other circumstances (Chapter Five). The sequence of reasoning above can support a risk assessment of relieving these constraints and thereby reducing the Army's dependence on contractors (Chapter Six). The form of such an analysis differs from that for a sourcing decision subject to constraint. The risks and information required to assess the implications of loosening a constraint also differ from those discussed here.

This sequence of reasoning identifies the information an Army decisionmaker must have to apply the standard Army risk assessment framework to a sourcing decision. The approach proposed here is not simple. Complexities discussed here directly reflect the complexity of operational art on the battlefield and of the multiple risks relevant to a sourcing decision. Application of the standard Army framework to more traditional operational questions is not simple either. Ideally, sourcing decisions in a particular contingency would be made as an integral part of operational planning for the contingency. But the same basic sequence of reasoning can help support decisions made at a higher level, elsewhere in the Army and outside the Army.

Where to Assess Risks Associated with Using Contractors

Where should risk assessment relevant to Army sourcing occur? Such assessment should support decisions that significantly affect Army use of contractors, wherever those decisions occur (Chapter Seven). Decisions in five distinct organizational locations or "venues" appear to be important.

Outside the Army

The size and OPTEMPO of the military force affect the use of contractors. As military end strength falls or OPTEMPO increases with a fixed end strength or monetary budget, the Army will likely rely more heavily on contractors to provide services that the military force simply cannot provide. Airlift capacity affects the use of contractors. As airlift—military or contractor—capacity increases, the Army will likely rely less heavily on contractors that use local nationals or forms of transport not available to the Army. Troop ceilings and policies on military presence in a theater affect the Army's use of contractors. As restrictions on the presence of military forces in-theater increase, the Army naturally turns to heavier use of contractors. Decisionmakers outside the Army choose the policies relevant to each of these factors, albeit with input from the Army. Historically, sourcing concerns in the Army have not shaped decisions made here. Perhaps they should.

Army Services Acquisition Venues

The policies the Army uses to choose contractors, design contracts and quality assurance plans, and oversee and support contractors in-theater heavily affect the residual risks associated with their use. Joint training of military and contractor personnel, application of these policies in-theater, and active integration of contractors into planning in-theater also affect residual risks. The more the Army uses the policies called for in its doctrine on the use of contractors on the battlefield, the more desirable contractors become relative to military personnel on the battlefield. This part of the Army's doctrine has emerged primarily from the logistics community. Decisions to apply the doctrine will occur there and in the operational community ultimately responsible for training the force and integrating logisticians with operators during contingencies. Formal risk assessment can help Army decisionmakers understand how such changes will likely affect the risks that the Army faces on the battlefield and the implications of these risks for Army use of contractors.

Force Design and Management Venues

The TAA determines which required CSS support activities the Army will resource from the active, Guard, and Reserve military components. These decisions affect the use of contractors. Diminished active component capability to perform an activity can encourage contractor use to alleviate rotation constraints. Diminished reserve component capability to perform an activity can encourage contractor use to avoid the political costs of repeatedly mobilizing a small number of units and personnel within these components. The Army uses O&M funds to get other support services, including contracting services. Decisions on how to use O&M funds occur in the PPBES and MACOM resource management processes. Such decisions on the application of O&M funds affect the Army's use of contractors directly. The sequence of reasoning offered here can help decisionmakers in the TAA, PPBES, and MACOM resourcing processes understand the effects of their decisions on Army risks and their implications for Army use of contractors on the battlefield.

System Design Venues

System requirements officials and program managers choose the support concept for a new or modified system. This encourages dependence on contractors when the support concept envisions a long interim contractor support period or requires highly skilled support personnel on the battlefield over the life of the system. More generally, officials use spiral development to field systems early and collect operational data on them from the battlefield to refine their designs over time. This encourages the presence of contractors on the battlefield. The sequence of reasoning offered here can help these decisionmakers understand the effects of their decisions on Army risks and the presence of contractors on the battlefield.

Specific Contingencies

Given the decisions made in the venues above, a COCOM calls on existing Army capabilities to assemble a force. The sequence of reasoning presented here flows directly from this decision setting and is likely to be easiest to apply in this setting. That said, this setting has received the most attention in recent Army doctrine on the use of contractors on the battlefield. Despite its direct applicability here, the sequence of reasoning above may well improve decisionmaking more in venues that have not received as much attention.

In each of these venues, the sequence of reasoning proposed here asks decisionmakers to assess risk by comparing the residual risk of using a contractor source, with appropriate mitigations, with the residual risk of using a military source, with appropriate mitigations. Unfortunately, the decisionmakers in each venue control only a portion of the mitigations relevant to their decisions. They must make assumptions about mitigations that other decisionmakers will apply. Standard Army guidance could help all decisionmakers coordinate their decisions against a common set of assumptions. In the absence of such guidance, the decisionmakers in individual venues are likely to apply their own priorities or plan for the worst, assuming mitigation will be inadequate elsewhere. The joint effect of such behavior could easily be underutilization of contractors and hence a higher level of risk on the battlefield than necessary. The approach suggested here would be grossly incomplete without Army-wide guidance to coordinate decisions in different venues.

Today, decisions are made in many of these venues relevant to Army use of contractors on the battlefield without regard to such an effect. In other places, decisionmakers recognize that their decisions affect the presence of contractors but do not use a risk assessment compatible with the Army's standard approach to risk assessment to address the effects of their decisions. The Army literature on using contractors on the battlefield and, most particularly, its doctrine on this topic recommends repeatedly to assess the risks of using contractors. We offer the sequence of reasoning in this report to help decisionmakers respond positively to that recommendation in every venue significant to the Army's use of contractors on the battlefield.

Can the Future Differ from the Past?

In the quotation that opens this report, LTC Donald Curtis captures the Army's central dilemma about using contractors on the battlefield when he says, "In each conflict, there is almost universal agreement that use of contractors versus military support forces was the necessary, but not preferred course of action" (Curtis, 2000, p. 10). This report suggests that this may have occurred throughout the Army's history in part because contractors have helped the Army mitigate the effects of specific policy and resource constraints. If enough airlift capacity were available, the Army would prefer to use military personnel. If troop ceilings were higher, the Army would prefer to use military personnel. If the Army had enough active military personnel to handle all of its deployment responsibilities, it would prefer to use military personnel. In the presence of these and many other constraints, however, it has been necessary to use contractors to reduce the unnecessary risks that the Army faced in each deployment. Because, in all likelihood, such constraints will persist, the Army will continue to use contractors, even though its leaders might prefer to use military personnel in many cases.

We believe a deeper problem underlies the Army's dilemma about using contractors. Disagreement persists in the Army about specific uses of contractors on the battlefield. That is because people in different parts of the Army, with different priorities and different perspectives, lack a common structure and language that they can use to present their concerns in comparable terms and reduce their disagreements. Without a common understanding of what affects the Army's use of contractors on the battlefield, many decisionmakers can continue to choose courses of action that increase the Army's dependence on contractors without even realizing it. Others who do understand their effects on the use of contractors have no Army-wide guidance to shape their decisions and so rely on their own priorities and assumptions about what mitigations will occur elsewhere to choose their own mitigations and sourcing decisions relevant to the use of contractors. When this occurs, people in one part of the Army can decry decisions being made elsewhere without having the power to improve those decisions from an Army-wide perspective.

This report offers a single, integrated model of how a large number of decisions affect the Army's use of contractors on the battlefield and of the principal factors relevant to these decisions. We hope this model and these factors can help shape a more constructive, precise, engaged discussion within the Army. As that discussion proceeds, it will become apparent which considerations are most important to differences in points of view. The Army can focus on collecting better empirical evidence about these considerations and use the evidence to improve its decisions about where, when, and how to use contractors on the battlefield. Over time, such a discussion should help Army leaders stop "grappling with the same issues their predecessors did when the nation was born" (Curtis, 2000, p. 10) and move on to other challenges.

APPENDIX A

Recent Policy Developments Relevant to the Use of Contractors on the Battlefield

Concern about relying on contractors on the battlefield is not new. In fact, the Army has relied on contractors to varying degrees ever since the Revolutionary War.[1] But the Vietnam War saw qualitative changes in the nature of support as manufacturer field technicians become a permanent fixture on the battlefield to support increasingly sophisticated equipment (Curtis, 2000, p. 7).[2] Since then, a number of Army and DoD actions have pointed to broader concerns about dependence on contract support during hostilities.

This appendix reviews a series of efforts over the last two decades to understand better the risks associated with using contractors on the

[1] Epley (1990) suggests that, with some variation in individual wars, one contract billet has supported about six military billets in American wars from the Revolution through the Vietnam War. Most contract employees worked in relatively safe portions of the theater of operations. Gutierrez (2001) and Schrader (1999) provide useful summary histories. Tomich (2001, Appendix C) offers a revealing set of direct observations on the use of contractors through the Army's history up to the Vietnam War. Tomich (2001, Appendix E) provides an excellent single source of information on contractor experience (under LOGCAP, described below) in eight deployments during 1992–1999. For additional information, see Brown (1999); Buhler (2000); Curtis (2000); Dibble, Home, and Lindsay (1993); Fortner (1999); Huston (1966); Lynn (1963); McDonnell (1996); O'Connor (1965); Schrader (1999); Stollenwerk (1999).

[2] Other support was also important. "Tactical operations in Vietnam could only begin in earnest with the help of the commercial sector. . . . 'In near desperation, the Army turned to RMK (Raymond-Morrison-Knudsen), a civilian construction firm' [Clow and Flavin, 1993, p. 4] with two years experience in Vietnam. RMK doubled its workforce *three* times in two years and worked (along with many other contractors) closely with military units and task forces of all sorts to quickly develop the theater and support military operations in the field with engineering, construction, transportation, and supply services" (Stollenwerk, 1999, p.12).

battlefield and to change policies to manage the negative effects of these risks more effectively.

A 1981 Defense Science Board (DSB) summer study, for example, examined the implications for operational readiness of growing military dependence on contractor support of high-performance systems. It concluded that "contractor civilian employees have become essential in the effective operation of many military systems. . . . DoD dependence on contractor civilian employees should and will steadily increase" (DSB, 1982a). Growing dependence was important to garrison and deployment operations. Shortly thereafter, another DSB study asked where contractors held mission-essential jobs supporting the DoD and what risks they posed (DSB, 1982b). It concluded that contractor employees have an outstanding record of reliability during crisis and actual combat. Only a small number were critical to sustaining military operations. DoD should monitor the activities they support and develop contingency plans to ensure their robustness during crises and combat. Refined contractual arrangements should be able to ensure performance by other contract employees (DSB, 1982b, pp. 2–5).

In 1984, a subcommittee of the House Committee on Government Operations held hearings on the effect that contract support can have on mission-essential activities (U.S. Congress, 1984, p. 6).[3] Its findings were disturbing. Most defense firms queried had not discussed the implications of hostilities with their employees. Some contractor personnel interviewed said there were no requirements for them to stay in-theater if a war began. Many said they would leave Europe if hostilities arose. Field maintenance technicians predicted that Hawk missile batteries in-theater would fail within five days without their support. At that time, Army planners gave Europe higher priority than any other theater as a potential site of future hostilities critical to U.S. security. The findings foreshadowed those of a less visible study 15 years later that found that a number of "developmental contractor personnel" supporting the Army's most techno-

[3] For a useful discussion, see Foster (1998).

logically sophisticated division, the Fourth Infantry Division, had "no desire or intention to support a real [outside the continental U.S.] operation" (CASCOM, 2001, p. 17).

A 1988 DoD Inspector General (1991) audit found that, when relying on contractors during hostilities, the armed services could not ensure continuity of service, compel contractors to perform, or enforce contractual terms. They had no central visibility of what emergency-essential services contractors provided or their readiness to provide those services in emergencies. In response to this audit, DoD developed an instruction to create better visibility of emergency-essential contractor activities and DoD plans to manage these activities.[4] A recent GAO study found that DoD has not been complying with this instruction and that poor visibility of mission-essential contract support and plans to ensure its performance during hostilities remain a serious problem.[5]

Meanwhile, in the mid 1980s, the Total Army Analysis identified shortfalls in logistics capabilities and pointed to increased use of contractors as one potential solution (Nichols, 1996). In 1985, the Army began to think about contingency contracting in a new way when it issued its regulation for the Logistics Civil Augmentation Program (LOGCAP) (Department of the Army, 1985). LOGCAP is an umbrella program in which a contractor develops plans for potential contingencies and stands ready to provide a wide range of in-theater services related to logistics, life support, and facility management when the Army calls. The Army chose a contractor for its LOGCAP program in 1992 and began using it to support contingencies almost immediately. LOGCAP has provided contract support for

---

[4] DoDI 3020.37, "Continuation of Essential DoD Contractor Services During Crises," November 6, 1990.

[5] For example, the logistics portion of the operations plan for the war in Iraq has no backup plans if contractors fail to perform. In the past, contractors have usually performed in hostile theaters. When they have not, DoD has substituted other contractors or military sources. The plan in Iraq in effect proposes a similar implicit backup plan. This is true even though the logistics supplement to the Joint Strategic Capabilities Plan, written in 2002, requires development of a mitigation plan to back up commercial support (GAO, 2003a, pp. 14–16). See also Phillips (2002, p. 5).

Army deployments and other contingencies ever since (Gally and Horne, 1996; GAO, 1997; Harris, 2000; Kolar, 1997; LMI, undated; Palmer, 1999; Thomas, 2000; Williamson, 1998). [6] Although the program has experienced "growing pains" and some believe it has given too little priority to cost consciousness, it is widely admired as an exemplar.[7] For example, it gives the Army high visibility of all activities conducted under its auspices and works to integrate contract services in any theater where the Army uses it. That said, even the arrangements of LOGCAP do not ensure continuity of service, compel contractors to perform, or enforce contractual terms for the Army.

LOGCAP had not directly supported any large combat actions before the recent wars in Afghanistan and Iraq, but the Army received support from 76 contractors during the first Persian Gulf War. About 9,200 American contract employees supported 541,000 military personnel at the height of that war (GAO, 1994, p. 5; Orsini and Bublitz, 1999, p. 131). For example, manufacturers' technical representatives were present to support TOW and Patriot missiles, Fox nuclear, biological, and chemical (NBC) warfare vehicles, Bradley

---

[6] For a particularly good overview, see Stollenwerk (1999). Tomich (2001, Appendix E) provides useful detail on contractor experience in eight deployments.

[7] "Once [they] tested [it] and found [it] to be good, some commanders overindulged in what the contractors brought to the table. To some observers, there were 'growing pains;' to others, it was a bit more serious. Without adequate planning and communication, the Army and other government agencies could inadvertently require the contractor to perform services outside the scope of the contract. In a contingency operations environment like Bosnia, this easily resulted in significant cost overruns, the type that captured the attention of General Accounting Office (GAO), Army Audit Agency (AAA), the Inspector General (IG), and Congress. The image of the LOGCAP contractor ran the gamut from 'money-grubbing profiteer' to invaluable resource. Nonetheless, the United States Army Europe (USAREUR) became enamored of BRSC's [Brown and Root's] performance. So much so that when the follow-on, less expensive contract was awarded to DynCorp, USAREUR severed ties with the prescribed Department of the Army (DA) LOGCAP contract in favor of a more expensive, more restrictive, but-already-in-place sole source contract with BRSC. However, it is important to recognize that the commander tested contractors on the battlefield and found it to be good—very good" (Young, 1999). Young (1999) attributes early problems with LOGCAP in the Balkans to "USAREUR's inexperience and lack of understanding of the LOGCAP contract, contractor's capabilities, and program management." See also GAO (1997, pp. 4–5); Harris (2000, pp. 1–2). This "already-in-place sole source contract with BRSC" is the Army's Balkans Support Contract (BSC). For a discussion of the BSC closely linked to many of the issues raised here, see Greenfield and Camm (forthcoming).

personnel carriers, M1 and M1A1/2 tanks, and OH-58D helicopters (Dibble, Home, and Lindsay, 1993; Hyde, 1991, p. 32). With a handful of exceptions, these contractors performed well.

Interest in how best to employ contractors on the battlefield has accelerated in recent years. During 1999–2000, the Army Training and Doctrine Command/Army CASCOM's Contractors on the Battlefield Integrated Concept Team (ICT) developed and published synchronized capstone doctrine and policy for using contracted support in Army operations.[8] Those publications are[9]

- Field Manual 100-10-2, *Contracting Support on the Battlefield,*
- Army Regulation 715-9, *Contractors Accompanying the Force,* and
- Field Manual 100-21, *Contractors on the Battlefield.*

These documents provide "comprehensive and detailed direction to commanders, contracting personnel, and contractors on what their roles and responsibilities are and how they should meet them." A GAO survey of Army personnel found that "officials . . . were generally aware of the Army's guidance."[10] These documents have also created a concrete forum for ongoing discussion of contractors on the battlefield in the Army that easily exceeds anything occurring elsewhere in DoD.[11]

In 2002, the Assistant Secretary of the Army for Acquisition, Logistics, and Technology issued memoranda relevant to the role and use of contractors on the battlefield. On January, he directed that contracts for development activities where support personnel could be deployed outside the U.S. will contain appropriate deployment guid-

---

[8] For a clear discussion of these efforts, see Fortner (2000a, 2000b).

[9] AR 100-10-2 (1999), AR 715-9 (1999), FM 100-21 (2000). These documents built on Army Pamphlet 715-16 (1998).

[10] Based on a review of Army personnel deployed in the Balkans and Southwest Asia (GAO, 2003a, p. 24).

[11] This discussion has generated an updated document on doctrine, Department of the Army (2003).

ance (Bolton, 2002a). On June 11, 2002, the assistant secretary directed that program executive offices and other program developers to devise support plans for new or modified weapon systems that would avoid a permanent contractor presence in the division area or equivalent (Bolton, 2002b).[12] Meanwhile, in efforts to define Army activities that were not core competencies and therefore appropriate for conversion to civilian sources in the Third Wave initiative, the Assistant Secretary of the Army for Manpower and Reserve Affairs (ASA [M&RA]) aggressively reviewed many support billets traditionally designated as military in the operating force (White, 2002).

The documents mentioned above and other recent statements about using contractors on the battlefield frequently refer to the value of assessing risks more systematically. Here is a representative sample:

- "In the end, the commander must weigh the risks, use good judgment and understand the law to determine the best course of action" (Mailander, 2002, p. 10). "Commanders at all levels must conduct risk analyses before deciding to use contractor support during such operations" (Nichols, 1996, p. 65). "MACOMs must evaluate each function, define the acceptable degree of risk, and balance its military and contractor support mix accordingly" (AR 700-137, 1985).
- Risk assessment is the first governing principle of contractor support: "To properly evaluate the value of contractors to a military operation, the requesting authority or designated supporting unit must make an assessment of the risk. This assessment evaluates the impact of contractor support on mission accomplishment and contractor safety to determine the most effective use of contractor support. Assessment also addresses potential degradation of contractor effectiveness during situations of tension or increased hostility" (FM 100-21, 2000, pp. 1-2–1-3).
- A failure to find any evidence that the Army had conducted a formal risk assessment of the use of contractors to support Army

[12] See also CASCOM (2001, p. 20).

aviation units, despite considerable effort, yielded a recommendation that the Office of the Deputy Chief of Staff for Logistics "commission a risk assessment to address the risks associated with employing civilian personnel in a combat zone" (Brooke, 1998, p. 26).

- A review of the final draft for FM 3-100.21, *Contractors on the Battlefield*, concluded that it "could become the primary source document for this area of study." It also observed that, although the draft manual recommended application of risk assessment, it was "weak in 'risk assessment.' A risk assessment model should be included in the manual" (Mailander, 2002, p. 7).
- DoD's guidance on how to classify activities in the "2003 Inventory of Commercial and Inherently Governmental Activities" calls for the services to conduct risk assessments to support two kinds of decisions: whether "use of DoD civilians or contract support constitutes an inappropriate or unacceptable risk" and "decisions about the number of military [or civilian] support elements necessary to provide a core capability." These assessments inform decisions to retain activities in-house because of their relationship to military operations, military support of operating forces, or civilian support elements in operating forces.[13]
- "We cannot stop the move to increased private sector involvement and can no longer limit the involvement to base operations or supply. Those functions are already significantly private sector provided. What leaders must do is drive further outsourcing, not by how many military it removes but based upon a risk assessment. The outcome of a wrong choice could well be measured in lives and possibly battles lost" (Zamparelli, 1999, p. 18).
- "'Imbedded contractors' are here to stay, and contractors on the forward area of the battlefield during conflict may indeed be the 'Wave of the Future' even with its inherent risks. However . . .

[13] Commonly referred to as the IGCA Inventory (Office of the Secretary of Defense, 2003, Secs. E1.1.1, E1.1.1.3, E1.1.1.4, E1.1.1.5, E1.1.3, E1.1.2, E1.1.3.2). This document has an enclosure on risk assessment that inventories in close detail the risks to consider.

> [we should] . . . not use more contractors until doctrine is clarified and risks identified. . . . Risking responsibly means . . . making sound and deliberate decisions on the best way to use contractors to accomplish the mission, the best way to enhance the use of available military personnel, and the best way to reduce risk. . . . The way we proceed with these critical decisions can mean the difference in contractor support being a force multiplier or a detractor—decisions that could tip the scales in favor of the enemy" (Foster, 1998, pp. 27–29).

Notable in these statements is how naturally they view contractors as an integral part of the force. Each statement implicitly recognizes that whoever assesses the risks associated with using contractors on the battlefield must integrate their assessment with broader assessments of the risks that the force as a whole faces and ask how the presence of contractors affects those risks. But none of them explains how to achieve this goal.

Recent comments capture another important point:

> The central theme to the privatization strategy as portrayed in the QDR [Quadrennial Defense Review] centers on changing the relationship between the DOD and commercial business. However, lessons of the past clearly point out the tenuous relationships forged between the warrior and the contractor. These new relationships will have to be built upon shared risk and a sense of mission. . . . This tolerance for risk and the establishment of trust and security is a challenge for the DoD. (Mailander, 2002, p. 5.)

Military planners are comfortable with risk. They know that it comes with the territory in combat and cannot be reduced too much without constraining the commander. They are also not comfortable with risks imposed by contractors. The idea of assessing such risks in the broader context of operational mission planning requires a better appreciation of how to create and sustain trust between the Army and its commercial supporters on the battlefield. The issue of how this occurs must be an integral part of any risk assessment.

APPENDIX B

Risks That Increase with Contractor Use on the Battlefield

This appendix draws on recent Army experience and knowledgeable commentary on that experience to identify the primary sources of risk relevant to using contractors on the battlefield.[1] The information presented here underlies the summary statements in Chapter Three.

Army personnel and other commentators have identified a wide variety of things that can go wrong with contract support.[2] In the Army's standard approach to risk assessment, these "things that can go wrong" become *hazards*—sources of risks that must be assessed. We group them in this appendix in the following categories:

- Contracting creates risks inherent in a "principal-agent relationship." The principal (Army) and agent (contractor) have different goals and values. Unless those goals and values are aligned through proper monitoring and incentives, the principal and agent can work at cross-purposes, endangering the success of the Army's mission. The risks are likely to be higher when the

---

[1] The Army's standard documents on using contractors on the battlefield raise many of these points. We believe the discussion below addresses all the points these documents raise that are relevant to this analysis, but we do not attempt to link specific Army documents to specific points. Footnotes in this appendix focus on sources other than official Army documents. The Army documents most relevant to the discussion in this appendix are the following: AR 700-137 (1985); Pamphlet 715-16 (1998); AR 100-10-2 (1999); AR 715-9 (1999); AMC Pamphlet 715-18 (1999); FM 100-21 (2000); FM 3-100.21 (2003). See also DoD (2001).

[2] For example, Singer (2003) is useful primarily as a compendium of bad things that have happened and that might happen in the future.

commander and his staff do not have experience using contractors on the battlefield.

- The chaos of the battlefield, which is increasing as combat becomes less linear, can create additional opportunities for contractors to evade effective oversight. The "fog of war" makes it easier for a contractor to pursue its own goals at the Army's expense, endangering the Army's mission success.
- The status of contract personnel on the battlefield under the international law of war is inherently uncertain. This can discourage contract personnel from entering and remaining on the battlefield, endangering the Army's mission success.
- A commander cannot simply force a contractor to do what he needs done. The commander must comply with specific rules to get performance, but even these do not guarantee performance. The Army can sue a contractor for nonperformance, but by then, a mission is likely to be over. A contractor's failure to perform as expected can endanger the Army's mission success.
- By demanding force protection and other support, contractors impose a burden on the Army in-theater. The contractor needs the Army's support to give the Army effective support in-theater. But providing support to the contractor diverts Army leadership attention and Army combat resources from the immediate fight, potentially endangering mission success.
- Status of forces agreements (SOFAs) and other agreements can limit the Army's access to contractors and increase their costs in-theater. In extreme cases, contractors expected in-theater are not allowed to enter, endangering the Army's mission success. When they enter, they can cost the Army more than expected, imposing risks associated with dollar costs, if not the mission itself.
- Moving from organic to contract support as a theater stabilizes is challenging. Any transfer of responsibility on the battlefield is tricky. One that changes the commander's mechanism of control from direct control to control through a contract adds complexity on the battlefield and can endanger the Army's mission success, particularly if the commander and his staff do not have experience using contractors on the battlefield.

- Because the Army contracts out to acquire capabilities not available in the Army, it puts these capabilities at risk when it imposes controls on a contractor. Inappropriate controls can stifle the benefits the Army initially wanted from a contract source—benefits it expected would increase the likelihood of mission success.
- Outsourcing permanently removes key capabilities from direct governmental control. Over the longer run, this can reduce the likelihood of mission success in future Army missions in a variety of ways. It can reduce the Army's ability to act as an effective principal on the battlefield. It can reduce the Army's ability to use organic capability to backstop a contractor, in case it fails to perform on the battlefield. It can reduce the availability of trained personnel relevant to future Army successes. It can expose key capabilities to future enemy attack or influence.

The Army has developed ways to mitigate almost all of these risks. This appendix offers methods used or considered to avoid, reduce, or manage the negative effects of each source of risk discussed. As will quickly become apparent, efforts to control negative effects often affect several sources of risk and have negative effects of their own. The principal concerns about these risks derive from the Army's persistent reluctance to take the actions required to mitigate these risks, even when it knows (or at least knowledgeable parts of the Army know) how to do so.

Contracting Raises Principal-Agent Problems

The common law of agency defines an explicit distribution of liabilities, rights, and duties that applies whenever a "principal" uses an "agent" to do or produce something that the principal values.[3] Dis-

---

[3] Black (1999, p. 62) defines agency as "a fiduciary relationship created by express or implied contract or by law, whereby one party (the *agent*) may act on behalf of another party (the

tinctions between the principal and agent on the battlefield raise two different kinds of issues.

First, in a formal contractual relationship between two different organizations, agency law makes it impossible to assign exactly the same roles and responsibilities to an agent and to a principal. As soon as the principal begins to rely on an agent to perform a task, the principal must be aware that formal aspects of the law will shape how that task is performed. This is particularly important when the principal is the federal government and the agent is a private party. In this case, the government has rights and responsibilities that it cannot convey to any private agent, even if that agent is executing a task under the direct oversight of the government to achieve a government goal. The Federal Acquisition Regulation captures the elements of these differences important to government contracting, and government-contracting officials are trained to recognize them. Commanders and their staffs, however, must work closely with their contracting officials to ensure that they appreciate how these differences affect their ability to rely on private contractors.

Second, and more broadly, when a principal relies on an agent to perform a specific task, the agent typically understands details about the task better than the principal and so has an advantage arising from this superior information. Knowing that the agent will use its information advantage to gain at the principal's expense, the principal seeks to design a relationship that encourages the agent to pursue the principal's goals as closely as possible.[4]

On the battlefield, a division commander might be the principal and a company commander the agent. The military uses a well-honed command and control system to align the company commander's interests as closely as possible with the division commander's interests, even if the company commander cares much more about her

principal) and bind that other party by words and actions." American Law Institute (1958) spells out the legal aspects of this relationship in detail.

[4] The principal-agent paradigm limned here is the standard tool that economists use to analyze bilateral relationships. Milgrom and Roberts (1992) provides a simple discussion of how to apply the principal-agent paradigm to relationships within organizations and between organizations. Singer (2003) applies it to the role of the contractor on the battlefield.

piece of the battlefield than the division commander does. Or the agent could be a contractor, with its own profit-related interests quite separate from the division commander's military performance concerns. The military can use a well-designed and practiced contract administration system to increase the contractor's profit if and only if the contractor performs to support the division commander's plan as closely as possible. Each approach involves different oversight mechanisms and costs.[5]

On the battlefield, then, the "principal-agent problem" is simply the challenge of ensuring that the commander gets what he expects from those who support him.[6] The commander wants performance that supports mission success at a reasonable cost; principal-agent problems pose threats to the commander's goals of mission success and low cost. On this point, contract sources present risks relative to organic sources for two reasons.

First, contractors and military organizations come from different cultures, with different values and expectations (Deal and Ward, 2001; Foster, 1998; Mailander, 2002, p. 16).[7] Public and private

---

[5] Donahue (1989) frames this as follows: "The profit seeker, in exchange for a *price*, agrees to *deliver a product*. The civil servant, in exchange for a *wage*, agrees to *accept instructions*." That is, the principal frames what is expected in very different terms in each case (quoted in Avant, 2001, p. 2. See also Singer, 2003, pp. 151, 152, 155). As Hennart (1993) emphasizes, of course, the world that buyers and sellers—and hence principals and agents—inhabit is rarely this simple.

[6] Some commentators conclude that privatization delegates public duties to private organizations, in effect giving for-profit organizations control over public policy. (See, for example, Markusen, 2001, p. 10; Singer 2003, p. 155.) While this danger exists, it is not inherent in privatization. Quite the contrary, when outsourcing or privatization is properly executed, it explicitly recognizes that the government remains the principal and that contractual relationships must to the full extent possible align any private-sector, for-profit agent with the public interest. The key to success lies in how well this alignment occurs, not in who provides support activities, day-to-day, on the battlefield. Singer (2003, p. 237) explains this key: "Most important, privatizing services does not mean turning over oversight. Links with the PMF [privatized military firm] must be established at the tactical, operational, and strategic level, to ensure that client interests are maintained."

[7] Campbell (2000, p. 4, quoted by Curtis, 2000, pp. 11–12) emphasizes the way these differences affect mutual trust: "Reliance and trust is based on military discipline and professionalism. If this is lost, or even put in doubt, a military mission may be put into peril. Will combat soldiers have the same level of confidence in civilian contractors providing support as they do soldiers? Why should they?"

"motivations, responsibilities, and loyalties" differ.[8] The Army can reduce the importance of this difference by developing habitual relationships with contractors and including them in standard peacetime training exercises to teach them the Army culture, by engaging contractors in planning and training to teach them more about the Army culture, and by choosing contractors with a history of association with the military or employees with a military background who already understand the military culture (Kolar, 1997; Mailander, 2002, p. 17). These strategies might not change how a contractor values alternatives internally, but they all increase the likelihood that the contractor will understand what a military principal wants and expects.

Second, the typical military commander has more experience getting performance from military sources than getting performance from contract sources.[9] And the Army's mechanisms for getting immediate performance from military sources are more mature, better tested, and more robust than those for getting immediate performance from a contract source. To address this basic gap, the Army can make contracting oversight an integral part of operational plan-

---

[8] In "the gray areas where the national interest is not clear," private firms can exploit the situation (Singer, 2003, p. 154).

[9] A military commander familiar with applying the Uniform Code of Military Justice (UCMJ) in a military setting simply cannot use the UCMJ to govern contractor performance. "Article 2 of the Uniform Code of Military Justice (UCMJ), makes the following persons subject to the UCMJ:

> (10) *In times of war*, all persons serving with or accompanying an armed force in the field.
>
> (11) Subject to the provisions of any treaty or agreement to which the United States is or may be a party or to any accepted rule of international law, all *persons serving with, employed by or accompanying the armed forces without the continental limits of the United States.*

Beginning in 1957, the Article 2(11) UCMJ jurisdiction over civilians serving with, employed by, or accompanying the armed forces overseas . . . during peacetime was held unconstitutional in a series of U.S. Supreme Court decisions, beginning with *Reid v. Covert*, 354 U.S. 1 (1957). . . . In *U.S. v. Averette*, 19 U.S.C.M.A. 363, 41 C.M.R. 363 (1970), the U.S. Court of Military Appeals . . . held that, for Article 2(10) jurisdictional purposes, the term 'in time of war' was limited to situations of congressionally-declared wars" (Reed, Barnes, and Smith, 2000).

ning in capstone documents on doctrine and general training exercises (Stollenwerk, 1999, pp. 42, 44).

Several practices can mitigate these risks by helping a commander and his staff induce effective contractor performance in-theater. First, understanding the contract administration processes in-theater well helps (Mailander, 2002, p. 6).[10] The commander and his staff should receive awareness training on contract administration (Phillips, 2002, p. 6).[11] More generally, as in all things, the more prior experience they have had motivating contractors to perform, the more likely they are to induce effective contract performance during a contingency (Kolar, 1997; Mailander, 2002, p. 16; Thomas, 2000, p. 7; Whitson, 2001, p. 15).[12] As this experience accumulates, the contracting mechanisms they use will get more exercise and will improve in their maturity and robustness. Contracting officer representatives (CORs) should complete COR training before assuming their responsibilities in-theater (GAO, 2003a, pp. S-1, 36; Singer, 2003, p. 154; Thomas, 2000, p. 7).

Second, well-organized processes integrated effectively with the commander's more general plans and operation processes help (Gutierrez, 2001, pp. 38–47).[13] Control through contract administra-

---

[10] For example, the U.S. Army commander in Kosovo initially had difficulty controlling contract employees because he tried to use standard military channels and methods. Confusion and poor field support occurred until the contracting authority resolved the problem (Buhler, 2000). As noted above, "USAREUR's inexperience and lack of understanding of the LOGCAP contract, contractor's capabilities, and program management created problems during deployment" (Young, 1999).

[11] Womack (2000) provides a useful, practical guide to contingency contracting from the perspective of the brigade or task force commander and his or her staff. See also Bond and Castrinos (1999) and Nash and Schooner (1992).

[12] "Successful use of privatized military support begins with key unit leaders facing the issues at their home station, rather than being introduced to them in the midst of a crisis" (Singer, 2003, p. 237). "For a variety of reasons, mostly cultural, military planners have not routinely planned extensively for the use of contractor augmentation and support in [the operation plan] and [concept plans]." One way to overcome this problem is to integrate contingency contractors into peacetime training exercises. "LOGCAP has had difficulty convincing MACOMs to include LOGCAP in their exercises" (Wynn, 2000, p. 7).

[13] Serious deficiencies have existed in deployments from Lebanon in 1958 to the current war in Iraq (LMI, undated; GAO, 2003a). Army experience in the Balkans has ultimately

tion works best when organized before deployment, as an integral part of contingency planning, and collocated with the supported command. It does not work as well when it operates at a distance from the theater.[14] Coordinating the multiple contracting authorities in-theater, directly responsible to Army Materiel Command, the Corps of Engineers, the Army Supporting Component Command in-theater, and potentially other parts of the Army, should be part of any such integration effort.[15] The commander should ensure that good relationships are established early between his operational staff, key contracting officers, contractors themselves, and military units benefiting from contract services (Kolar, 1997, p. 5; Singer, 2003, p. 153; Thomas, 2000, p. 7). The commander should ensure that adequate funding is available before a contingency to avoid the need for incremental tasking and funding, which can both cause delays in performance (Mailander, 2002, p. 17; Thomas, 2000, p. 7; Wynn, 2000).

Third, familiarity with the specific terms and conditions of the contracts they rely on to get contract performance helps (Nelson,

---

allowed the development of effective logistics command and control for contractors in-theater. For useful, detailed lessons learned from that setting, see Young (1999) and Greenfield and Camm (forthcoming).

[14] "How do we integrate contractors into the commander's operation plan (OPLAN)? The success of contractors on the battlefield requires cooperation, support, and advance planning from the joint force commander's (JFC's) staff. . . . Contract administrators and contractor personnel should be involved early in planning to enhance mission success and generate realistic cost estimates. . . . The JFC does not have the option of going to war . . . with an all-military team" (Young, 1999). Young offers detailed suggestions on such planning. For additional details, see also Chiarotti (2000, p. 13), Schenck (2001), and Whitson (2001, p. 16).

[15] CASCOM (2001, p. 18) found that "there is a general expectation a U.S. Army Materiel Command (AMC) Logistics Support Element (LSE) will manage system support contractor personnel during a 4ID deployment. However, research did not identify any substantive systems support planning involving systems contractors, 4ID, and AMC." Wynn (2000) saw it this way: "It is critical that the administrative contracting officers (ACOs) communicate directly and frequently with the Task Force Commander so that the contractual capabilities and the contracting officers' authorities are clearly understood by the maneuver force. With so many participants, there is plenty of room for misunderstanding, especially in the harried days when a deployment is fresh." For a good discussion of how DCMA has coordinated its activities with LOGCAP deployments (and the challenges faced), particularly in the Balkans, see Thomas (2000). Young (1999) suggests that the Joint Logistics Support Command, which AMC, DCMC, and USACE formed together in Haiti, offers valuable lessons on how to integrate contract administration in-theater. See also Harris (2000, p. 2).

2000, p. 7).[16] Increased standardization of these terms and conditions should simplify the commander's oversight responsibility and increase the likelihood that all contracts have the terms and conditions that the commander needs before a contingency starts (GAO, 2003a, pp. 26–28). Reducing the number of contracting firms in-theater by bundling tasks can also simplify oversight, improve integration of support services, and help the commander and his staff focus on the operational aspects of the operation in-theater (Harris, 2000, p. 5; Kolar, 1997; Mailander, 2002, pp. 7, 17).[17]

Fourth, over the longer term, sustained competition to improve the Army's leverage in relationships likely to support the warfighter in a contingency helps.[18] Formal competition is problematic during a contingency—it takes too long. Competitions completed *before* a contingency give the Army an opportunity to review carefully an offeror's past performance in a contingency and its capabilities for operating in future contingencies. The Army should conduct competitions to discourage the traditional contractor practice of over-promising and then using contractual modifications to get well over the course of the contract.[19] An unavoidable tension, however, exists

---

[16] Commanders have only a limited understanding of all contractor operations in their areas of operations. Central visibility of all contract support in any specific location is practically nonexistent except in Bosnia, where a concerted effort has occurred to identify all contract support (GAO, 2003a, p. 3). Bondanella et al. (1994, p. 12) found that, in the first Gulf War, "there was no central cognizance of who was in theater, en route, or who had left." Thomas (2000) nominates DCMA as a logical place to establish full visibility of contracts and offers details on how to do that.

[17] "One contractor with several hundred employees is easier to manage than a hundred small contractors with a few employees each" (Young, 1998, p. 14).

[18] Markusen (2001, pp. 3, 17) emphasizes the ability of competition to control costs and increase quality and innovation but warns that contractors can game competitions.

[19] Singer (2003, pp. 155, 159–161) warns of the danger of "ex post rent extraction" when contracting. See also Donahue (1989); Helper, MacDuffie, and Sabel (1999); Laffont and Tirole (1992, pp. 55–84); and Schmitz (2001). Acquisition reform in DoD has given close attention to this problem and encourages the use of nonprice source-selection criteria, particularly those based on reputation and past performance, to suppress this behavior. Properly framed award fees can also help. See, for example, Anderson (1999) and Camm, Blickstein, and Venzor (2003). Markusen (2001, p. 19) warns against relying on past performance to choose among offerors, but does not explain why.

between sustaining competition and sustaining habitual relationships with contractors.[20]

Acquisition reform is pursuing efforts to attract nontraditional contract sources to work with defense buyers and to apply new commercial forms of acquisition practices to get better performance from these new sources. Over the long term, these changes offer substantial opportunities for improved performance in the Army. Trying to apply these commercial mechanisms in a combat setting, however, could exacerbate the principal-agent problem raised here. New contractors unfamiliar with combat or military values and military personnel unfamiliar with the values that underlie new commercial services acquisition methods could easily run afoul of one another. Over time, the Army should be able to overcome this problem, but it should expect additional risk associated with commercial contracting on the battlefield until all parties have come to a common understanding of one another's priorities.[21]

A Chaotic Battlefield Allows Contractors to Evade Effective Oversight

By increasing the level of uncertainty about the enemy's intentions and actions, the "fog of war" increases the level of risk faced by the force as a whole, including any contractor-provided components of the force. It also masks many errors and indiscretions, potentially giving agents room to maneuver relative to their principals (Avant, 2001, p. 3; Singer, 2003, p. 154).[22] Because enemy actions can affect

---

[20] Camm (2002) examines this tension at greater length.

[21] This paragraph offers a perfect example of the challenge of balancing current and future goals. Unless current sourcing makes room for innovative contracting, despite the associated risk, the Army cannot achieve the promise that acquisition reform holds for the future. In the limit, the Army simply "can't get there from here." Chapter Five discusses this challenge in a broader context.

[22] In a formal analytic principal-agent context, this chaos effectively increases the information asymmetry in the relationship by limiting the principal's monitoring capability. This reduces the value of repeated games or reputation effects as means to overcome information

outcomes, accountability is more difficult to establish than in peacetime, for military and contract sources (Singer, 2003, p. 157). An agent may ask whether it is better off pursuing its own immediate interest or pursuing the interests of the commander. In the fog of war, it may conclude that it can shirk without getting caught and so profit from its action. A contracting firm really can create profits for its owners; a company commander may "shirk" simply to increase the safety of her personnel more than the operational plan envisioned.

Three points are worth noting. First, both contract and organic sources can exploit the fog of war to shirk their responsibilities. However, the cultural difference between contract and organic sources makes it more likely that shirking by a contract source will increase risk by compromising the commander's goals.

Second, shirking serious enough to threaten the mission threatens everyone in-theater. As a result, the combat setting may place limits on how much shirking an agent would attempt to get away with.

Third, contractors in-theater are not only sources of services but also demanders of Army services. Their customer touches them in the "front" and the "back." The more integrated a contractor is with the military customer in-theater, the more likely a shirking contractor is to get caught and the more likely the shirking would have unanticipated negative consequences for the contractor. Integration via formal information systems and interpersonal relationships presumably make shirking increasingly difficult.

These points do not say shirking will not occur in-theater. But they suggest that shirking in a mutually hazardous environment is more complex and challenging than it is likely to be in the standard principal-agent setting, where principal and agent sit firmly at arm's length from one another with no dependencies outside their formal contract.

---

asymmetry because it is simply harder for the principal to know whether an agent is cheating or shirking and hence harder to discipline the agent in a future game or even to change its image of the agent's reputation.

A Commander Cannot Simply Force a Contractor to Perform

Unless Congress declares war, a military commander cannot apply the UCMJ to contractors in-theater (Curtis, 2000, p. 11; Epley, 1990, p. 30; Phillips, 2002, p. 2). Even if Congress did declare war, some question remains about whether current interpretation of the Constitution would allow the military to force a private citizen to perform. Several points are important.

First, a commander breaks the law if she demands that a contractor perform services outside the statement of work for a contract. The commander is outside the chain of command with the authority to obligate funds and write or modify a contract to allow execution of a task not specified in the original contract. To prevent a commander from unknowingly overreaching, the Army must ensure that its commanders and their staffs understand how support contracts work in general (Buhler, 2000, pp. 15–16). Commanders in specific circumstances should be familiar with the statements of work for the contracts they rely on so that they can make quick, well-informed decisions about how to integrate contract sources into their operational plans. Thinking longer term, more broadly written statements of work can reduce this problem, giving the commander greater flexibility and less to worry about (Buhler, 2000, p. 12; Castillo, 2000).[23] More broadly written contracts tend to shift risk to the government, particularly with regard to cost, but this may be worthwhile to give the commander greater flexibility.[24] Such an approach allows the Army to balance risks associated with mission performance and cost, allowing a potential increase in cost in exchange for improved command and control of the contractor and hence better mission performance.

---

[23] Problems with contractual scope affected the success of the Operational Support Agency (OSA) during the first Gulf War (Dyche, 1995, p. 186).

[24] Greenfield and Camm (forthcoming) explains why this issue is central to questions about the design and implementation of the Army's Balkans Support Contract.

Second, for activities within the scope of the contract, new government directives must still flow through the government-contracting officer to ensure that the directives are authorized (Castillo, 2000; Nash and Schooner, 1992; Phillips, 2002, p. 6; Zamparelli, 1999, p. 17). The contracting officer can delegate some authority to a COR to sustain contractor responsiveness and flexibility, but such delegation must be clearly defined in advance (Foster, 1998, p. 19). In practice, arrangements can be set up to allow quick government-contractor communication and response for activities within the scope of the contract. The Army commander and his staff must understand, however, that these arrangements differ from traditional command and control arrangements.[25] Practice and experience with effective contracting arrangements help in this regard.

Third, whether a new directive is within scope or not, no government person can give a direct order to an individual contractor employee. Rather, such an order must come through contract channels, from the contract officer on the government side to the appropriate supervisor on the contractor side, who then directs the employee. This is standard practice in all contract relationships, between private firms and between the government and a contractor. In practice, arrangements develop to get the customer what is needed. As above, the commander and staff must know how these relationships work and what to expect from individual contract employees.

Fourth, the challenges of control multiply when a subcontractor provides services (Mailander, 2002, p. 14). The government has "privity of contract" only with the prime contractor and must rely on the prime to ensure the performance of the subcontractor. Orders must go through the contracting officer to the prime contractor to the supervisor in the subcontractor to the subcontractor's employees. When arrangements are properly set up, this works well, but the commander must ensure that such arrangements exist and that he knows how to use them.

---

[25] As noted above (footnote 10), the commander in Kosovo had initial difficulty controlling contract employees because he tried to use standard military channels and methods (Buhler, 2000).

Fifth, of particular concern is the behavior of contractor employees outside the traditional workplace.[26] Unless a contract specifies that contractor employees must obey general orders in-theater, the commander technically cannot directly restrict employees' behavior off post, even during periods of high hazard. The Military Extraterritorial Jurisdiction Act of 2000 offers a useful step toward simplifying this problem, but problems remain.[27] The commander cannot control legal behavior, like drunkenness or lewd behavior, that presents the U.S. in an unfavorable light in a sensitive region. The easiest way to reduce this risk is to ensure that a contract gives the military commander the authority to restrict employee behavior in-theater. An alternative available to a commander is to prohibit specific individuals access to U.S. facilities, effectively forcing them to withdraw from the theater. Advance arrangements give a commander more subtle options to apply.

Sixth, and of greatest concern, even if the government has every right to expect performance, the commander cannot force immediate performance. The contractor can simply breach the contract (Gutierrez, 2001, pp. 56–59, 69–70; Mailander, 2002, p. 16; Nelson, 2000, p. 11; Singer, 2003, p. 152).[28] The government can sue for damages

---

[26] "Knowing the location of all soldiers 24 hours a day and restricting off-post activities were key elements in force protection during Task Force Eagle. Hostile elements would have loved to kidnap or kill unsuspecting American soldiers found in an off-post restaurant or motel" (Department of the Army, undated). The same reasoning applied to U.S. contract personnel, who are much harder to control. For example, Brown and Root Services employees in Bosnia often violated off-post restrictions and so were exposed to risks. Fortunately, this never led to a crisis (Foster, 1998, pp. 20–22). See also Gutierrez (2001, pp. 49–54, 68).

[27] The law covers only felonies punishable by confinement of at least a year. Regulations have not been completed to implement it, and so the law has not been tested in practice (Gutierrez, 2001, pp. 33–34, 86–91; Phillips, 2002, pp. 2, 10).

[28] A possibly apocryphal story from the first Gulf War tells of a firm that withdrew its employees from the theater when the ballistic missile threat to rear areas became clear. DoD attempted to discourage the firm from leaving by offering to pay more. The firm claimed that no price increase could change its mind. DoD threatened the firm's access to future defense contracts. The firm responded that its commitment to the safety of its own employees was higher than its commitment to DoD—without loyal employees, the firm would have no future in which to seek additional defense work. Even if apocryphal, the story illustrates well the basic arguments at issue.

or even performance over the longer term but not within the timeframes relevant to activity in-theater during hostilities. The Army can do a number of things to reduce the likelihood that this occurs, but it cannot prevent it. The Army can choose a provider with a strong record of performance under duress in the past. It can require that each contractor employee sign an agreement in advance to serve under specified circumstances in-theater.[29] It can require the use of employees with certain kinds of characteristics. It can protect the contractor effectively in-theater or use the contractor only in safe portions of the theater to reduce any incentive for the contractor to leave the theater. It can place heavy penalties for nonperformance in the contract. It can limit future contracting opportunities for firms that fail to perform. Even if the Army does all these things, a contractor can still breach an agreement and settle the consequences later. To deal with this eventuality, a commander can develop alternative sources on the battlefield and backup plans to employ them if needed (Buhler, 2000, p. 16; GAO, 2003a, p. 10; Kaiser and Fabbro, 1980, p. v; Robinson, 2002, p. 40; Whitson, 2001, p. 14).

The Status of Contract Personnel on the Battlefield Under the International Law of War Is Inherently Uncertain

The status of contract employees under the international law of war affects whether the enemy will treat them as prisoners of war (POWs) if it captures them and whether the law allows the enemy to target them during hostilities.[30] If the contract employees have the status of

---

[29] DSB (1982b, pp. 2–9) offers examples of agreements to consider. The National Security Agency (NSA), for example, used a condition of employment agreement and declaration of intent agreement. In 20 years, only one employee broke such agreements. E-Systems suffered from contract penalties if contract employees left their duty post without permission. E-Systems required its employees to agree to reimburse the firm for such costs as a condition of employment.

[30] For good discussions of these issues, see Gutierrez (2001); Phillips (2002); Sarnoski (1994); and Sumser and Hemingway (1995).

lawful combatants, international law requires that they be treated as POWs if captured and allows the enemy to target them. If contractors are noncombants that the Army formally recognizes as accompanying the force, international law requires that they be treated as POWs if captured and prohibits the enemy from targeting them during hostilities. If the contractors are noncombatants not recognized by the U.S. Army as accompanying the force, international law does not require that they be treated as POWs but prohibits the enemy from targeting them. If the contractors are not lawful combatants, international law allows the enemy to try them for war crimes, execute them for murder, and target them during hostilities. If these distinctions apply in practice, they are obviously critically important to contract employees (Thomas, 2000, p. 7; Tomich, 2001, p. 19).

Unfortunately, it is not possible today to assure contract employees that these rules will apply and that all participants to a conflict will view them as lawful noncombatants with POW status and protection from attack. Three considerations are important.[31]

First, a lawful noncombatant accompanying the U.S. Army force must abide by certain specific rules. If a contract employee wears a uniform, it must be distinguishable from a distance from a military uniform. The employee can only carry or use certain firearms. The employee must have an identification card that certifies the Army's agreement that the employee is lawfully accompanying the force. Some ambiguity exists about these rules, but contractors have found it fairly easy to allow their employees to comply with the rules and thereby allow them the opportunity to be treated as lawful noncombants accompanying the force (Sarnoski, 1994, p. 29).[32] Work-

---

[31] Related concerns about Army obligations to contract personnel remain unresolved. Should the Army leave wounded or dead contract employees behind in combat, or should they risk their lives to treat them the same way they would treat military personnel in combat? If a contract employee is killed in-theater, who is responsible for handling the remains? What should happen to the remains (Foster, 1998, p. 21)?

[32] These conditions are defined in a series of the Hague and Geneva Conventions that define important elements of the international laws of war. Of most direct relevance are Article 1 of the Regulations respecting the laws and customs of war on land appended to the Hague Convention IV of 1907 ("the Hague Regulations"), Article 4A(2) of the 1949 Geneva POW

ing together, the Army and its contractors can effectively avoid this source of risk.

Second, legal experts disagree about what support activities are compatible with lawful noncombatant status accompanying the force.[33] Some traditional support activities, such as cooking or laundry, are distant enough from the warfighter to allow an easy judgment that a contractor is a lawful noncombatant accompanying the force. But what about a contract employee who flies an unmanned aerial vehicle (UAV); fuses intelligence from multiple sources and transmits, in real time, the product to a shooter; reprograms the flight program for a cruise missile immediately before launch to hit a time-sensitive target; or fine-tunes the software on jammers used to blind the enemy electronically during an assault?[34]

> Never has there been such a reliance on nonmilitary members to accomplish tasks directly affecting the tactical success of an engagement. This has blurred the distinction between soldier and civilian. . . . The requirements of warfare have dramatically changed the scope and relevance of the support tasks they provide, thus making their distinction as noncombatants less obvious. (Zamparelli, 1999, pp. 11–12.)

Opinions differ on where to draw the line, but most agree that it is impermissible under international law for contractors to engage in some of these "support" activities. Some U.S. military observers are far more conservative and would call all of them impermissible

---

Convention, and Articles 42 and 43 of Additional Protocol I of 1977 to the 1949 Geneva Conventions. Phillips (2002) discusses these at greater length.

[33] The problem arises because, as Phillips (2002, p. 7) notes, under Article 51(3) of the "Additional Protocol I of 1977 to the 1949 Geneva Conventions (which is not in effect for the United States but the United States apparently has no objection to this Article being considered as part of customary international law), . . . civilians enjoy their protected status 'unless and for such time as they take a direct part in hostilities.'" "Direct part in hostilities" is not well defined anywhere. "A different term, 'active part in the hostilities,' is used in Article 3 of the Geneva POW Convention [of 1949], leading to even more confusion" (Phillips, 2002, p. 7).

[34] For problematic examples from the first Gulf War, see Dibble, Home, and Lindsay (1993).

(Castillo, 2000; Gutierrez, 2001, pp. 54–56).[35] Of greater practical importance is how an enemy, willing to abide by international laws of war but eager to disarm the U.S.'s technological superiority wherever possible, would draw the line. We cannot predict how such an enemy would behave, but we can state that a continuum exists and that a contractor is likely to remain safer the farther contractor employees stay from warfighter tasks on that continuum.

Third, the enemy need not honor the laws of war.[36] The distinctions drawn above may simply be meaningless to some enemies. Enemies who have ambiguous status themselves under the law—for example, transnational military groups operating without formal state sponsorship—may see no reason to acknowledge the law. The Army cannot directly affect such behavior. Historically, the Army has favored treating enemy personnel according to a strict interpretation of international law to build precedent that U.S. personnel should be treated in a similar manner. But nothing forces a new enemy to react favorably to such a reciprocal argument.

Contractors Impose a Burden on the Army In-Theater

Contractors are not self-sufficient in-theater, especially during hostilities. Unlike contracting in a normal peacetime setting, where it is reasonable and often even desirable to give a contractor as much freedom to execute as possible, a number of factors tie the contractor

---

[35] For examples, see Buhler (2000, pp. 8–9) and Mailander (2002, p. 11). The Working Symposium on the Roles of Civilians during Military Operations recommended drawing as bright a line as possible between contractor activities that are permissible and those that are not. For example, while providing operational maintenance would not be permissible, providing intermediate maintenance would. Although providing base operating or rear-area logistics support would be permissible, providing any kind of intelligence, surveillance, or reconnaissance service would not (Phillips, 2002, p. 8).

[36] Deal and Ward (2001, p. 53) explores an important variation on this theme. Increasing military dependence on commercial services, such as commercial communications, invites an enemy to attack what is essentially commercial infrastructure in-theater. This military focus could have mortal ramifications for personnel who have no awareness whatsoever that they are essentially supporting an American military operation.

directly to the Army in-theater, forcing the Army to commit real resources on the ground, as well as funds, to ensure access to contract services.

The most important factor is force protection. The Army has a moral obligation to protect civilians it has placed in harm's way. It typically has a legal and contractual obligation as well. Because international law limits a contractor's ability to defend itself, contracts often carry language spelling out the Army's responsibility to protect contractor personnel in-theater. The Army also has practical reasons to defend its contractors—it will get better service from them if they are better protected (CASCOM, 2001, p. 23; Mailander, 2002, p. 12; Robinson, 2002, p. 40. Thomas, 2000, p. 7; Tomich, 2001, p. 19; Young, 1998, p. 6).[37] Needs for force protection change as the environment of hostilities changes in-theater.[38] In addition to the troops committed to protection, the Army must commit leadership attention to tracking contractor needs and ensuring that they are met. This has proved to be difficult to do well in the past (Curtis, 2000, p. 12). Even if the Army has planned for these needs in advance, in-theater, these requirements compete with other requirements for the scarce resources and leadership attention available (Young, 1999). The easiest solution is to use contractors where they are not directly exposed to enemy action.[39] The effects of such force protection

---

[37] GAO (2003a, p. 25) recently highlighted a conflict in DoD policy on force protection. Joint Publication 4-0, Chapter Five, states, "force protection of DoD contract employees is a contractor responsibility, unless valid contract terms place that responsibility with another party." FM 3-100.21 (2003) is compatible with the statements in the text above. It says, "protecting contractors and their employees on the battlefield is the commander's responsibility." Although this conflict must be resolved, no ambiguity exists within the Army.

[38] The situation in Somalia required military escort for contractors most of the time. Little or no escort has been required in Hungary, Bosnia, and Croatia (Young, 1999). But even in the Balkans, the Army has adjusted the protection given to Brown and Root as circumstances have changed over time.

[39] For example, support activities particularly ill suited to contract provision include construction tasks and NBC detection and cleanup in hostile areas. It is highly desirable in both cases for the technicians performing tasks to provide their own protection (Curtis, 2000, p. 13). Over the longer term, efforts to reduce the logistics footprint in-theater with more reliable systems and reach-back logistics support systems can take military and civilian personnel

measures on operational effectiveness deserve close attention.[40] In a nonlinear battlefield, "safe" portions of the battlefield are increasingly difficult to define (Nelson, 2000, p. 17; Robinson, 2002, p. 40). As noted above, coordination of force protection needs potentially gives the Army additional insight into a contractor's operations that it can use to oversee contractor performance. The Army must create appropriate channels of communication to take advantage of this opportunity.

A closely related issue is that contractor personnel cannot provide reserve or buffer combat capability that the commander can call on in emergencies (Tomich, 2001, p. 19). To some extent, a commander can count on military cooks to defend themselves or call them to the front lines as supplemental infantry if necessary. The commander cannot do this with contractors. In effect, the presence of contractors on the battlefield forces the commander to create and preserve reserve combat capabilities elsewhere. The cost these additional reserves impose on the Army—in terms of their own support and oversight and the billets they absorb within a troop ceiling—can be attributed to the Army's use of contractors. The cost may be particularly significant in the presence of troop ceilings. The need to maintain a military reserve that might otherwise have resided in military support troops reduces the effective military capability that the commander can project with a given total number of military personnel.[41] The Army must consider this burden when choosing to rely on contractors and plan for it.

When a large number of forces enter a region and compete with one another for local capabilities—labor, raw material, services, and so on—the forces can easily place inflationary pressures on the scarce

out of the theater, reducing the need for all forms of force protection (Fontaine, 1997–1998; Peltz, 2003).

[40] For example, during the first Gulf War, DoD housed C-21 maintenance contractors in downtown Riyadh to separate them from military targets. This placed them farther from the aircraft they supported, degrading their effectiveness. It also complicated their personal security (Dyche, 1995, p. 175, quoted in Nelson, 2000, p. 14).

[41] On net, of course, under a ceiling, using contractors in-theater can still free military forces to perform core military tasks in-theater.

local resources available (Foster, 1998, p. 24).[42] The Army will inevitably pay for such inflation, either through pass-through cost-plus and economic price adjustment arrangements or fixed prices that anticipate such inflation. The Army can limit this cost by centralizing access to local resources and using nonprice means to allocate scarce resources among the many contractors and military organizations that demand them in-theater. This responsibility imposes an additional burden on the Army. In principle, a single contractor can provide access to local resources, but the Army must still adjudicate access to these resources. Ideally, adjudication will reflect priorities relevant to the commander's operational plan. The Army would benefit from such a central capability even if it had no contractors in-theater. Their presence complicates provision of the capability because adjudication of demands must be carefully coordinated with the terms of each contract. The Army can plan for such a capability and provide the resources in-theater to achieve it.

Individual contracts can impose additional burdens. They may require the Army to provide inter- and intratheater transportation; access to Army supply systems; water and electric power; facilities and food; security clearances; medical care and mortuary services; postal and morale, welfare, and recreation (MWR) services; religious services; and so on (CASCOM, 2001, p. 23; Castillo, 2000; Tomich, 2001, p. 30).[43] The variety of terms in contracts imposes a burden in itself. The Army must understand this variation and plan for it (Fos-

---

[42] In Operation Joint Endeavor, "the number of contracting organizations, contracting officers, interests, and agencies grew to be nearly counterproductive as these contracting interests competed against each other for limited local resources and increased the costs of goods and services (Harris, 2000, p. 4).

[43] Young (1999) finds that it is generally most effective for contractors to take responsibility to get their employees to the theater, although this can be costly. Food, lodging, and medical care are generally cheaper if the government provides them. Such support must be planned for, especially medical care. Contractors can acquire their own facilities, but such efforts should be centrally coordinated to manage competition for scarce resources. Foster (1998, p. 25) reports that, "in Bosnia, commanders found that many contractors were not physically capable of withstanding the harsh environment." As a result, if the Army provides medical care to contractors, as is likely, contractors could draw disproportionately on the medical system.

ter, 1998, p. 24; Phillips, 2002, pp. 4–5). The Army can simplify this burden by developing standard terms for use in contracts that anticipate services in-theater.[44] It can also ensure that the commander's staff has easy access to a complete file of the terms in all contracts to support planning, operations, and adjudication of disputes about the goods and services that contractors demand in-theater (Castillo, 2000).

International Agreements Can Limit the Desirability of Using Contractors

SOFAs closely shape the conditions under which U.S. contractors can operate in a foreign country.[45] They identify what activities U.S. contractors can perform. They place conditions on the contractors' use of local resources of all kinds. They define contract employees' status under local laws and regulations. They define what taxes, tariffs, and other fees contractors and their employees must pay while they operate in a foreign country.

The United States has negotiated 109 SOFAs, but only five contain language that, directly or by implication, include contractors or their civilian employees in the definition of the "civilian component"—the civilian personnel accompanying an armed force. Existing SOFAs could be clarified to ensure that contractor employees are

---

[44] Army policy currently says that "the Army will provide or make available, on a reimbursable basis, force protection and support services commensurate with those provided to DoD civilian personnel to the extent authorized by law." Unfortunately, no management system exists to capture what those costs are. Such a management system is likely to be important to support any more detailed Army standards in this area (Foster, 1998, p. 26).

[45] For example, in Operation Joint Endeavor, the LOGCAP contractor, Brown and Root Services, had difficulty bringing foreign nationals into Hungary until Hungary saw employment opportunities for many Hungarian nationals. Initially, Hungary made Brown and Root subject to its value-added tax and its employees subject to the Hungarian income tax, even though the U.S. government was exempt from any taxes. Hungary required Brown and Root to get permits for many activities where it would not have required the U.S. Army to get permits. Subsequent negotiations gave Brown and Root and its employees the same treatment that the U.S. government received (Young, 1999). See also Castillo (2000), Gally and Horne (1996, p. 7), Gutierrez (2001, pp. 36–37), Thomas (2000, p. 7), and Young (1999).

covered by terms relevant to the "civilian component" of the U.S. force (Phillips, 2002, p. 3). The Working Symposium on the Roles of Civilians during Military Operations recommended that a SOFA template be developed, with model language on "contractor liability for or exemption from customs, taxes, licenses, immigration, and similar problems" (Phillips, 2002, p. 4).

When the U.S. enters a country where it has no SOFA in place, contractors must comply with any existing international agreements. A SOFA often specifies a range of capabilities and resources that the country will provide, with or without U.S. payment, through host nation support. Once this is defined, a SOFA typically simplifies contractor operations across the board and reduces their costs—costs typically passed on to the Army in cost-plus agreements or fixed prices chosen to reflect local circumstances. A SOFA can broaden the range of capabilities a U.S. contractor can bring into the country, immunize the firm and its employees against certain local laws and regulations, and limit taxes, tariffs, and fees. Army planning for the use of contractors on the battlefield can give close attention to the conditions a SOFA is likely to define once it is in place.

Negotiating a SOFA takes time. Its terms probably depend on specific circumstances associated with a particular contingency. As a result, complete, up-to-date SOFAs become more common as a contingency becomes more likely. Negotiating a SOFA at the last minute before deployment can place the United States at a disadvantage, but earlier negotiations can be hard to justify. In this setting, contractor support is likely to be easier to provide after serious planning for a contingency begins. The Army can recognize this by planning for military support for activities most affected by a SOFA, followed by contract support once a SOFA is in place.

Moving from Organic to Contract Support over Time Is Challenging

One way to deal with the risks identified above is to rely on military support in the most hazardous portions of the battlefield and to increase reliance on contractors as the theater stabilizes and the general level of hazard falls (Curtis, 2000, pp. 12–13; Epley, 1990, p. 30; Whitson, 2001, p. 15). Contractors normally do not perform services in the first 30 days of a violent contingency. In a peaceful setting, they can normally simply ramp up their operational tempo (Foster, 1998, p. 17). Such a strategy

- reduces the importance of differences in military and commercial culture,
- reduces the effects of the fog of war on oversight,
- reduces the importance of a contractor's status under international law,
- reduces the contractor's incentive to breach a contract,
- reduces the Army's need to provide force protection, and
- gives the U.S. additional time to improve the terms of SOFAs.

This strategy requires that the Army maintain capabilities in-house to perform tasks not suited to contractors. It also requires commanders to be comfortable accessing similar support services in two fundamentally different ways in different parts of the battlefield or at different times during a contingency.

The challenge is likely to be greatest when a commander switches from one type of support to the other. Military support activities must maintain a capability to hand off as seamlessly as possible to contract support activities, giving them access to information about the state of the commander's priorities at the handoff point, the status of requests for services and inventories, the more general state of play in the theater relevant to each contract, and so on. For this reason alone, it may be appropriate to delay such a handoff until the commander and his staff can take their focus off combat and turn to the challenging, but less dynamic, issue of stabilization.

In fact, unless rapid deployment is written into a contract and advance arrangements made to get U.S. contract personnel through individual deployment sites and into their operational positions in-theater quickly, large numbers of U.S. contract employees will not normally arrive early in a contingency, requiring some degree of

Army self-sufficiency early in a deployment, followed by an orderly handoff (Foster, 1998, p. 18). The Army has demonstrated its ability to do this in specific cases. But the demand for such transitions simply increases the challenges that a commander faces when relying on contractor support in-theater.

The Army Puts Contractor Capabilities at Risk When It Imposes Controls

Another way to deal with the risks identified above is to place specific conditions on a contractor that address the concerns above. In the early 1980s, for example, the military services suggested that "contractor employees be made subject to some form of military compulsion in order to insure that they will remain at their assigned duty stations" (DSB, 1982b, p. 1).[46] The most far-reaching condition would require a contractor to hire only personnel in the Army Reserve.[47] Then, when the Army told the contractor to deploy to the theater, the Army could mobilize the contractor's employees so that they entered theater as military personnel. This would allow the commander to apply the UCMJ to these employees, effectively changing the nature of the principal-agent problem in-theater, protecting all employees' status under international law, and ensuring compliance with the terms of the contract. Such a proposal raises important concerns (DSB, 1982b, pp. 1, 22–24).

First, requiring contract employees to be members of the Reserve severely restricts the pool of labor the contractor can draw on. This could be a good thing if it ensured the military orientation, physical health, and readiness to deploy of the employees (Curtis, 2000, p. 12). But it would complicate the contractor's ability to perform in peacetime without peacetime benefits.

---

[46] For a useful legal discussion of recent efforts to do this, see Gutierrez (2001).

[47] The United Kingdom considered such a "Sponsored Reserve" program for selected contractors. The Working Symposium on the Roles of Civilians during Military Operations recommended that DoD consider such an approach as an option (Phillips, 2002, pp. 3–4).

Second, in all likelihood, a contractor would have to pay more for labor under such circumstances. Again, this could be a good thing. Employees would clearly understand the importance of the requirement to deploy. The labor market would screen candidates for jobs and offer more pay for those who clearly expressed their readiness to deploy.

Third, varying Army demands for Reservists would have to be deconflicted during a mobilization. Ideally, the Reservists would serve as members of a unit associated with an individual contractor and would mobilize as a unit. This approach would support continuity from peacetime to wartime.

Fourth, matching a reserve unit to a contract organization is likely to limit severely how the contractor organizes production. The temptation would be high to assign a Modified Table of Organization and Equipment (MTOE) to the contract organization, imposing a standard military organizational form and production approach on the contractor. This approach would, at a minimum, severely limit the benefits that the Army could garner from commercial innovation, training, and so on.

In its most extreme form, such a scheme simply militarizes a contractor organization, placing military personnel in a contractor's facilities.[48] The contractor or the government could own capital assets in the activity. The main advantage such an organization would offer over a standard military unit would be its ability to pay employees more than current standard and special military pays allow. If this is the primary benefit, the Army might instead consider revisiting the special pays it currently uses to compensate military personnel with high-value, hard-to-retain skills.

More-limited proposals require contractors to use standard military information systems, rely exclusively on government-furnished material and equipment, conduct activities according to exact Army

---

[48] For example, problems with discipline, control, and responsiveness during the Korean War ultimately led to a decision to militarize the Korean Civil Transport Corps into the Korean Service Corps. Such actions have been exceptional in U.S. Army history (Epley, 1990, p. 34).

templates, and so on. Each of these proposals represents a trade-off; it substitutes a mechanism designed to give the Army greater control over a contractor or greater assurance that the contractor will perform as expected for the freedom that allows contractors to innovate and provide capabilities simply unavailable within the Army (Everly, 2001, p. 4).

A priori, we cannot say what trade-offs are most appropriate. We can certainly say that optimal trade-offs will differ for different activities—activities that occur in different parts of the battlefield, subjecting contractors to different levels of hazard, and activities that affect the performance of warfighters more or less directly and so are more or less critical to the Army's success in a contingency.

Outsourcing Permanently Removes Key Capabilities from Direct Government Control

Moving capabilities out of the Army can have unintended and unanticipated negative consequences later. For the most part, unlike the issues above, these concerns are as important off as on the battlefield. They also appear to present less serious, more easily managed problems than the issues discussed above. Because they often arise in discussion of the use of contractors on the battlefield, however, we include them here.

Observers cite the following concerns. First, the Army can lose the expertise it needs to oversee external providers (Markusen, 2001, p. 4).[49] An ongoing debate about the characteristics of a "smart buyer" sets two alternative views against one another. The first states that a buyer must understand a provider's processes well to oversee them reliably. The best way to acquire such understanding is for personnel who will oversee processes later in their careers to work inside

---

[49] Markusen (2001) expects this effect to be most severe when a single external source controls a capability the Army needs but gives up, in effect limiting the Army's ability to use competition to discipline the source and learn about the alternatives available to the Army. See also Camm (1993).

the processes earlier in their careers (Wong et al., 2000). The second view states that an effective buyer focuses on stating what it wants from a provider in performance terms and leaves the details of how the providers meets these terms to the provider's staff. The second view favors training personnel who will oversee external providers as program managers, not specialists in the functions they will oversee (Camm, 2002). As in most debates of this kind, each side has some merit. Observers fearful that the Army will lose its capability to oversee contractors favor the first view. The Army can address this concern by retaining enough work in-house to develop the senior-level skills it will expect in contract monitors. It can also consider hiring experts from the outside to support this oversight activity, either as employees or as third-party advisors. Alternatively, the Army can change its basic approach to acquiring services by training services acquisition personnel as program managers, using a career track similar to the one it uses to prepare its personnel to oversee weapon system development and production contracts (Anderson, 1999).

Second, the Army loses the ability to reconstitute a capability if external sources cannot perform satisfactorily (Castillo, 2000; Zamparelli, 1999). Over the long run, once the Army gives up a capability, the start-up costs may simply become too high to justify bringing it back in-house, even if it should never have left in the first place. In the short run, if the Army suddenly discovers in a particular contingency that no contract source is available, it does not have the time to reconstitute the capability in-house, regardless of the cost.[50] The Army can approach this problem by retaining a broad range of capabilities as backup to capabilities that it expects from its contractors. Such a capability addresses concerns about monitoring contractor performance mentioned above as well. Carrying such a capability in peacetime will incur an additional cost. The Army could reduce this

[50] Observers often point out that LOGCAP "lacked the ability to serve as an initial entry force" at the beginning of the Balkan contingencies. Army V Corps G3 concluded, "We do not have an expeditionary force capability in Brown and Root" (Curtis, 2000, p. 9; Brown, 1999). In that case, the Army drew on civil engineering capabilities in the Air Force and Navy to provide the services it expected from its contract and could not provide itself. In the past, the Army could have performed this work in-house without help.

cost by placing such capability in the Reserve, but Reserve support poses its own risks.

Third, when external sources provide services, Army personnel lose training opportunities they need to develop mission-critical skills. This problem is most severe when contractors work on the battlefield (Brooke, 1998, p. 26). When contractors do the hands-on work, opportunities for on-the-job training diminish. Over the longer term, as a commander becomes more dependent on contractors, she is more likely to give their employees priority in formal, off-site training, further diminishing opportunities for military personnel. The Army can discourage such outcomes by including training as an integral part of the contractor's support task.[51]

Fourth, contractors currently rely heavily on former military personnel to staff work performed for the Army. If the Army stops doing relevant work in-house, it will also stop developing skilled personnel that its contractors can hire (Mailander, 2002, p. 14). In effect, the Army continues to benefit from the technical training, which it initially provided to skilled technicians, when they remove their uniforms and report as civilians. It also continues to benefit from access to workers who understand the military and will have less difficulty aligning their work with the commander's goals. Their past military experience is likely to be of particular importance in a hazardous environment in-theater. The technical skills will still be available to the Army if it ends its training; it will simply pay contractors, directly or indirectly, to provide training rather than paying for it directly. Workers can still "grow up" working with the military, potentially in hazardous settings, over the course of their careers. But the Army should be prepared to alter its contract oversight mecha-

---

[51] Leech, Campbell, and Goodman (2002) discusses a successful contract in which senior Lockheed Martin technicians fully integrated themselves with an aviation maintenance unit, providing informal and formal training for the maintenance technicians and even helping the commander devise a new maintenance plan that significantly improved the performance of the aircraft that the unit supported. This occurred precisely because the unit conceived the contract from the beginning with training in mind and chose a contractor who was well prepared to provide the training services demanded.

nisms to recognize a somewhat wider cultural gap between its contractors and itself than it has known in the past.

Fifth, capabilities that reside in external sources are more vulnerable to enemy attack or influence (Singer, 2003, p. 168). Because the Army does not control them directly, they may be less visible to the commander and so receive a lesser priority in general force protection. Such generic services as telecommunications and electric power may lie completely beyond the commander's military concerns. Telecommunications infrastructure offers new opportunities for the application of information warfare (Deal and Ward, 2001, p. 52).[52] More subtly, an enemy might seek to compromise an external source by acquiring control over it (Deal and Ward, 2001, p. 51).[53] The Army can review the ownership of firms providing key material, but ownership changes often, ownership can be masked, and efforts to avoid such exposure could easily eliminate opportunities worth a great deal more than the costs of exposure.

---

[52] Singer (2003, pp. 163–164) offers an egregious example of a contractor that used standard commercial television frequencies to transmit classified imagery. This could easily have been compromised by an enemy seeking to plant misinformation. It could also easily have been avoided with a properly framed contract.

[53] During the war in Iraq, an executive of the Swiss Swatch Group AG delayed delivery of subcomponents critical to the production of precision munitions and grenades, apparently in response to opponents of the war. An enemy with similar financial control could easily have achieved a similar outcome (Gertz, 2003).

APPENDIX C

Using Contractors to Reduce Risks on the Battlefield

For the most part, the Army has used an increasing number of contractors on the battlefield during the last 15 years because to do so is the best choice available to the Army *within the constraints that it faces*. This appendix summarizes statements by Army personnel and other knowledgeable commentators that explain this pattern of use. The information presented here underlies the summary statements in Chapter Three.

The unifying idea that lies behind the explanations given below is simple: despite the many fears that Army leaders have had about using contractors on the battlefield, in specific circumstances, it is the best option given a decisionmaker's existing resource and policy constraints. There is no doubt that this occurs only in certain circumstances and that the Army has on occasion used contractors inappropriately in the past. It is also clear that opportunities exist to use contractors to relieve the effects of a wide variety of constraints.

The following list summarizes the major reasons that Army personnel and other commentators have given recently for using contractors on the battlefield.

- With a smaller organic force and more deployments, the Army has less organic capability to support deployments than it did during the Cold War (CASCOM, 2001, p. 4; GAO, 2003a, p. S-1; Peters, 1996; Robinson, 2002, p. 40; Singer, 2003, p.

231).[1] In this case, the resource constraint that the Army faces takes a particular form—a military end-strength constraint on organic capability per se. Given this constraint, applying resources still available to contract sources can mitigate the effects of the hazard that the Army faces.

- Contractors offer capabilities that the Army cannot sustain cost-effectively in-house and options that the Army cannot easily exercise within its legal, political, and diplomatic constraints. Low-density, high-demand skills offer a particularly attractive opportunity to use contract support (Curtis, 2000, pp. 10, 13; Epley, 1990, p. 30; Gally and Horne, 1996, p. 7; Mailander, 2002, p. 17; Thomas, 2000, p. 7).[2] With the limited resources available, the Army can reduce the level of risk associated with military hazards by applying its resources to contract sources rather than organic sources. Contract sources offer better mitigation of the effects of the hazard than organic sources.
- Generic activities with close analogs in the commercial sector can easily be available at lower total ownership cost or higher performance levels from contract sources than from military sources.[3] As the Army defines its core competencies more

---

[1] Smith (2002–2003) proposes a dramatic expansion in reliance on contractors in response to the mismatch between the demands on the military and the military's ability to meet the demand with organic capabilities. He proposes the use of "private military corporations," particularly in peacekeeping and humanitarian operations that require skills beyond DoD's traditional core competencies. Although this report does not attempt to address such a use of contractors directly—Smith contemplates much greater delegation of authority to contractors than we address here—many of the arguments offered here could apply in that setting.

[2] The Army Guardrail surveillance aircraft is entirely contract supported because it is not cost-effective to support in-house (GAO, 2003a, pp. 1, 9). USAREUR reported that the use of Brown and Root Services and other contractors resulted in significant cost savings in Operation Joint Endeavor (Schrader, 1999). Outsourcing does not always result in cost savings. See Markusen (2001) for examples of where it does not. Formal public-private competitions offer one way to sort opportunities where outsourcing can reduce costs, but they are rarely appropriate for application to support activities on the battlefield.

[3] Empirical studies comparing the cost and performance of public and private sources for comparable commercial goods and services strongly favor private providers. Megginson and Netter (2001) and Shirley and Walsh (2000) provide recent surveys of the empirical literature.

clearly, contracts can offer access to commercial providers with core competencies in activities outside the Army's core capabilities.[4] Given the limited resources available, such contract sources offer better mitigation of the effects of the military hazard that the Army faces than organic sources.

- Much of the Army's organic support capability lies in its reserve components. Using contractors allows the Army to avoid the politically unattractive option of mobilizing reservists often and for long periods.[5] Here the constraint takes another form. The President pays a political price when calling up the reserves and, in response, limits the organic manpower resources available to the Army. Under these circumstances, the Army can apply budgetary resources that are still available to contract sources and thereby mitigate the effects of the hazard that the Army faces.
- When rapid deployment is desirable, contract support can allow the Army to allocate scarce airlift assets to combat forces (Curtis, 2000, p. 7; Pagonis and Cruikshank, 1992, p. 107).[6] Contractors can use local resources in-theater to provide support and can use airlift assets not available to the military (Curtis, 2000, p. 10; Epley, 1990, p. 30; Gally and Horne, 1996, p. 7).[7] Here,

---

[4] Stollenwerk (1999 pp. 24–27, 37–40) offers a useful discussion of core competencies relevant to work on the battlefield. See also Epley (1990, p. 30). In Operation Desert Strike, contractors recommended and provided Mylar for guardhouse windows. Contractors provided asphalt, hazardous waste disposal, custodial services, fencing, construction equipment, escort, personnel bunkers, concrete revetments, guard facilities, and resupply via DHL and FedEx. DoD has outsourced most of its transportation support (88 percent for the Army, 50 percent for the Air Force, 68 percent for the Navy). FedEx gets supplies to deployed forces fast (Robertson, 2000, p. 10).

[5] Three-quarters of the Army's military combat service support lies in its reserve components (Russell, 1997, p. 19; Mailander, 2002, p. 17; Wynn, 2000).

[6] Military history has shown that armies are more maneuverable when not tied to large volumes of base supply (Mailander, 2002, p. 4). But see Mailander (2002, p. 12) for an alternative point of view offered by Major General B. D. Bates, Army Forces Korea.

[7] Contingency contracting personnel write contracts on the ground as a contingency unfolds. They arrive with the combat troops and arrange for life support and other services until Army CSS and LOGCAP can arrive. The first Persian Gulf War demonstrated the ability of contingency contracting to increase and decrease support services in-theater quickly

the resource constraint is imposed by a shortage of airlift, a perennially underfunded military capability. Given that the Army must accept the airlift that the COCOM allocates to it in a particular contingency, it can apply available budgetary resources to contract sources that do not place demands on military airlift and mitigate the effects of the military hazard that it faces in the contingency.

- As the Army relies on increasingly sophisticated weapon systems, the skills required to support them are increasingly difficult to retain within the Army (CASCOM, 2001, pp. 4, 23; DSB, 1982b, p. 2; Epley, 1990, p. 30; GAO, 2003a, p. S-1; Mailander, 2002, p. 14; Nelson, 2000, p. 6; Peters, 1996; Thomas, 2000, p. 7; Zamparelli, 1999, p. 14).[8] This is especially true before contractors stabilize their support concepts and develop technical orders that organic personnel can use to maintain new equipment (Curtis, 2000, p. 10).[9] Here, the operative constraint is likely to involve Army policy more than resources. Personnel management policies make it impossible for the Army to train and retain enough personnel with the skills it needs to support complex and immature technologies on the battlefield. A policy that allowed the Army to pay specialists to remain in uniform

---

(Harris, 2000, p. 4). When transportation fails to sustain military effort, leveraging local economies can compensate for materials in short supply (Fortner and Jaeckle, 1998). Thomas (2000, p. 7) worries that the reliability of host nation support varies across and even within countries. U.S. contractors can provide a hedge against such unreliability, but such a strategy then places them in competition with the military for transport and other resources in short supply early in a contingency. General Bates of Army Forces Korea (quoted in Mailander, 2002, p. 12) notes that a commander cannot always rely on local markets for support. Also, indigenous workers can pose a security threat, particularly when they work on post. This can pose a direct military threat and a threat to performance when the post is locked down under security restrictions, not allowing entry to all workers (Mailander, 2002, p. 16).

[8] Robinson (2002, p. 40) notes that virtually all high-technology defense systems require contractor support in the field.

[9] It was unusual when DoD deployed the developmental JSTARS in the first Gulf War. Years later, contractor personnel manned stations for the JSTARS in Operation Joint Endeavor over Bosnia. JSTARS could not have operated effectively without them (Air Force Background Papers, 1997, p. 105, quoted in Nelson, 2000, p. 4). With spiral development, this pattern is expected to become more common.

might allow the Army to think more carefully about the relative desirability of using contract and organic specialists on the battlefield, but until DoD allows the Army to adopt such a policy, the Army simply faces a shortage of trained personnel on the battlefield. Given this shortage, applying available budgetary resources to contract sources mitigates the effects of the military hazard that the Army faces on the battlefield by increasing the availability and sustainability of its best weapon systems.

- Decisions to field equipment still in development, or to keep equipment in development longer to increase capabilities, delay the date at which mature technical orders become available, allowing maintenance work to come in-house.[10] The constraint here results from a variation on the policy that drives the point above. By bringing weapons to the battlefield earlier in their development phase and extending that development phase well into production, new DoD policy extends the period during which the Army needs personnel of the kind it cannot retain. As long as these two policies persist, side by side—increased demand for highly skilled technicians on the battlefield and no special personnel policies to keep them in uniform—applying available resources to contract sources mitigates the effects of the military hazard that the Army faces on the battlefield.
- The Army, following DoD guidance, is increasing its reliance on life-cycle contractor logistics support. When the Army uses such support, it never develops organic support capability for a system and relies on continuing contractor support through the system's lifetime, even on the battlefield. The problem would be less severe if a system's support concept envisioned simple remove-and-replace activities for faulty components that military technicians could perform when deployed and life-cycle

[10] Because no military support capability was available for the systems, about 60 contract employees (representing one-third of the total number of contractors sent to Iraq with the 4ID) deployed to Iraq with the 4ID to support high-technology command and control (C2) systems still in development (GAO, 2003a, p. 8).

CLS-supported diagnosis and repair of components outside the theater.

- Congressional and presidential troop ceilings limit the number of military personnel allowed in a theater (Castillo, 2000; Curtis, 2000, p. 10; Epley, 1990, p. 30; GAO, 2003a, p. S-1; Gally and Horne, 1996, p. 7; Peters, 1996; Stollenwerk, 1999, p. 13; Thomas, 2000, p. 7). Under such restrictions, contractors can substitute for support troops, allowing the Army to field more combat capability within a given ceiling. As long as these political mandates persist, applying available budgetary resources to contract sources mitigates the effects of the military hazard that the Army faces on the battlefield.
- More generally, contract support allows the United States to maintain a lower military profile in-theater and to direct resources at local nationals (Mailander, 2002, p. 17; Wynn, 2000).[11] Both actions can support American diplomatic and political goals in sensitive theaters. This point is a variation on the point above.

---

[11] On the other hand, Robinson (2002, p. 40) notes that contractors in-theater can actually make U.S. military operations more visible if enemy forces follow the contractors to the military forces themselves.

APPENDIX D

How the Approach Proposed Here Compares with Alternative Approaches

The Army uses a variety of concepts and tools to think about sourcing decisions today and is considering others. This appendix relates the approach in the text to the most important of these alternatives.

"Core," "Inherently Governmental," and "Military Essential" Capabilities

Most discussions of sourcing in DoD begin by excluding from potential outsourcing any "core," "inherently governmental," or "military-essential" activity. For example, the Army's Third Wave was explicitly structured around a Non–Core Competencies Working Group, which started seeking candidates for competitive sourcing by excluding "core" Army activities (White, 2002). Efforts to identify candidates for military-to-civilian conversion in TAA-13 started with a clear definition of "militarily essential" and considered only billets that were not.[1] The easiest way to integrate the checklist that appears in Table 5.1 with standard Army practice would be to screen such activities from consideration before beginning, and that may be appropriate. Unfortunately, interpretations of these terms in DoD

[1] A "military-essential" billet is defined as one that must be occupied by a person with recent, current, direct, hands-on experience in a military billet in the operating force. TAA-11 Generating Force Requirements Council of Colonels, Leesburg, Va., August 20–27, 2003. The interpretation of "military essential" used in this case was not conservative.

have tended to be conservative. Conservative interpretations could prematurely choose military sources for many CSS activities on the battlefield.[2]

The checklist offered in Table 5.1 avoids the terms above, not because they are irrelevant but because it seeks to address the issues they raise from a different direction to limit inappropriately conservative assessments of these terms. It deliberately starts with the opportunity a contract source offers and then looks for valid reasons to avoid using a potentially attractive source. Traditional application of the terms above does the opposite. If, for example, a contract source offers attractive opportunities to maintain, on the battlefield, the weapon systems most important to the Army's mission success, the traditional view of the Army's *core* activities will immediately reject such contractor provision. Such activities could also be viewed as inherently military-essential. Current Army practice with many weapon systems raises questions about whether such an immediate rejection is appropriate. Similarly, if a contract source offers attractive capabilities for managing inventory on the battlefield, the traditional interpretation of "inherently governmental" could easily reject these capabilities, noting that such management inherently involves requirements determination and so is inherently governmental.[3]

Elements implicit in the framework offered here pick up these concerns in a different way. Outsourcing support activities too close to activities involving policy discretion and obligation of funds, for example—factors integral to any formal definition of what is inher-

---

[2] For example, GAO (2003b, p. 3) recently found that "definitions of core remain somewhat broad and subjective" in DoD. GAO also noted that the Army had found that once it had "determined that a function is not core to an agency's missions, other factors that are not currently covered in DOD's guidance must be considered, such as risk and operational considerations" (GAO, 2003b, p. 3).

[3] The FAIR Act of 1998 provides a formal definition of "inherently governmental." It states that only a government official may bind the United States with respect to taking an action by contract, policy, regulation, authorization, or otherwise; undertake military or diplomatic action, civil or criminal judicial proceedings, or contract management; significantly affect the life or property of private persons; appoint, direct, or control officials of the United States; or control the acquisition, use, or disposition of the property of the United States. In practice, application of this definition has typically allowed considerable discretion.

ently governmental—would not allow acceptable contract oversight (Question 5 in Table 5.1) and would not comply with procurement laws and regulations (Question 14). Outsourcing support activities with direct control over the application of violence on the battlefield would leave contractor employees explicitly unprotected by the international law of war, imposing unacceptable risks on employee safety (Question 4); federal law also reserves such activities for government personnel only (Question 14). If recent, current, direct experience in a military billet in the operating force is the key attribute relevant to filling a "military-essential" billet, Question 5 can easily exclude any such billet from contractor control. The definition of *core* is more ambiguous. The checklist seeks to challenge traditional definitions where contract sources appear to offer attractive opportunities for the Army.

The IGCA Inventory Approach to Risk Assessment

OSD's guidance for an Inherently Governmental/Commercial Activity (IGCA) Inventory submission also provides a list of sources of risk that could be characterized as a checklist (OSD, 2003, Enclosure 8). The IGCA list and the list that underlies the analysis here look remarkably similar. But the treatment of the two lists is profoundly different.

- The approach here addresses risk explicitly as one of four kinds of failures—failures relevant to military mission, the safety of contractor personnel and equipment, cost, or federal policies, of which federal acquisition policy is prominent. "Sources of risk" or hazards are relevant explicitly because they can induce one or more of these types of failure. The IGCA Inventory approach lists many potential sources of risk without clearly defining what risk is relevant to assessment for sourcing purposes—and hence why these sources of risk are relevant.
- The approach here seeks to understand how these sources of risk are related to the risks they induce and to one another. Some

result from efforts to mitigate the effects of other sources of risk—efforts that, on net, reduce risks to the Army. This is most evident when the Army uses contractors to relieve policy and resource constraints, but it occurs through many of the channels of influence in Figure 5.1. In contrast, the IGCA Inventory approach tends to allow any one source of risk to eliminate an activity as a candidate for contract sourcing without asking how it affects the residual risk relevant to choosing among types of sources.

- The approach here recognizes that, at any point in time, only a portion of the missions that the Army's CSS activities will service is expected to face heavy combat or highly dynamic circumstances in an unpredictable theater. As a result, only a portion of the Army's capability to provide CSS services must be robust enough to perform well in such an environment. In contrast, the IGCA Inventory approach implicitly suggests that if any portion of an Army CSS capability must face danger in combat, all parts of that capability should be treated as though they would face danger as well.
- The IGCA Inventory approach classifies an activity as "military-essential" and so exempt from contract sourcing if "continued, proper, and timely execution of the function under combat conditions has to be assured or safeguarded through UCMJ authority and discipline and military training."[4] This view simply shifts the burden of defining "military-essential" to defining what must be assured through UCMJ authority. The IGCA Inventory approach offers no guidance on when UCMJ authority is required. The approach offered here does not directly invoke the UCMJ. Rather, it focuses on the considerations likely to create a high enough level of risk to require military discipline—type of activity, nature of contingency, location on the battlefield, and so on.

---

[4] This quotation echoes many similar statements throughout OSD (2003, Enclosure 8). It occurs in Section E2.2.5.1.1.2.

- The IGCA Inventory approach uses a view of inherently governmental activities inconsistent with the formal definition offered in the FAIR Act, which, as noted above, defines inherently governmental activities in very narrow terms. In effect, the IGCA Inventory approach cannot utilize the formal legislative definition of "inherently governmental" as a separable consideration relevant to sourcing. The approach offered here makes no reference to "inherently governmental" directly but captures its appropriately narrow, legislative interpretation in its treatment of failure to comply with federal laws and regulations as an important risk that deserves attention.
- The differences above strongly suggest that the IGCA Inventory approach will exempt more Army CSS activities from potential contract sourcing than the approach offered here. The basic perspective is quite different in the two approaches. The approach offered here considers a contract source only when it offers the Army a potential benefit of some kind. It then prohibits a contract source only if the risks associated with using the contract source are likely to outweigh the benefits. The IGCA Inventory approach gives no formal or explicit attention to any benefit that a contract source might offer. If it can identify any relevant source of risk, that one source can be enough to prohibit using a contract source, regardless of its benefits. And by treating the definitions of "inherently governmental" and "military-essential" so broadly, the IGCA Inventory approach tends to foreclose many of the factors considered here before they even arise.
- Finally, once it has identified a potential source of risk, the IGCA Inventory approach tends to rely on subjective expert judgment to determine its importance without any formal guidance on how to assess the importance. Recognizing that subjective judgment is unavoidable in risk assessments relevant to sourcing on the battlefield, the approach offered here attempts to provide a coherent, objective structure in which to assess the many subjective judgments relevant to any assessment. Although such an approach cannot wash out subjective judgments, it can

make them more visible, more transparent, and more easily subject to improved analytic attention over time.

Analysis Supporting Current Competitive Sourcing Studies

The Army can use formal public-private competitions to determine whether to use a contract or military source. The Army uses the Office of Management and Budget's (OMB's) Circular A-76 to structure such competitions (OMB, 2003). [5] Until May 2003, the Army had the option of using competitions defined by Circular A-76 to determine whether or not to outsource activities currently performed by military personnel. Following a major rewrite of Circular A-76 in May 2003, the Army may be required to use such competitions before it can convert an activity from a military to a contractor source (*Federal Register*, 2003). Because no competitions have been completed under the new version of Circular A-76, it is too early to verify whether this interpretation is correct or not. If it is, Congress requires that, in such a competition, any choice between a military (or other government) source and a contract source be determined on the basis of the relative costs of the public and private options.[6] Under such circumstances, what role could a risk assessment approach like that outlined here play in choosing between a military and contract source?

The approach offered here can play two roles. First, it can help the Army decide which activities to offer as available for competition

---

[5] For a useful discussion of how Circular A-76 has evolved and how it works today, see GAO (2003b).

[6] "Except as otherwise provided by law, the Secretary of Defense shall procure each supply or service necessary for or beneficial to the accomplishment of the authorized functions of the Department of Defense (*other than functions which the Secretary of Defense determines must be performed by military or Government personnel*) from a source in the private sector if such a source can provide such supply or service to the Department at a cost that is lower (after including any cost differential required by law, Executive order, or regulation) than the cost at which the Department can provide the same supply or service" (10 U.S.C. 2462[a]) (emphasis added).

and hence subject to the rules that Circular A-76 and Congress provide for conducting public-private competitions. The FAIR Act provides guidelines for defining what activities should be available for competition.[7] The approach offered here could help the Army implement these guidelines by assessing the risks associated with military and contract sources. In particular, our approach could help the Army understand which support activities are so subject to risk on the battlefield that they should not be classified as commercial and hence made available for potential outsourcing. Second, once the Army has decided which activities are available for public-private competition, it must decide which activities to compete first. The approach offered here can help the Army rank activities to suggest where competition is likely to give the Army the greatest payoff.

Viewed in this way, the approach offered here is completely compatible with congressional guidance on sourcing and Circular A-76. It helps the Army implement the guidance that ultimately leads to competitions based on the rules in Circular A-76.[8]

Drill-Down Analysis

The checklist works from a set of inputs to a final assessment that identifies the relative residual risks associated with contractor and military sources. It starts with empirical data and subjective judgments available today to make statements about what might happen in the future. Can it support an effort to go the other direction? That is, can it start with specific instances of contractor performance on

[7] FAIR Act, 1998.

[8] The approach offered here may best be applied within the context of the economist's formal principal-agent paradigm. Under the traditional principal-agent paradigm, the Army as principal chooses institutional arrangements with the foreknowledge that an agent will attempt to maximize its own well-being within this framework. In the present setting, the Army as principal decides whether or when to offer an activity for public-private competition with the foreknowledge that an agent—this time OMB's Circular A-76—will choose the source that looks best under its own rules. That is, *given* how Circular A-76 works, the Army asks what the relative risks are of classifying an activity as available or unavailable for competition and then of pursuing competition immediately or delaying competition to the future. The assessment of risks in the approach offered here could be explicitly framed to consider the relative residual risks associated with using Circular A-76 to make sourcing decisions.

the battlefield and ask what factors account for that high or low level of performance—with regard to mission success, employee safety, resource cost, compliance with the law, or whatever? Such a capability is often called a "drill-down" capability because it allows an analyst to drill down through all the factors that could have influenced an outcome until it identifies the key factors.[9]

Speaking broadly, the two ideas are closely related. The checklist traces a variety of assumptions about factors relevant to a sourcing decision, through channels of influence with assumed properties, to statements about the relative value of a contract source in particular circumstances. A drill-down analysis could use the same channels of influence, with the same assumed properties, to trace an outcome back to the underlying factors that provide the "root causes" for the outcome.[10] In fact, methods exist to use such drill-down analysis to collect empirical information that can be used to sharpen our understanding of the channels of influence and so improve the Army's ability to make reliable, well-informed sourcing decisions on the battlefield.[11]

As a practical matter, then, drill-down methods are likely to be useful in the refinement of such an approach as the one proposed here. That said, the basic sequence of reasoning underlying the approach presented here, as summarized in Figure 5.1, could serve as a starting point for the architecture of a drill-down approach.[12]

---

[9] See also Peltz et al. (2002).

[10] Greenfield and Camm (forthcoming) illustrates how to apply a fault tree to explain the observed outcomes for a specific Army contract that provides support to deployed forces—the Balkans Support Contract. A fault tree starts with a set of proximate failures and considers each of the intermediate failures that could have caused these. It provides a systematic mapping that an analyst can use to walk through these intermediate failures to the root causes of a proximate failure.

[11] See, for example, Vesely et al. (1981). The "Bayesian networks" used to organize knowledge for use in inference engines provide clear, formal ways to use a single set of channels of influence to go in either direction—from assumptions about causes to probable outcomes or from observed outcomes to probable causes. For an introduction, see Jensen (1996).

[12] Appendix A looks at the use of contractors on the battlefield from a broader perspective and illustrates how a single model can potentially be used to look in either direction.

Balanced Scorecard

When the Chief of Staff approved the development of the Strategic Readiness System in March 2002, the Army embarked on a broad effort to build a balanced scorecard for the Army as a whole and for all major activities within the Army (Burlas, 2002; Cox, 2002). A balanced scorecard helps an organization translate its high-level strategic goals into specific resource decisions that promote those goals.[13] The checklist does something similar by helping analysts characterize specific sourcing decisions on the battlefield in terms of risks relevant to high-level strategic goals. By doing so, it can support Army efforts to "translate" those strategic goals into specific sourcing decisions on the battlefield. This makes the checklist sound similar to a balanced scorecard.

This is not the place to discuss the nuances of a balanced scorecard.[14] But suffice it to say that a scorecard is primarily a *process* designed to develop and sustain a consensus among the high-level leaders of an organization on the key factors relevant to the organization's success. We offer the checklist described here primarily as the conceptual basis for an analytic *tool* that the Army could use to improve sourcing decisions that affect who performs support activities on the battlefield.

That said, the Army planners responsible for supporting such decisions could use the checklist offered here in a context resembling the one relevant to a balanced scorecard. It might work as follows:

- Use the checklist as the basis for building a model of the channels of influence that describe the principal sources of risk and mitigations relevant to sourcing decisions on the battlefield.
- Use the model to support consensus-building among planners about these sources of risk and mitigations and how they are likely to work in practice.

---

[13] The standard reference for a balanced scoreboard is Kaplan and Norton (1996). For a discussion of how a balanced scorecard might work in an Army setting, see Camm, Eden, and Peltz (forthcoming).

[14] See the references in the previous footnote.

- Capture this consensus in doctrine on the use of contractors on the battlefield.
- Use the model to structure information collected from ongoing experience with contractors on the battlefield. Use this information to refine the model and to sustain the consensus among planners about the risks, mitigations, and their representation in the model.
- Update Army doctrine periodically to keep it as current with available information as possible.

How to do this goes well beyond the immediate concerns of this report but the development of such a process to build and sustain consensus could be the most powerful and useful product of such an approach as the one offered here.[15]

---

[15] This approach is common in many complex areas where great uncertainty persists about key assumptions relevant to policy or scientific outcomes. For example, the Energy Modeling Forum has, for many years, provided standard structures in which to test alternative assumptions and clarify the issues that require the most empirical analytic effort in the future. Atmospheric chemists maintain similar forums to structure and facilitate ongoing research on global warming. For details, see http://www.stanford.edu/group/EMF/home/index.htm, accessed October 31, 2003.

APPENDIX E

Measuring the Readiness of Contract Services

When the Army plans to use contract services on the battlefield, what level of performance can the Army reasonably expect? How much time will it take to provide the level of performance needed? These are questions the Army asks about military units on a regular, systematic basis.

When contract services become critical to the Army's success on the battlefield, the Army needs answers about contract services that are as reliable and informative as those about its own military units. This report provides insights that should help the Army get relevant answers about using contractors. Asking whether a contract will ensure performance on the battlefield as expected is in effect asking for an assessment of the residual risk associated with a contractor's effect on mission success. Asking how long it will take a contract service to be ready can be framed in terms of a planning horizon that allows mitigations to occur. How long does a planning horizon have to be to allow a contract source of services to improve enough to make it a reliable and preferred source on the battlefield?

The text of this report has emphasized that the performance of contract services depends not just on the contractor but also on the governance structure that the Army uses to ensure that the contractor performs. Army measurement of unit readiness carefully distinguishes the readiness of the unit itself from its contribution to mission success on the battlefield; a unit's readiness is only one of many factors that contribute to mission success. To find a suitable contract analog for Army unit readiness reporting, we need to focus on the contract source itself and draw a line around that source that is comparable to the line the Army draws around a military unit when it assesses its readiness. Doing this leads to important differences in readiness measurement based on basic differences in the way the Army governs military units and contractors.

This appendix starts by summarizing how the Army judges the readiness of its own units to provide a benchmark. It then examines how the Army could get comparably useful information on contract sources.

Readiness of Military Units

"The Army defines unit readiness as the ability of a unit to deliver the output for which it was designed" (*How the Army Runs*, 2001, p. 8-2).[1] The Joint Staff collects information relevant to this ability through its Global Status of Resources and Training System (GSORTS). The unit status report (USR) is the Army's monthly input to GSORTS. The USR provides

> HQDA and all levels of the Army's chain of command with the current status of U.S. Army units and necessary information for making operational decisions. The USR is designed to measure the status of resources and training level of a unit at a given point in time. . . . The USR provides a timely single source document for assessing key elements of unit status. . . . Detailed reviews of problems are conducted using other data systems. . . . [HQDA] uses the USR in conjunction with other personnel and logistics reports to improve resource management of people, equipment, and the programming of facilities and training areas/exercises to increase the combat effectiveness of subordinate elements. (*How the Army Runs*, 2001, pp. 8-10, 8-12; AR 220-1, 1997.)
>
> Reporting units are required to submit a USR covering their resource and training status levels. The overall category level (C-

[1] This subsection is based on Chapter Eight of this document.

1, C-2, C-3, C-4, C-5) indicates the degree to which a unit has achieved prescribed levels of personnel and equipment, the training of those personnel, and the maintenance of the equipment. These levels reflect the status of the unit's resources and training measured against the resources and training required to undertake the wartime mission for which the unit is organized or designed. *Category levels do not project a unit's combat ability once committed to action. The overall unit category level will be based only upon organic resources and training under the operational control of the reporting unit or its parent unit.* (*How the Army Runs*, 2001, p. 8-12 [emphasis added].)

The USR includes the following information:

- Personnel. It compares available strength, available MOS-qualified strength, and available senior grade strength against wartime requirements. It documents assigned strength and personnel turnover.
- Equipment on hand. It compares the fill of selected equipment to wartime requirements. Wartime and actual levels are determined for all of an MTOE unit's primary items of equipment, including weapons and major support equipment.
- Equipment serviceability. It documents what portion of on-hand reportable equipment is fully mission capable, by item type.
- Training. It indicates the current ability of the unit to perform assigned wartime missions. It also identifies shortfalls that prevent attainment of a training tempo necessary to achieve or maintain proficiency.
- Mission accomplishment estimate. This is the unit commander's subjective assessment of the percentage of wartime mission that the unit could accomplish if the unit were alerted/committed within 72 hours of the date of the report.
- Overall unit status level. The commander normally assigns the lowest level recorded in any of the unit's individually measured resource areas of personnel, equipment on hand, equipment

serviceability, and training. The commander can also upgrade or downgrade the unit's overall status.

In sum, the Army starts with a unit's specific wartime mission, translates that into a set of skills and assets needed to achieve it, and combines objective and subjective data to assess monthly the unit's ability to execute its mission. It focuses on the unit and the things under its control.

Readiness of Contract Sources

In principle, the Army could apply a similar regimen to its contract sources, but two issues get in the way. First, the Army rarely has enough knowledge about *how* a contractor would operate in wartime to know exactly what resources and training it should have to achieve a mission. The contractor may not even maintain personnel and equipment under its direct control until a deployment mission is well enough defined to determine what resources it actually needs. In fact, the Army sometimes relies on a contractor precisely to get access to its ability to subcontract quickly for reliable goods and services, using second-tier sources that the government has little knowledge of. Second, even if the Army had all the information above, it would not be enough. Because the Army controls a contractor through a contract, the terms of the contract itself deserve close attention. Several other issues also deserve attention. Consider each in turn.

Information on Resources and Training

The prior existence of a Table of Organization and Equipment (TO&E) for every military unit dramatically simplifies the application of the USR. It tells the commander exactly what skills and equipment to look for and defines the wartime goal well enough to allow quantitative assessments of resources and a solid assessment of other aspects of readiness. No similar document exists for most contractors. If the Army wanted to apply an approach similar to the one used in the USR, it would have to start by putting the equivalent of a

TO&E in each contract to be monitored. Of course, the Army would have to pay someone to prepare such a document.

Under performance-based contracting, which is now the dominant mode of services acquisition in DoD, an Army buyer does not tell a contractor *how* to produce a service provided. Rather, the Army tells the contractor *what* to provide and monitors the quality of *what* the contractor provides. From this perspective, a TO&E-equivalent document is problematic. It requires a level of visibility over the contractor that is increasingly rare in DoD services contracts.

That said, performance-based contracting must take a different form when the Army applies it to a service provided routinely in peacetime and when the Army applies it to a service that, in effect, maintains a wartime capability for use when needed. A performance-based contract can directly monitor the adequacy of routine peacetime output without any information about the resources used to generate the output. To monitor in peacetime the adequacy of a service maintaining wartime capability, a performance-based contract must rely on something other than routine peacetime capability. Possibilities include the following:

- Use peacetime performance as a surrogate for wartime performance of the elements of a service that can be provided without changing the location of performance or level of workload.
- Assess the contractor's plan to change workload level or location of performance.
- If plans depend on skills or equipment not readily available in current commercial markets, require the contractor to make specific arrangements to get such skills and equipment, in serviceable status, within specified deadlines. Assess the contractor's ability to do this. If necessary, require ownership and monitor the status of these skills and assets but do not assume that this is the only option.
- In an extreme measure, pay the contractor to prepare a TO&E-equivalent document, check it for reasonableness, and use this document as a point of reference for ongoing readiness measurement.

- Test the contractor periodically by changing workload level or changing performance location, perhaps to support an Army exercise.

The primary risk in question here is mission performance. Each of these options offers insight into the level of that risk. Each option gives the Army information that it can use to ensure that the contractor is complying with its agreement to be ready to provide services while, at the same time, not providing those services. Access to that information helps the Army maintain accountability that reduces the probability that the contractor will not deliver the service promised when and where needed and, if it does fail to deliver, limits the impact of that failure on mission success.

These arrangements do not dictate how to perform in peacetime or wartime. They leave this decision to the contractor. Once the contractor has made this decision, however, these alternatives require the contractor to verify periodically that it is doing what it promised to do—maintain a wartime capability in peacetime. From this perspective, it might well be appropriate during a source selection to ask offerors to suggest a method for monitoring readiness for wartime tasks during peacetime and make the monitoring plan a deliverable in the contract. Such an approach would be compatible with an increasingly common practice today, which is to ask offerors to provide quality assurance plans during the source selection and to choose a source in part on the basis of the plan offered.

Contracts that use award fees provide a process that the Army might use to measure readiness. In fact, it would be natural to integrate readiness assessment with the award fee process and make a portion of the award fee contingent on the level of readiness measured. This is natural if readiness for wartime is in fact a distinct deliverable in addition to peacetime support. An award fee is a bonus paid to a contractor several times a year for performance during an earlier period. Contracts with award fees typically pay a contractor such fees three or four times a year based on performance over a three- to four-month period.[2]

The personnel involved in an award fee determination can include customers, contract administrators, and military officials who observe the performance of the military units supported, as well as others. They have good insight into current performance but may also have valuable insight into likely performance in wartime, based on their ongoing experience with a contractor. They are the people who come closest to embodying the habitual relationship that the Army seeks with a contractor. That said, readiness measurement is likely to require collection of information other than that typically used in an award fee determination today. This might suggest the participation of additional Army personnel to judge the readiness of the contractor.

The administrative cost of determining an award fee is nontrivial. That is why the Army awards them only once every three or four months. The cost of measuring readiness might be equally high, warranting measurement quarterly or even less often, rather than monthly. Coordinating readiness measurement with the performance measurement that goes into the award fee, however, should significantly limit the incremental cost of readiness measurement. The Army would have to decide whether the value of more frequent reporting warranted more frequent measurement.

Part of this determination will depend on how much the status of a source can change in a short period. From this perspective, it is worth noting an important distinction between the goals of contract and military sources. While the primary goal of the contract source is to provide services, the military also must train personnel who turn over frequently. This training is an integral part of what any military unit does in peacetime. Contracts, on the other hand, typically do not

---

[2] Such contracts dictate an award fee process that collects data from as many players as deemed appropriate, brings those data to a fee determining official, and then announces the award to the contractor, sometimes (but not always) with an explanation of how the fee was determined. The contract must clarify the general grounds that will be used to award a fee, but a contractor cannot appeal the fee awarded. The Army must budget for a 100 percent fee award even if it does not make such an award each period.

include training or skill levels of their own personnel as deliverables to the Army. Contractors tend to use personnel who are more experienced and who require substantially less on-the-job training in basic skills. That is not to say that training is not important in a contractor setting—contractors must learn how to meet the Army's needs. Once they have learned these skills, however, the skills do not decay as rapidly as skills decay in a military unit because contractors typically experience much lower turnover. This difference suggests that it may make sense to measure contractors less frequently than military units. Less frequent measurement would make it easier to do more in-depth measurement whenever it occurs.

Any Army effort to seek new information about contractors, through any of these means, could trigger the Paperwork Reduction Act of 1995. The Act requires that any agency, including the Army, not initiate any new information collection before it has conducted a formally defined review of the utility and cost of the collection, received public comment on its collection methods, verified that the approach cannot be improved, and received approval for the collection from OMB (Sec. 3507 of the Act). The Act gives the director of OMB broad discretion over an agency's right to collect new information. The Act can apply even if the Army collects new data through its formal contracts and pays contractors for the full cost of the collection.[3]

In sum, even if the Army wants to know exactly the same thing about military and contractor sources, the process of measuring contractor readiness must be aligned with contracting requirements. Such alignment is likely to yield differences, potentially significant, in readiness measurement between contract and military sources. It is likely that the approach to readiness measurement will vary more

---

[3] This became apparent in the Army's efforts to collect very simple information on contractor employees as part of a recent DoD Business Initiative Council (BIC) described in Aldridge (2002). Data collection could not occur without OMB approval, even though the Army sought the data to fulfill a congressional reporting requirement (Brown, 2002). Any initiative to collect the more complex and complete data discussed above could similarly evoke OMB interest, even if it were motivated by serious concerns about the readiness of contract sources.

across contractors than across military units. Given relative costs of measurement, it could well be that measurement should occur less frequently for contractors than for military units.

Information on Contract Terms

Because a commander can only ask for support specified in a contract, a review of the terms of a contract should be an integral part of any assessment of a contractor's readiness.[4] If a contract does not arrange for deployed support or does so inadequately, this by itself could prevent a contractor from providing services required in-theater.

The Army understands this problem well. The U.S. Army Materiel Systems Analysis Agency (AMSAA) and CASCOM studies described in Chapter One highlight the extent of this problem (McGauley, 2001; CASCOM, 2001). Recent Army doctrine on using contractors on the battlefield gives a great deal of attention to what terms should appear in Army support contracts (AR 700-137, 1985; Pamphlet 715-16, 1998; AR 100-10-2, 1999; AR 715-9, 1999; AMC Pamphlet 715-18, 1999; FM 100-21, 2000; DoD, 2001; and FM 3-100.21, 2003).[5] They argue that, for contractors to be ready for deployment, contract terms should address the following types of issues[6]:

- A clear statement of the work scope for the contract. Ideally, this would be stated to allow enough flexibility to accommodate the surprises that inevitably occur in wartime. Flexibility is likely to be enhanced by contract line items that can be written in a cost-

---

[4] See also OSD (2003) on readiness reporting, past performance, and availability of key personnel (E2.2.1); flexibility of personnel (E2.2.5.1.1.2); and a clear statement of work (E2.3.2).

[5] The bulleted list in the text is simply a more detailed version of the second bullet in the "standard contracting improvement package" discussed above on p. 101. Each of these is an integral part of a plan to mitigate risks associated the principal-agent problem the Army must solve to maintain effective control over a contractor during deployment.

[6] For more information about how large defense support services contracts use such terms today, see Greenfield and Camm, forthcoming; Camm, Blickstein, and Venzor, 2003.

based form to ensure that the government bears the cost risk for add-on work that it wants done under a contract.

- Readiness to support a deployment, from a different location and with a different level of workload if appropriate, should be an explicit deliverable.
- How readiness measurement will occur. All formal information needed should be deliverables that the Army pays for. The process used to measure readiness should be included as a part of the quality assurance plan.
- Incentives to encourage a contractor to perform during a deployment. These can include higher prices, less demanding performance requirements, and equitable adjustment for unexpected expenses during a deployment. They should specify who pays various taxes, tariffs, and local government fees in-theater. They should include penalties for failing to perform during a deployment. An award fee or award term can be useful, especially if the contract formally identifies performance during a deployment as an award criterion.
- Mechanisms to ensure that employees are aware of the possibility of deployment and are prepared to deploy if called. These could include signed statements of agreement from employees to deploy if called, bonuses or special pays for deployment, and explicit penalties if they fail to deploy. They should include conditions on employees to ensure that deployment is feasible. These might include explicit statements about health status. They could include requirements that relevant insurance arrangements cover personnel before a deployment is announced and assist employees in getting access to government-subsidized insurance where it is available.
- What support the Army will give the contractor in-theater. This covers any appropriate preparation, including training and provisioning with standard NBC protective gear and other equipment; medical preparation, including vaccinations and physicals; transportation of personnel and equipment to the theater; induction into the theater; life support, facility support, and provision of equipment and materiel and other services in-

theater; force protection; and anything else relevant to effective contractor execution of its mission.

This list could provide the basis for a standard template that the Army could use in two ways. Contracting professionals could use it to write contracts. Those responsible for tracking readiness could use it to judge the readiness of the terms of a contract. The template could support the development of a specific measure of readiness that might be used to check whether the terms of a contract are compatible with how critical the contract services are to mission success.

Other Issues

Funding. A contracting officer requires a specific fund citation before he can obligate funds to a contract. Without such a citation, the Army cannot ask a contractor for services. This suggests that the level of funding available is a natural item to check during a readiness check. It is not under the direct control of the contractor or the contractor's contracting officer but is as important as any item in the USR checklist when predicting the availability of a specific contractor's services to any Army organization.

Recent Experience in a Similar Activity. Perhaps the best surrogate for training when talking about a contractor's readiness is its recent experience in a similar activity. As formal arrangements for assessing past performance in source selection show, two factors are important: (1) How similar was the activity to the contractor's wartime mission? (2) How recently did it occur? The Army has formal templates it can use to measure each of these, and it could easily apply them to a readiness assessment. For example, in omnibus contracts, source selections can continue through the life of a contract to determine the source for new task orders.[7] These source selections can assess past performance, which changes over the course of a contract as a contractor's performance changes, under the contract at hand and elsewhere in related activities. From this perspective, we can

---

[7] The Army Rapid Response program works this way. For details, see Camm, Blickstein, and Venzor (2003).

think of a new deployment as a new task order in a contract that provides a new opportunity to assess readiness in terms of past performance. This could be useful even if no new source selection occurs or even if no new deployment or task occurs. The assessment could simply help the Army update its assessment of the contractor's likely ability to execute a new deployment or task if one occurred in the near future.

Broader Reputation. Reputation has proven to be one of the most important factors used in choosing among sources during formal source selections. Past performance is one measurable element of reputation. General financial, managerial, and technological capacities are also important elements of many source selections. In the commercial sector where less transparency can be tolerated in source selections, a more subjective assessment of reputation can be an important criterion. The Army can draw on instruments that DoD has used successfully in services acquisition to assess corporate capacity broadly writ and, in particular, to assess the level of risk associated with that capacity. Some variation on such an assessment could be applied periodically through the course of a contract to ensure that the capacity measured in the initial source selection was still in place. These assessments are costly and could not occur as often as, say, an award fee determination. They could be scheduled as part of a readiness measurement that occurred annually, every other year, or at major milestones in a contract, as when an award term is scheduled to extend the term of the contract beyond its initial length.

Discussion

Traditional unit readiness reporting attempts to determine whether "a military unit can deliver the output for which it was designed." The analogous problem when using a contract source is to determine whether the contract can deliver the output for which it was designed. Required skills and equipment are an integral part of the design of a unit. They may be important to the design of a contract as well, but other factors may be more important. In a principal-agent problem, the Army principal anticipates what will motivate a contractor agent and designs a contract and associated relationship to motivate the contractor to give the Army *what* it wants. That is precisely what contracts attempt to do. The contractor works the details on *how* to do what the Army wants done.

Given that the Army designs a military unit and its operations, it is natural for the Army to measure its readiness in terms of the unit's ability to comply with the Army design. From this perspective, it is natural to think of measuring the readiness of a contract in terms of the contract's ability to comply with a standard design for Army contracts. The discussion above suggests that such a standard design could consider the following factors:

- Does the contract have the standard terms that the Army uses for contractor activities that have some level of critical importance to mission success? Contractor activities with more critical effects on the mission should presumably have a more complete set of the terms reviewed.
- Is the contract funded at a level adequate to ensure appropriate Army access through the course of a deployment?
- Does the contractor continue to display the level of performance on similar activities and more general financial, management, and technological capacity that the Army observed when the Army chose this specific contractor as its preferred source to operate on the battlefield?

More traditional resource-oriented measures of readiness, of the type used in the USR, may also be useful if they provide the only reliable way to verify peacetime readiness to provide wartime services at a different workload level or from a different location than the contractor provides peacetime support. This is particularly true if the Army asks offerors to recommend ways to measure peacetime readiness to provide wartime services, and the winning offeror chooses such an approach. That said, such an approach needs to be tailored to the ways that peacetime and wartime operations differ and focus on the differences and such an approach should not replace the bulleted questions above. Rather, it should complement them by providing a continuing check on the realism of the contractor's proposed way to make the transition to wartime.

Such an assessment can use manpower level, equipment status, and training assessments if these appear to be the best criteria available to judge likely future performance of a contractor. It is revealing that source selections use such information to assess the realism of a proposal but do not focus on such resource-oriented measures and tend to emphasize a number of other criteria as more useful.

Criteria associated with past performance on similar activities and, more generally, broad capacity to perform tend to receive greater attention in services-acquisition source selections. Past performance on similar activities can do double duty by motivating contractors to perform on the battlefield today to build their opportunities for future work on the battlefield. This experience in services acquisition suggests that such measures could be useful in readiness measurement as well.

The approach to measuring the readiness of a contractor offered here does not predict the contractor's performance once committed to action. A measure that did that would have to take into account all of the factors discussed earlier in the report, particularly the Army's arrangements to oversee and support the contractor and integrate it with the rest of the force. As with the approach used in the USR, the approach suggested here focuses on the performance of the contractor itself and the equivalent of its "parent unit," which for a contractor includes the provider of funds for the contract and the contracting officer.

Bibliography

Air Force Background Papers 1997, *Operational Forces Course Book*, Maxwell AFB, Ala.: Air University Press, 1997.

Aldridge, E. C., Jr., "Business Initiative Council's (BIC) Approval of Initiatives," memorandum, BIC, Department of Defense, Washington, D.C., September 13, 2002.

American Law Institute, *Restatement of the Law Second, Agency*, 8 vols., Philadelphia, 1958.

Anderson, Brig. Gen. Frank J., Jr., USAF, *A Plan to Accelerate the Transition to Performance-Based Services: Final Report of the Section 912(c) Working Group for Review of the Acquisition Training, Processes, and Tools for Services Contracts*, AF903T1, USD (AT&L), Washington, D.C., June 1999, available at http://www.acq.osd.mil/dpap/Docs/servrpt.pdf, accessed May 2003.

Army Materiel Command, *AMC Contracts and Contracting Supporting Military Operations*, AMC Pamphlet 715-18, Alexandria, Va., June 16, 2000.

Avant, Deborah, "Selling Security: Post–Cold War Private Security Services in Historical Perspective," paper prepared for delivery at the 2001 Annual Meeting of the American Political Science Association, San Francisco, August 30–September 2, 2001.

Black, H. C., *Black's Law Dictionary*, seventh edition, Dordrecht, the Netherlands: Kluwer Academic, 1999.

Bodilly, Susan, Frank Camm, and Richard Pei, *Analysis of Past Air Force Aircraft Multiyear Procurements, with Implications for the B-2*, Santa Monica, Calif.: RAND Corporation, R-3990-ACQ, 1990.

Bolton, Charles, Jr., "Contractor Systems Support During Contingency Operations," memorandum, Assistant Secretary of the Army (Acquisition, Logistics, and Technology), Washington, D.C., January 28, 2002a.

_____, "Contractor Support Restrictions," memorandum, Assistant Secretary of the Army (Acquisition, Logistics and Technology), Washington, D.C., June 11, 2002b.

Bond, Brig. Gen. William L., and Maj. Anthony L. Castrinos, "Contingency Contracting: Strengthening the Tail," *Army Logistician*, May–June 1999, p. 6.

Bondanella, John, Edward Keating, William Spencer, Lucille Horgan, and Edison Cesar, "Army Civilians and Contractor Employees in Contingency Operations: Developing a Shared Vision between Planners, Leaders, and Participants," Santa Monica, Calif.: RAND Corporation, DRR-857-A, 1994.

Bramblett, Lt. Col. Howard T., "Prime Vendor Support," unpublished paper, Carlisle Barracks, Pa.: U.S. Army War College, DTIC Document ADA342256, March 11, 1998.

Brooke, Col. J. Lynton, "Contracting: An Alarming Trend in Aviation Maintenance," unpublished paper, Carlisle Barracks, Pa.: U.S. Army War College, DTIC No. 19980522 012, April 16, 1998.

Brown, Brig. Gen. John S., "Contractors on the Battlefield: An Historical Survey from the Civil War to Bosnia," memorandum, Assistant Secretary of the Army (Force Management, Manpower, and Resources), Washington, D.C., June 30, 1999.

Brown, Reginald J., "Annual Congressional Report on Civilian Work Force Management," memorandum, Assistant Secretary of the Army (Manpower and Reserve Affairs), Washington, D.C., June 19, 2002.

Buhler, Maj. Carl A., USAF, "When Contractors Deploy: A Guide for the Operational Commander," unpublished paper, Newport, R.I.: Naval War College, February 2000.

Burlas, Joe, "New Scorecard Gives Holistic Readiness Picture," *ArmyLINK News,* Washington, D.C., July 24, 2002, available at http://www.dtic.mil/armylink/news/Jul2002/a20020724srs0423.html, accessed August 2002.

Camm, Frank, *DoD Should Maintain Both Organic and Contract Sources for Depot-Level Logistics Services*, Santa Monica, Calif.: RAND Corporation, IP-111, 1993.

_____, "Strategic Sourcing in the Air Force," in Zalmay Khalilzad and Jeremy Shapiro, eds., *Strategic Appraisal: United States Air and Space Power in the 21st Century*, Santa Monica, Calif.: RAND Corporation, MR-1314-AF, 2002, pp. 397–435.

Camm, Frank, Irv Blickstein, and Jose Venzor, "Recent, Large Service Acquisitions in the Department of Defense: Lessons for the Office of the Secretary of Defense," Santa Monica, Calif.: RAND Corporation, DRR-3062-OSD, 2003.

Camm, Frank, Rick Eden, and Eric Peltz, "A Candidate Framework for Assessing the Health of the Logistics System," Santa Monica, Calif.: RAND Corporation, forthcoming.

Campbell, Gordon L., "Contractors on the Battlefield: The Ethics of Paying Civilians to Enter Harm's Way and Requiring Soldiers to Depend on Them," paper for Joint Services Conference on Professional Ethics 2000, Springfield, Va., January 27–28, 2000, available at http://www.usafa.af.mil/jscope/JSCOPE00/Campbell.html, accessed June 2003.

CASCOM, "Systems Contractor Support of the 4th Infantry Division," Acquisition Liaison Office, U.S. Army Combined Arms Support Command, Fort Lee, Va., August 1, 2001.

Castillo, Lt. Col. Lourdes A., USAF, "Waging War with Civilians: Asking the Unanswered Questions," *Aerospace Power Journal*, Fall 2000, available at http://www.airpower.maxwell.af.mil/airchronicles/apj/apj00/fal00/castillo.htm, accessed August 2002.

Chiarotti, Charles G., "Joint Contractor Logistics Support Doctrine: Ensuring Success on the 21st Century Battlefield," unpublished paper, Newport, R.I.: U.S. Naval War College, 2000.

Clow, Kenneth H., and William J. Flavin, "The Logistics Civil Augmentation Program: Status Report," unpublished paper, Carlisle Barracks, Pa.: U.S. Army War College, February 22, 1993.

Cox, Col. Robert E., "Strategic Readiness System Army Scorecard," briefing, Headquarters, Department of the Army, Washington, D.C., March 2002.

Crocker, Keith J., and Kenneth J. Reynolds, "The Efficiency of Incomplete Contracts: An Empirical Analysis of Air Force Engine Procurements," *RAND Journal of Economics,* Vol. 24, 1993, pp. 126–146.

Curtis, Lt. Col. Donald R., Jr., USA, "Civilianizing Army Generating Forces," unpublished paper, Carlisle Barracks, Pa.: U.S. Army War College, April 2000.

Dahlman, Carl, and David Thaler, "Ready for War but Not for Peace: The Apparent Paradox of Military Preparedness," in Zalmay Khalilzad and Jeremy Shapiro, eds., *Strategic Appraisal: United States Air and Space Power in the 21st Century*, Santa Monica, Calif.: RAND Corporation, MR-1314-AF, 2002, pp. 437–481.

Deal, Col. John C., and James H. Ward, "Second Thoughts on Outsourcing for the Army," *Army*, May 2001, pp. 49–54.

Defense Science Board (DSB), "Report of Summer Study on Operational Readiness with High-Performance Systems," Office of the Under Secretary of Defense for Research and Engineering, Washington, D.C., April 1982a.

_____, "Report of the Task Force on Contractor Field Support During Crises," Office of the Under Secretary of Defense for Research and Engineering, Washington, D.C., DTIC document AD A129747, October 1982b.

Department of Defense (DoD), "Continuation of Essential DoD Contractor Services During Crises," DoDI 3020.37, Washington, D.C., November 6, 1990.

_____, Inspector General, *Audit Report on Civilian Contractor Overseas Support during Hostilities*, Report No. 91-105, Washington, D.C., June 26, 1991.

_____, "Contractor Support in the Theater of Operations," Acquisition Deskbook Supplement, Washington, D.C., March 28, 2001, available at http://web2.deskbook.osd.mil/New_Pubs/CLSSupplement.htm.

Department of the Army, *Logistics Civil Augmentation Program (LOGCAP)*, Army Regulation (AR) 700-137, Washington, D.C., December 16, 1985.

_____, *Total Army Analysis,* AR 71-11, Washington, D.C., 1995.

_____, *Unit Status Reporting,* AR 220-1, Washington, D.C., 1997.

_____, *Contractor Deployment Guide*, Pamphlet 715-16, Washington, D.C., February 27, 1998.

_____, *Risk Management*, Field Manual (FM) 100-14, Washington, D.C., April 1998.

_____, *Contracting Support on the Battlefield*, AR 100-10-2, Washington, D.C., August 4, 1999.

_____, *Contractors Accompanying the Force*, AR 715-9, Washington, D.C., October 29, 1999.

_____, *Contractors on the Battlefield*, FM 100-21, Washington, D.C., March 26, 2000.

_____, *Risk Management*, FM 3-100.12, Washington, D.C., February 2001.

_____, *Operations*, FM 3-0, Washington, D.C., 2001.

_____, *Contractors on the Battlefield*, FM 3-100.21, Washington, D.C., January 2003.

______, "Task Force Eagle After-Action Report," Carlisle Barracks, Pa., December 28, 1995–November 10, 1996, undated.

Dibble, George B., Charles L. Home III, and William F. Lindsay, *Army Contractors and Civilian Maintenance, Supply, and Transportation Support During Operations Desert Shield and Desert Storm, Vol. I*, Bethesda, Md.: Logistics Management Institute, Study Report AR113-01RD1, June 1993.

Donahue, John, *The Privatization Decision*, New York: Basic, 1989.

Dyche, Lt. Col., David D., "Making Operational Support Airlift Ready for War," Maxwell AFB, Ala.: Air University Press, Research Report No. AU-ARI-93-11, 1995.

DynCorp, "Logistics Civil Augmentation Program (LOGCAP), Worldwide Management and Staff Plan," 2001.

Eggleston, Karen, Eric A. Posner, and Richard Zeckhauser, "Simplicity and Complexity in Contracts," John M. Olin Law and Economics Working Paper No. 93, Second Series, University of Chicago Law School, January 18, 2000, available at http://www.law.uchicago.edu.

Epley, Maj. William W., "Civilian Support of Field Armies," *Army Logistician*, November–December 1990, pp. 30–35.

Everly, Col. J. Reid, USA (Ret.), letters, *Army*, July 2001, pp. 4–5.

Federal Activities Inventory Reform (FAIR) Act, 112 STAT 2382, P.L. 105-270, 1998.

Federal Register, "Revision to Office of Management and Budget Circular No. A-76, 'Performance of Commercial Activities,'" Vol. 68, No. 103, pp. 32134–32142, available at http://www.a257.g.akamaitech.net/7/257/2422/14mar20010800/edocket.access.gpo.gov/2003/03-13457.htm, accessed May 2003.

Fontaine, Yves J., "Strategic Logistics for Intervention Force," *Parameters*, No. 20, Winter 1997–1998.

Fortner, Joe A., "Information Paper on Contractors on the Battlefield," February 11, 1999, available at http://www.cascom.army.mil.

_____, "Institutionalizing Contractor Support on the Battlefield," *Army Logistician*, July–August 2000a, available at http://www.almc.army.mil/ALOG/issues/JulAug00/MS570.htm.

_____, "Managing, Deploying, Sustaining, and Protecting Contractors on the Battlefield," *Army Logistician*, September–October 2000b, p. 4, available at http://www.almc.army.mil/ALOG/issues/SepOct00/MS571.htm, accessed July 2002.

Fortner, Joe A., and Ron Jaeckle, "Institutionalizing Contractors on the Battlefield," *Army Logistician,* Vol. 30, No. 6, November–December 1998, pp. 11–13.

Foster, Susan C., "Contractors on the Battlefield: Force Multipliers or Detractors?" unpublished paper, Carlisle Barracks, Pa.: U.S. Army War College, April 1998.

Gally, David R., and Charles L. Horne III, *LOGCAP Support in Operation Joint Endeavor: A Review and Analysis*, McLean, Va.: Logistics Management Institute, LG612LN1, September 1996.

Gebman, J. R., D. W. McIver, and H. L. Shulman, "A New View of Weapon System Reliability and Maintainability," Santa Monica, Calif.: RAND Corporation, R-3604/2-AF, 1989.

General Accounting Office (GAO), "DoD Force Mix Issues: Greater Reliance on Civilians in Support Roles Could Provide Significant Benefits," Washington, D.C., GAO/NSIAD-95-5, October 19, 1994.

_____, "Contingency Operations: Opportunities to Improve the Logistics Civil Augmentation Program," Washington, D.C., GAO/NSIAD-97-63, February 1997.

_____, "Contingency Operations: Army Should Do More to Control Cost in the Balkans," Washington, D.C., GAO/NSIAD-00-225, September 2000.

_____, "Defense Budget: Contingency Operations in the Balkans May Need Less Funding in Fiscal Year 2003," Washington, D.C., GAO-02-1073, September 2002.

_____, "Military Operations: Contractors Provide Vital Services to Deployed Forces but Are Not Adequately Addressed in DoD Plans," Washington, D.C., GAO-03-695, June 2003a.

_____, "Defense Management: DOD Faces Challenges Implementing Its Core Competency Approach and A-76 Competitions," GAO-03-818, Washington, D.C., July 2003b.

Gertz, Bill, "Swiss Delay of Military Parts Sparks 'Buy American' Push," *Washington Times*, July 24, 2003, available at http://www.washingtontimes.com/national/20030724-113347-4214r.htm, accessed October 1, 2003.

Glennan, Thomas Keith, Susan J. Bodilly, Frank Camm, Kenneth R. Mayer, and Timothy Webb, *Barriers to Managing Risk in Large-Scale Weapons System Development Programs,* Santa Monica, Calif.: RAND Corporation, MR-248-AF, 1993.

Greenfield, Victoria A., and Frank Camm, *Risk Management and Performance in the Balkans Support Contract*, Santa Monica, Calif.: RAND Corporation, MG-282-A, forthcoming.

Gutierrez, John T., "Contracted Logistics Support in Operational Environments: The Legal Issues and Their Effects on the Decision to Outsource," thesis, Naval Postgraduate School, Monterey, Calif., December 2001.

Harris, Marilyn, "LOGCAP: The Nation's Premier Contingency Contracting Program for Force XXI," unpublished paper, Carlisle Barracks, Pa.: U.S. Army War College, April 2000.

Helper, Susan, John Paul MacDuffie, and Charles Sabel, "Pragmatic Collaborations: Advancing Knowledge While Controlling Opportunism," paper for conference on "Make Versus Buy: The New Boundaries of the Firm," Columbia Law School, New York, May 1998, revised March 1999.

Hennart, Jean-Francois, "Explaining the Swollen Middle: Why Most Transactions Are a Mix of 'Market' and 'Hierarchy,'" *Organization Science*, Vol. 4, No. 4, November 1993, pp. 529–547.

How the Army Runs: A Senior Leaders Reference Handbook, 2001–2002, 23rd edition, Col. Edward J. Filiberti, ed., Carlisle Barracks, Pa.: U.S. Army War College, 2001.

Huston, James A., *The Sinews of War: Army Logistics 1775–1953*, Washington, D.C.: Office of the Chief of Military History, 1966.

Hyde, James C., "Defense Contractors Serve on the Front Lines of Operation Desert Storm," *Armed Forces Journal International*, March 1991, p. 32.

Jensen, Finn V., "Bayesian Network Basics," *AISB Quarterly*, Vol. 94, 1996, pp. 9–22, 1996, available at http://www.cs.auc.dk/research/DSS/abstracts/jensen:96b.html, accessed on October 13, 2003.

Kaiser, Robert D., and Richard M. Fabbro, *DoD Use of Civilian Technicians*, Logistics Management Institute, McLean, Va., July 1980, available as AD A093154 from DTIC.

Kaplan, Robert S., and David P. Norton, *The Balanced Scorecard: Translating Strategy into Action*, Boston: Harvard Business School Press, 1996.

Kern, Lt. Gen. Paul J., "Prime Vendor Support: Wave of the Future," *Army RD&A*, January–February 1998, p. 5.

Kolar, Nicholas J., Jr., "LOGCAP: Providing Vital Services to Soldiers," *Engineer Magazine*, March 1997.

Laffont, Jean-Jacques, and Jean Tirole, *A Theory of Incentive in Procurement and Regulation*, Cambridge, Mass.: MIT Press, 1992.

Leech, Capt. Jack R., III, Lt. Col. Kyle D. Campbell, and Maj. Robert L. Goodman, "Aviation Contract Maintenance: A True Combat Multiplier," *Army Logistician*, May–June 2002, available at http://www.almc.army.mil, accessed September 2002.

Lewis, Leslie, and Roger Allen Brown, "What We Really Know About an Uncertain DoD Budget," paper for conference at Army War College, Carlisle Barracks, Pa., 2001.

Logistics Management Institute (LMI), "Contracting in Contingency Operations: Insights for the BCA Working Group," briefing, undated.

Lynn, John A., "The History of Logistics and Supplying War," in John A. Lynn, ed., *Feeding Mars: Logistics in Western Warfare from the Middle Ages to the Present,* Boulder, Colo.: Westview, 1963, p. 17.

Mailander, Commander David J., USN, "Battlefield Contractors: Assessing the Benefits and Weighing the Risks," unpublished paper, Carlisle Barracks, Pa.: U.S. Army War College, March 2002.

Markusen, Ann, "The Case Against Privatizing National Security," working paper, Council on Foreign Relations, New York, January 2001.

Masten, Scott E., "Contractual Choice," Topic 4100 in B. Boukaert and G. De Geest, eds., *Encyclopedia of Law and Economics*, Northampton, Mass.: Edward Elgar Publishing, 1999.

Megginson, William L., and Jeffry M. Netter, "From State to Market: A Survey of Empirical Studies on Privatization," *Journal of Economic Literature*, June 2001.

Milgrom, Paul, and John Roberts, *Economics, Organization, and Management*, Englewood Cliffs, N.J.: Prentice-Hall, 1992.

McDonnell, Janet A., *U.S. Army Corps of Engineers in the Persian Gulf War*, Alexandria, Va.: USACE Office of History, 1996.

McGauley, Dick, "Determining the Extent of Contractors in the Battlespace: Final Report," U.S. Army Materiel Systems Analysis Activity, Aberdeen Proving Ground, Md., July 2001.

Nash, Ralph C., Jr., and Steven L. Schooner, *The Government Contracts Reference Book*, Washington, D.C.: George Washington University, 1992.

Nelson, Maj. Kim M., "Contractors on the Battlefield: Force Multipliers or Force Dividers?" research report, Maxwell AFB, Ala.: Air Command and Staff College, Air University, AU/ACSC/130/2000-04, April 2000.

Nichols, Maj. Camille M., "The Logistics Civilian Augmentation Program," *Military Review*, March–April 1996.

O'Connor, Charles M., "Vietnam: How Business Fights the War by Contract," *Business Week*, No. 1905, March 5, 1965, pp. 58–62.

Odierno, Brig. Gen. Raymond T., "Army Materiel Command (AMC) Logistics Civil Augmentation Program (LOGCAP)," briefing, Headquarters, Department of the Army, DCSOPS, Washington, D.C., May 21, 2001.

Office of Management and Budget (OMB), "Performance of Commercial Activities," Circular A-76 (revised, including technical correction made by OMB Memorandum M-03-20), Washington, D.C., May 29, 2003, available at http://www.whitehouse.gov/omb/circulars/a076/a76_incl_tech_correction.html, accessed November 2003.

Office of the Secretary of Defense (OSD), "DoD Inventory of Commercial and Inherently Governmental Activities: Guide to Inventory Submission," Washington, D.C., October 2003.

Orsini, Eric A., and Lt. Col. Gary Bublitz, "Contractors on the Battlefield: Risks on the Road Ahead?" *Army Logistician*, Vol. 31, No. 1, January–February 1999, pp. 130–132, available at http://www.almc.army.mil/alog/JanFeb99/MS376.htm, accessed July 2000.

Pagonis, William G., and Jeffrey Cruikshank, *Moving Mountains: Lessons in Leadership and Logistics for the Gulf War,* Boston: Harvard Business School Press, 1992.

Palmer, Herman T., "More Tooth, Less Tail: Contractors in Bosnia," *Army Logistician*, September–October 1999, available at http://www.almc.army.mil/alog/sepoct99/ms408.htm.

Paperwork Reduction Act, P.L. 104-13, U.S. Code, Title 44, Chapter 35, 1995.

Peltz, Eric, *Equipment Sustainment Requirements for the Transforming Army*, Santa Monica, Calif.: RAND Corporation, MR-1577-A, 2003.

Peltz, Eric, John M. Halliday, and Aimee Bower, "Speed and Power: Toward an Expeditionary Army," Santa Monica, Calif.: RAND Corporation, MR-1755-A, 2003.

Peltz, Eric, Marc L. Robbins, Patricia Boren, and Melvin Wolff, *Diagnosing the Army's Equipment Readiness: The Equipment Downtime Analyzer,* Santa Monica, Calif.: RAND Corporation, MR-1481-A, 2002.

Peters, Kathryn McIntire, "Civilians at War," *Government Executive*, July 1996, pp. 24–27.

Phillips, Walter D., "Report of the Working Symposium on the Roles of Civilians During Military Operations," January 14–16, 2002, Air Force Judge Advocate General School, May 23, 2002.

Poppo, Laura, and Todd Zenger, "Substitutes or Complements? Exploring the Relationship Between Formal Contracts and Relational Governance," Social Science Research Network, April 27, 2000, available at http://www.papers.ssrn.com.

Quinn, James Brian, and Frederick G. Hilmer, "Make Versus Buy: Strategic Outsourcing," *McKinsey Quarterly*, No. 1, 1995, pp. 48–70, available at http://www.mckinseyquarterly.com.

Reed, Robert E., Brig. Gen. Joseph R. Barnes, USA, and Brig. Gen. James B. Smith, USAF, "Statement on the Military Extraterritorial Jurisdiction Act," before the Subcommittee on Crime, Committee on the Judiciary, U.S. House of Representatives, Second Session, 106th Congress, Washington, D.C., March 30, 2000, available at http://www.house.gov/judiciary/smit0330.htm, accessed November 2003.

Resetar, Susan A., Frank Camm, and Jeffrey A. Drezner, *Environmental Management in Design: Lessons from Volvo and Hewlett-Packard for the Department of Defense*, Santa Monica, Calif.: RAND Corporation, MR-1009-OSD, 1998.

Robertson, Cynthia M., "Outsourcing: An Impact on Readiness?" unpublished paper, Maxwell AFB, Ala.: Air Command and Staff College, Air University, March 22, 2000.

Robinson, Linda, "America's Secret Armies," *U.S. News and World Report*, November 4, 2002, pp. 38–43.

Russell, David W., "Understanding the Application of the Army's Logistics Civil Augmentation Program (LOGCAP)," unpublished paper, Carlisle Barracks, Pa.: U.S. Army War College, 1997.

Samaniego, Francisco (workshop chair), *Reliability Issues for DoD Systems: Report of a Workshop*, Washington, D.C.: National Research Council of the National Academies, 2002.

Sarnoski, Lt. Cmdr. Stephen R., JAGC, USNR, "The Status Under International Law of Civilian Persons Serving with or Accompanying Armed Forces in the Field," *The Army Lawyer*, DA PAM 27-50-260, July 1994, pp. 29–34.

Schenck, Richard G., "Contractors: A Strategic Asset or Achilles' Heel?" strategic research project, Army War College, Carlisle Barracks, Pa., July 20, 2001.

Schmitz, Patrick W., "The Hold-Up Problem and Incomplete Contracts: A Survey of Recent Topics in Contract Theory," *Bulletin of Economic Research*, Vol. 53, No. 1, January 2001, pp. 1–17.

Schrader, Charles R., *Contractors on the Battlefield*, Landpower essay series, No. 99-6, Arlington, Va., Institute of Land Warfare, Association of the U.S. Army, May 1999.

Shirley, Mary, and Patrick Walsh, "Public Versus Private Ownership: The Current State of the Debate," unpublished paper, Washington, D.C.: World Bank, June 2000.

Singer, Peter W., *Corporate Warriors: The Rise of the Privatized Military Industry*, Ithaca, N.Y.: Cornell University Press, 2003.

Smith, Eugene B., "The New Condottieri and U.S. Policy: The Privatization of Conflict and Its Implications," *Parameters*, Winter 2002–2003, pp. 104–119.

Stollenwerk, Maj. Michael F., "LOGCAP: Can Battlefield Privatization and Outsourcing Create Tactical Synergy?" School of Advanced Military Studies, U.S. Army Command and General Staff College, Fort Leavenworth, Kan., 1999.

Sumser, Raymond J., and Charles W. Hemingway, "Emerging Importance of Civilians and Contractor Employees to Army Operations," Landpower Essay Series, No. 95-4, Association of the U.S. Army, Arlington, Va., 1995.

Thomas, Col. Dwight E., "Contract Management Strategy for the 21st Century," Strategy Research Project, U.S. Army War College, Carlisle Barracks, Pa., DTIC 20000613 119, 2000.

Tolar, Larry L., "Civilians on the Battlefield," *Army Logistician*, November–December 1994.

Tomich, Kevin S., *Study Historical Experiences of Contractors in Theater Operations (SHECITO)*, Center for Army Analysis, Fort Belvoir, Va., 2001.

U.S. Code, Title 10, Sec. 2462, "Contracting for Certain Supplies and Services Required When Cost Is Lower," available at http://www4.law.cornell.edu/uscode/10/2304.html, accessed November 2003.

U.S. Congress, House of Representatives, Subcommittee of the Committee on Government Operations, "Essential Civilian Support of DoD Front-line Weapon Systems Is Not Assured," 98th Congress, Second Session, August 2, 1984.

Varian, Hal R., *Intermediate Microeconomics: A Modern Approach*, sixth edition, New York: W. W. Norton, 2002.

Vesely, W. E., F. F. Goldberg, N. H. Roberts, and D. F. Hassl, *Fault Tree Handbook*, U.S. Nuclear Regulatory Commission, Washington, D.C., NUREG-0492, January 1981.

Vick, Alan, David T. Orletsky, Bruce Pirnie, and Seth G. Jones, *The Stryker Brigade Combat Team: Rethinking Strategic Responsiveness and Assessing Deployment Options*, Santa Monica, Calif.: RAND Corporation, MR-1606-AF, 2002.

White, Thomas E., "Non–Core Competencies Working Group and the Third Wave," memorandum, Secretary of the Army, Washington, D.C., October 4, 2002.

Whitson. Maj., Anthony K., USA, "Logistical Contractors on the Peacekeeping (PKO) Battlefield: A Guide for the Operational Commander," unpublished paper, Newport, R.I.: Naval War College, February 2001.

Williamson, Darrel A., "Contracted Logistics in Bosnia," *Army Logistician*, May–June 1998, available at http://www.almc.army.mil/alog/mayjun98/ms286.htm.

Womack, Maj. John Shannon, "Contingency Contracting—A Commander's Logistics Force Multiplier," *Armor*, July–August 2000, pp. 35–37, 56.

Wong, Carolyn, Kenneth P. Horn, Elliot I. Axelband, and Paul Steinberg, "Maintaining the Government's Ability to Buy Smart," *Acquisition Review Quarterly*, Vol. 7, No. 3, Summer 2000 (also available as RP-919, RAND Corporation, Santa Monica, Calif., 2000).

Wynn, Col. Donald T., "Managing the Logistics Support Contract in the Balkan Theater," Training Techniques, Center for Army Lessons

Learned, fourth quarter, 2000, available at http://www.tac.usace.army.mil/news/wynn042000.html.

Young, David L., "Operational Planning for Contractors on the Battlefield," unpublished paper, Newport, R.I.: U.S. Naval War College, 1998.

_____, "Planning: The Key to Contractors on the Battlefield" *Army Logistician*, May–June 1999, available at http://www.almc.army.mil/ALOG/issues/MayJun99/MS344.htm, accessed September 2002.

Zamparelli, Col. Steven J., USAF, "Contractors on the Battlefield: What Have We Signed Up For?" *Air Force Journal of Logistics*, Vol. 23, No. 3, Fall 1999, pp. 10–19.